A VILLAGE OF OUTCASTS
Historical Archaeology and Documentary Research at the Lighthouse Site

Kenneth L. Feder
Central Connecticut State University

Mayfield Publishing Company
Mountain View, California
London • Toronto

Library of Congress Cataloging-in-Publication Data

Feder, Kenneth L.
    A village of outcasts : historical archaeology and documentary
  research at the Lighthouse Site / Kenneth L. Feder.
        p.   cm.
    Includes bibliographical references and index.
    ISBN 1-55934-255-2
    1. Lighthouse Site (Barkhamsted, Conn.) 2. Lighthouses-
-Connecticut--Barkhamsted--History. 3. Excavations (Archaeology)-
-Connecticut--Barkhamsted. 4. Barkhamsted (Conn.)--Antiquities.
5. Barkhamsted (Conn.)--Social life and customs.   I. Title.
F104.B2F44 1993
974.6'1--dc20   93-1441
                                                    CIP

Manufactured in the United States of America
10 9 8 7 6 5 4 3 2 1

Mayfield Publishing Company
1280 Villa Street
Mountain View, California 94041

Sponsoring editor, Janet M. Beatty; production editor, Lynn Rabin Bauer; manuscript
editor, Colleen O'Brien; text and cover designer, Susan Breitbard; cover photograph,
Kenneth L. Feder; manufacturing manager, Martha Branch. The text was set in 10/12
ITC Garamond Light and printed on 50# Butte des Morts by Banta Company.

PREFACE

This book presents a case study in historical archaeology. Specifically, it presents the story of the archaeological and documentary investigation of the Lighthouse site in the town of Barkhamsted, Connecticut. It is intended for students in courses in archaeology, anthropology, ethnography, and history, as well as those readers with a general interest in archaeology and history.

A case study in archaeology must work on a number of levels. It should show implicitly by example and explicitly through a detailed discussion of method how an archaeological research project is conducted. In an example such as the subject of this book, the interplay of archaeological fieldwork and documentary analysis also should be detailed. Most important, perhaps, is the discussion of the site itself. After all, it is the story of the people who lived out their lives in the village rather than the discussion of field methodology or deed research that will engage readers. With a story that is by itself compelling, a discussion of methodology becomes more interesting. It seems far easier to encourage interest in how archaeologists do their work when the reader is absorbed in the story that results from that work.

It is difficult not to be drawn into the lives of the inhabitants of the eighteenth- and nineteenth-century Lighthouse village of northwestern Connecticut. I have attempted to use the story itself to convey to the reader how archaeologists go about the tasks of discovery, data collection, analysis, reconstruction, explanation, and, ultimately, understanding a people now long since passed away.

Included in this case study are chapters on the methodology of documentary research (Chapter 5) and archaeological analysis (Chapter 7). For the reader with minimal background in archaeology, these chapters provide the basics for such analyses. For the student in anthropology, archaeology, or history courses where this book may be used as an adjunct to a primary text, these chapters reinforce the discussion of method presented in such courses. To assist readers, I've placed important terms in italic in the text and defined them in a glossary that appears after the narrative.

There is at least one additional level to the telling of this story and to the writing of the book illuminating process and result. The Lighthouse site is important in the history of Connecticut in particular, and of the United States in general. It has recently (1991) been placed on the National Register of Historic Places, a national "honor roll" of important sites in American history and prehistory. As a multitcultural, multitracial settlement, the Lighthouse is a part of American history that remains largely unwritten. Though couched in legend and myth, the Lighthouse was a real place with real inhabitants. Their story, preserved primarily in the archaeological and documentary records, deserves telling. I can only hope that in the researching of their lives, and in the telling of their story, this book does them justice.

Acknowledgments

An archaeological project like the one described represents the coordinated efforts of many people; I'd like to acknowledge here those who helped illuminate the story of the Lighthouse.

First, thanks are due to all the kind people of Barkhamsted and New Hartford who shared their knowledge of the Lighthouse legend. I especially would like to thank Douglas Roberts, town historian of Barkhamsted. Mr. Roberts has always been generous with his time and extensive historical knowledge of the region in general and the Lighthouse in particular. Thanks as well go to Mark Aaron, Nina Farrell, Beverly Ganung, Walt Landgraf, Mary Nason, Beatrice Osden, and Ben Warner for sharing their knowledge of the Chaughams, Peoples State Forest, and other local lore.

Thanks as well go to the Chaugham descendants who contacted me to help in my investigation. A special thanks is due to Raymond H. Ellis, a seventh-generation descendant of James and Molly. I greatly appreciate the information Mr. Ellis supplied, and I'm glad that it was my work that got him finally to visit the home of his fascinating ancestors.

I also thank the clerks in various town halls throughout Connecticut for their help in tracking down the primary documents associated with the inhabitants of the Lighthouse. Of special note was the kind and generous assistance of Nancy Winn, town clerk of Barkhamsted. Thanks are also due to the staff of the Connecticut State Library, Genealogical Division, as well as the staff of the Connecticut Historical Society.

Without the support and cooperation of the State of Connecticut, the Lighthouse project would have been impossible. Thanks to David Poirier of the Connecticut Historical Commission, Connecticut State Archaeologist Nick Bellantoni, and Anthony Cantele of the Department of Environmental Protection for granting permission to excavate the site and for all of their assistance and support. The original project in 1986 during which I first encountered the Lighthouse was supported by a Preservation and Planning Survey Grant from the U.S. Department of the Interior, administered by the Connecticut Historical Commission.

Thanks are also due to Arts and Sciences Dean George Clark and Vice President of Academic Affairs Karen Beyard, both of Central Connecticut State University, for supporting my research in spirit as well as through research release time and financial assistance.

I cannot forget the many students who contributed their time and labor to excavating the Lighthouse site, analyzing the material culture recovered there, and assisting in the documentary research. They all made important contributions, each in his or her own way. Thanks to the 1986 team involved in initially surveying the site: Marc Banks, Barbara Calogero, Dan Childers, Mark Dunacusky, Tina Thivierge, Marina Mozzi, and Bill Murdoch. Thanks to the field crew of 1990 for their work in the preliminary excavation: Joy Ambruso, Ron Breeze, John Danbury, Donna Davis, Fran Ellisio, Linda Ely, Barbara Gribbon, Rita Mushinsky, Rick Pullman, Emily Rushin, Sheila Szabo, Joe

Walczyk, and Dot Zyzo. Thanks to the field crew of 1991 for their work in the major excavation of the site: Amanda Avalone, Amy Belanger, Jeff Dahlstrom, Donna Davis, Myron Dytiuk, Joshua Max Feder, Fred Fenn, Nell Filippopoulos, Sonja Gray, Carol Keesling, Cathy Labadia, Shawn Lucas, Rachel Mancini, Kathy McGillis, Mick Mimo, Jim Nevins, Karin Rasted, Robin Ross, Mike Sealander, Sheila Szabo, and Jeff Widem.

Additionally, I would like to thank those individuals who assisted in specific elements of the research. Amy Dowe and Cathy Labadia did terrific work in town halls too numerous to mention. Sonja Gray is responsible for the work tracking down James Chaugham on Block Island. Newman Hall generously supplied me with information on the Elwell family. Shawn Lucas spent many hours poring over the faunal remains and Jim Nevins contributed much of his time to the analysis of smoking pipes. Larry Tallman generously provided his expert's eye in the examination of the coins found at the site. Thanks also to Tina Thivierge and Dan Childers for producing the original site map and to Regina Klonis Dardzienski for her fine work on the final site map. Roy Temple of the Central Connecticut State University Center for Instructional Media provided much needed assistance with black-and-white photography.

I wish to especially thank historical archaeologist Robert F. Gradie for his enormous contribution to the analysis of the material culture at the Lighthouse. Bob is the most experienced and knowledgeable person I know concerning seventeenth-, eighteenth-, and nineteenth-century European-American material culture. Bob spent more than a year making the long trip from his home in eastern Connecticut to my New Britain campus lab to go over the more than 12,000 artifacts recovered at the Lighthouse. Without his assistance, the analysis of the Lighthouse artifacts would have been impossible.

Thanks as well to colleague Kevin McBride whose insights into the culture of seventeenth-, eighteenth-, and nineteenth-century Native Americans played a crucial role in helping me understand the lives of the people who lived at the Lighthouse.

Once again I owe a debt of gratitude to the folks at Mayfield. This is my third book with Mayfield, and the magic they accomplish in taking a rough manuscript and transforming it into a polished book never ceases to amaze me. Thanks to sponsoring editor Jan Beatty, production editor Lynn Rabin Bauer, and copy editor Colleen O'Brien. Thanks also to my colleagues who reviewed the manuscript and whose suggestions contributed greatly to this work: Christopher R. DeCorse, Syracuse University; William A. Turnbaugh, University of Rhode Island; and W. H. Wills, University of New Mexico.

Finally, after writing a book about a remarkable family, I wish to thank my own remarkable family. My wife Melissa is my gentlest critic, my most understanding partner, my most patient sounding board, and my best friend. Our son Josh helped at the site, showed interest in what I was devoting so much of my time to, and is the only one who actually wears the field school T-shirt ("My Life Is in Ruins," indeed!) And I must not forget to thank Jacob, whose recent birth reminded me that we each are part of our own "generations speeding onward."

CONTENTS

Chapter 7

DIGGING IN THE DIRT: A BRIEF INTRODUCTION TO ARCHAEOLOGICAL METHODOLOGY AND ANALYSIS   111

Chapter 8

DIGGING IN THE DIRT: ARCHAEOLOGY AT THE LIGHTHOUSE SITE   131

Chapter 1

ENCOUNTERING
THE LIGHTHOUSE

A true "lighthouse" is a beacon directing the lost to safe harbor. Its light shines to guide the return of sailors and fishermen to their homes. The settlement that is the focus of this book, though so named, was not a lighthouse at all, at least not in the ordinary sense. It was, instead, a rural, pioneer village made up of a fascinating mixture of Native Americans (Indians), whites, and descendants of African-American slaves. The lives of the inhabitants of this multiethnic/multicultural/multiracial village—and the procedures employed in illuminating their lives—are the focuses of this book.

After spending 15 straight days in the field at the archaeological site created by the inhabitants of the legendary "Lighthouse" village (Figure 1.1), I employed the final four weeks of the summer of 1990 laying the groundwork for the documentary research of the lives of the Lighthouse inhabitants. Early in this phase of the research I worked in the vault of the Barkhamsted town hall where local historical records—tax lists, deed transferals, and *vital records* (births, deaths, and marriages)—are housed. This was decidedly the cleaner part of the research, not to mention the cooler. Nevertheless, this was a crucial part of the investigation, and I was, in a very real sense, "digging" in the documents (see Chapters 5 and 6).

As a branch of the social science of *anthropology, archaeology* focuses not on the admittedly fascinating objects we unearth—the ancient burials, spear points, pots, or jewelry; nor on the remarkable documents we examine—the hieroglyphic texts or cuneiform records. Our primary desire is not to fill museums with fabulous treasure but to contribute to an understanding of the human species by examining the lives of people who have long since

1

Figure 1.1   Archaeology at the Lighthouse site. Archaeologists search for the material evidence of human activities. It is this physical evidence that enables us to study the lives of those who left no written record documenting their own existence and to assess the veracity of records left by those who did.

passed into the dim mists of time. We accomplish this by recovering and examining the objects and records left by these people.

Archaeologists do not study artifacts and written records just because we find them interesting; we spend so much of our time searching for, recovering, and analyzing these things because we are caught in a quandary: If we wish to know more about people who lived in the past, virtually all we have left are the things they made and used, and, if they were a literate people, the documentary records they left behind. Of course such things as ancient cave paintings, flaked stone tools, and poetry inked onto sheets of papyrus are intrinsically fascinating. So you will not hear archaeologists complain too loudly or too often about the kinds of data we are "stuck" with.

As a result, archaeologists admit—perhaps grudgingly—that, although our work bears little resemblance to that of Indiana Jones, there is nonetheless a visceral element to our enterprise that goes deeper than our righteously held scientific objectivity. No archaeologist can, or should, deny the remarkable feeling that comes with the work. There is something quite extraordinary about holding an object just unearthed or perusing a document just encountered. These things resonate with the lives of long-dead people and create, even in the most hardened of us, a feeling that transcends time and objectivity. A human being who lived hundreds, thousands, or even millions of years ago, a human being in many ways like you or me, with hopes, fears, aspirations, and loves, made and used a tool, wrote a letter, or left an official record of his or her passing. The tool was lost, the letter hidden away, the document filed and forgotten. Now, that human being is gone and all that remains to mark his or her existence is the tool that you now hold in your hand, the fragment of a letter, or the official record of birth or death. And yet, although that person is gone, he or she is not forgotten, and the object recovered by the archaeologist, the letter recovered from oblivion, or the documentary record left unexamined for so many years seems to us to reverberate with the life of that long-gone individual.

With each discovery at the Lighthouse site in that first season of archaeological research, we were making just that sort of contact. (See Chapters 8 and 9.) But nothing prepared me for what I was to encounter at the Barkhamsted, Connecticut town hall vault when our field season was over.

Primarily a prehistoric sites archaeologist, I had become somewhat inured to discovering an object created so many years ago and being the first human since to touch it and ponder the life of its creator. Perhaps I had become blasé because my prehistoric finds were always anonymous. On that summer afternoon in the Barkhamsted town hall vault, however, for me the people of the Lighthouse were to forever lose their anonymity.

I glanced down the listing of births in Barkhamsted for 1858. (See Chapter 6.) Reviewing the records had been an extremely tedious job. The old index for the vital records was incomplete. This necessitated my carefully examining each page of the old volume and looking for names that I recognized from Lewis Mills's legendary account of the village (Chapters 3 and 4). The vital records were all handwritten, the pages yellowed and brittle; there were ink stains, water stains, and rips, and some sections were missing entirely.

The records were arranged in a series of columns. These columns organized the information considered to be significant by the record keepers of nineteenth-century Connecticut: date of birth, names of parents, baby's name, sex of the child, "color" of the parents, "color" of the child, and place of parents' residence. I spent several hours skimming the columns of the birth records, looking for any clues about the inhabitants of the Lighthouse.

I was not enormously confident that I would find anything significant. The people who lived at the Lighthouse were far out of the mainstream, outside the reach, I feared, even of regular record keeping. Yet, surprisingly, names I recognized from the Lighthouse legend began to turn up in the vital records. And there, on the page listing Barkhamsted births in May of 1858, was the most interesting of all the records I had yet seen (Figure 1.2).

A baby was born in Barkhamsted on May 14, 1858. Solomon and Mary Webster were listed as the parents. On a previous page, Solomon's father,

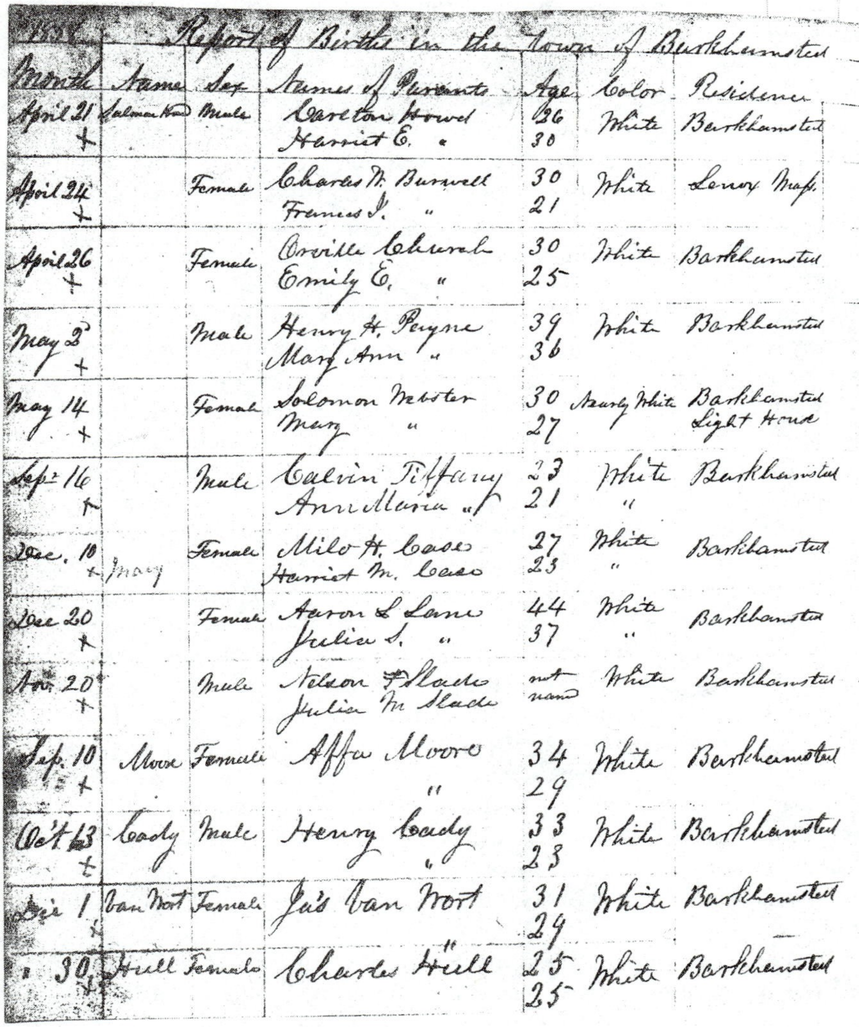

1858	Report of Births in the Town of Barkhamsted					
Month	Name	Sex	Names of Parents	Age	Color	Residence
April 21 +	Salmon Howd	Male	Carleton Howd Harriet E. "	26 30	White	Barkhamsted
April 24 +		Female	Charles N. Burwell Frances J. "	30 21	White	Lenox Mass.
April 26 +		Female	Orville Church Emily E. "	30 25	White	Barkhamsted
May 2 +		Male	Henry H. Payne Mary Ann "	39 36	White	Barkhamsted
May 14 +		Female	Solomon Webster Mary "	30 27	Nearly White	Barkhamsted Light House
Sep. 16 +		Male	Calvin Tiffany Ann Maria "	23 21	White "	Barkhamsted
Dec. 10 +	Mary	Female	Milo H. Case Harriet M. Case	27 23	White "	Barkhamsted
Dec 20 +		Female	Aaron L Lane Julia S. "	44 37	White "	Barkhamsted
Nov. 20 +		Male	Nelson F Slade Julia M Slade	not nam	White	Barkhamsted
Sep. 10 +	Moore	Female	Affa Moore "	34 29	White	Barkhamsted
Oct 13 +	Cady	Male	Henry Cady "	33 23	White	Barkhamsted
Dec 1 +	Van Wort	Female	Jas Van Wort	31 29	White	Barkhamsted
" 30 +	Hull	Female	Charles Hull	25 25	White	Barkhamsted

Figure 1.2 Official list of births for the town of Barkhamsted, Connecticut between April and December 1858. Note the listing for the birth of Solomon and Mary Webster's "Nearly White" baby on May 14. Their place of residence is officially listed in these town records as "Barkhamsted Light House."

Montgumery Webster, was listed and his color was given as Mohegan, an Indian tribal name in southern and eastern Connecticut. Solomon's mother, Sibel, was listed as being Creole. Sol's wife Mary, as we shall see, was a direct descendant of the original settlers of the Lighthouse village—Molly Barber, a white woman, and James Chaugham, her Narragansett Indian husband.

Under the column heading "Color," most of the babies on the page bore the designation "White." On other pages, babies bore the designation "Negro," and there were a few labeled "Creole," or mixed. Sol and Mary's child bore none of the common designators for its color. In fact, its racial category was unique in the entire volume of Barkhamsted's vital records: Sol and Mary's baby was listed as "Nearly White."

But it was the column for parental residence that so astonished me. The town of Barkhamsted is one of 169 incorporated Connecticut towns. Within many of these towns are smaller entities with names but little or no political significance. Within the boundaries of the town of Barkhamsted in 1858, for example, were the villages of Pleasant Valley and Hitchcocksville (now called Riverton). In the parental residence column in the town's vital records, most parents were listed as living in Barkhamsted. A few were listed as living in Pleasant Valley, a few in Hitchcocksville. Just as the Webster baby bore a unique listing for its race, Sol and Mary Webster had a unique designation for their place of residence. It was given as "Barkhamsted Light House." This was the first official document I had seen that listed the Lighthouse as an actual, recognized community (see Figure 1.2).

Through the discovery of a 132-year-old, handwritten entry on the brittle page of a town record, an initially enigmatic settlement name taken from a legend had become for me a concrete reality where real people had lived out their lives. The artifacts we had been excavating were no longer merely archaeological data to be used in the scientific examination of a historical legend; they could no longer be just means to an end—satisfying my curiosity about the historicity of a legend. I began to understand on an emotional level what I had always known on an intellectual level: These were the belongings of real people from a real place. We were no longer excavating just "data" from anonymous individuals. These artifacts had been the meager possessions of Mary and Sol, of James and Molly, of Isaac and Samuel, and of all the others we were to meet in our study of the Lighthouse village.

This book details the archaeological and documentary study of the inhabitants of the fascinating place called the Barkhamsted Lighthouse and presents both the process and results of our investigation of the site. As a case study in *historical archaeology,* this book must first place the research conducted within the context of historical archaeology in general. Chapter 2 focuses on the nature of the archaeology of our own historical period.

Chapter 2

THE ARCHAEOLOGY
OF HISTORY

Perhaps the great satirist Ambrose Bierce said it best in his *Devil's Dictionary* when he defined "history" as "an account mostly false, of events mostly unimportant, which are brought about by rulers mostly knaves, and soldiers mostly fools" (Bierce 1911:57). To be fair, we should add that he defined "prehistoric" as "belonging to an early period—and a museum" (Bierce 1911:103).

Others have defined history similarly. Archaeologist James Deetz has characterized the historical record as "the story of wealthy, white males" (Deetz 1980). In a similar vein, a common cliché maintains that "history is written only by the winners." Winston Churchill expressed this same perspective in a personal manner: "History will be kind to me for I intend to write it." For Voltaire, "History is a pack of cards with which we play tricks on the dead." Napoleon Bonaparte is supposed to have said, "What is history but a fable agreed upon?"

The point being made by these various thinkers, if somewhat exaggerated, is well taken. Particularly in the centuries preceding our own, history, as reflected by the written record, concentrates on the lives and accomplishments of "important" people. These are Bierce's knavish "rulers"—kings and pharaohs, emperors and princes, presidents and premiers—and his foolish "soldiers"—the generals responsible for implementing the military dictates of those rulers. For the most part, common people—peasants, farmers, factory workers, and slaves—were ignored. These ordinary people, who in every period constitute the majority of the population, are barely visible historically. People on the margins of society, ordinarily not accounted for by the ruling group, even for purposes of administration, taxation, or conscription, are virtually invisible.

6

A RATIONALE FOR HISTORICAL ARCHAEOLOGY

This leads us to a justification for doing historical archaeology in the first place. On the one hand, it is easy to validate prehistoric archaeology and understand its rationale. Prehistorians deal with cultures that left no written record of their histories and lifeways. The only way to learn directly about these nonliterate societies of the past is by excavating the physical remains of their habitations and attempting to reconstruct their lives through analysis of the recovered residue. In the case of nonliterate societies of the past, there simply is little choice other than examination of their material remains through the discipline of archaeology.

Historical archaeology is something else again. It is defined as that branch of archaeology that focuses on societies that left a written record of their passing. For many, it is hard to understand why, beyond the desire to fill museums with interpretive material, archaeologists would need to conduct excavations to learn about people who left perfectly comprehensible written records detailing their own cultures and lives. Wouldn't such an enterprise be redundant? How could archaeology possibly contribute to our further under-standing of a society that wrote about itself?

James Deetz, a well-known and respected historical sites archaeologist, has characterized the skepticism about the value of historical archaeology implied in such questions through a satirical definition: "Historical archaeolo-gy is the most expensive way in the world to learn something we already know" (Deetz 1991). Such a definition grossly (and intentionally, by Deetz) overestimates the quality of the historical record and underestimates the con-tribution historical archaeology can make to our understanding of the recent past.

As Deetz and others have pointed out, we should not have such faith in the veracity nor in the exhaustive or all-inclusive character of the docu-mentary record. Simply because a people left a written record about them-selves that we can read does not signify that we truly understand them. As Bierce implied in his sarcastic definition of history, the history writers did not record all important information, nor did they always tell the truth. Although written history may have a distinct bias toward "great men," the material record is far more democratic and encompasses all of us. This tangible record of broken pots, stone walls, house foundations, trash dumps, buttons, pipes, and all the other detritus of everyday living is the province of the archaeologist.

It is because of this tangible record that historical archaeology can make a consequential and distinctive contribution to our understanding of the recent past, the past for which we already have information in the form of written records. Historical archaeology can and should be a part of the sci-entific study of the human past, using many of the same methods and testing many of the same hypotheses that prehistorians use and test. Historical archaeologist Stanley South's (1977) pivotal book, *Method and Theory in*

Historical Archaeology, perhaps more than any other publication, pushed the discipline in a more scientific direction, where the goal became understanding the historical past rather than simply providing artifacts for colonial restorations. South's approach was anthropological and his methodology deductive. Testing hypotheses about our own recent history was emphasized and the potential of quantitative methods was explored. South's work has been criticized, but even more than 15 years after the publication of his major text, historical archaeologists continue to build on his approach.

THE UNIQUE CONTRIBUTIONS OF HISTORICAL ARCHAEOLOGY

As historical sites archaeologist Kathleen Deagan characterizes it, the most. important contribution of historical archaeology lies in its ability "to tell us things about America's past that we could learn in no other way" (Deagan 1991:103). Following Deagan (1991:104–105), we can catalog the areas in which historical archaeology can give us information about our past that we cannot obtain from documentary records or history books. She lists five such domains, and we can add a sixth category she did not include in her discussion. They are:

1. the colonization process
2. understanding the physical world of the historical past
3. examining health and nutrition of the historical past
4. documenting the lives of the disenfranchised and the oppressed
5. documenting illicit or illegal behaviors
6. evaluating and revising historical accounts of known events

Some projects in the archaeology of history make significant contributions to our understanding of the recent past in one or several of these categories of knowledge.

The Colonization Process

Beginning in the fifteenth century, explorers, colonists, and missionaries left written accounts of their experiences in the New World, as well as in other places where European societies expanded their influence and their populations. Explorers needed to provide written accounts of their discoveries to their benefactors back home in Europe (Campbell 1988). Although we may today emphasize the romantic aspects of the discovery and colonization of the New World—and celebrate holidays in remembrance of the accomplishments and sacrifices of those involved—we should remember that the rationale for exploration was economic. Columbus, Verrazzano, Weymouth, De Soto, Champlain, and the myriad other explorers sent to the New World by European monarchies were funded for sound economic reasons. For some, the expectation was that a "northwest passage" or route through the New World to the Orient would be discovered, providing a shortcut to the wealth of Asia and a possible trade monopoly for whichever nation discovered it. Once it was shown that there was no such shortcut, the New World itself became the treasure trove of resources that would fill the coffers of those who could lay claim to the riches present there.

With so many Europeans traveling to the New World, exploring its lands, exploiting its riches, and laying claim to its territory, determining who owned what became difficult. The Spanish claimed La Florida, whose northern border they placed as far north as modern Virginia. The Dutch claimed New Amsterdam, whose border extended east to the Connecticut River. The British claimed New England, whose western border they drew at the Hudson River. A simple perusal of a modern map can show the extraordinary degree of overlap in the territories claimed in the New World by various European nations.

It became important, therefore, for each European nation to solidify its territorial claims. One way to accomplish this was to establish colonies in the claimed territories. It was one thing for a British explorer like Martin Pring to journey to New England in 1606, claim territory, collect furs and sassafras, and then return home to the nation that funded the expedition. It was quite another thing to send English subjects to New England and have them establish an actual beachhead in the territory, as the Pilgrims did in Plimoth (now spelled Plymouth) in 1620. A line drawn on a map can easily be erased, a flag planted to mark a territorial claim can readily be pushed aside, but a colony of settlers who, by their very presence, make such a claim of land ownership quite concrete cannot be so easily dispensed with. Colonies made sense as economic investments, and they began to appear along the eastern seaboard of the United States in the seventeenth century.

Explorers and settlers alike left written accounts of the New World, its native population, and their own adjustment to life in the colonies. The first settlers at the Plimoth colony produced a work usually referred to as *Mourt's Relation* (1622). It is unclear precisely who "Mourt" was or if (as is more likely) he was an amalgam of authors. This book details the story of the journey of these first English settlers of New England, their exploration of the coast of New England, their settlement in Plimoth, and their adjustment to life in the New World.

In the case of *Mourt's Relation*, as well as in the subsequent description of life in Plimoth written by Governor William Bradford (Davis 1971), we have the perspective of the colonists only. The local natives could not provide us with their view concerning the colonizing of their territory because they could not write. Moreover, in producing works like *Mourt's Relation* and Bradford's journal, the colonists were providing a description of their experiences for a particular audience—the people back home. The narratives of explorers and colonial authors were anything but dispassionate, objective accountings of the colonial experience. These written works had, at least implicitly, the goal of convincing the Old World authorities to provide more support for the colonists as well as to inspire more people to migrate to the New World.

As a result of this hidden agenda, the historical works colonial authors produced are incomplete, imperfect, and often inaccurate sources of information concerning their lives and the colonial experience. This is why, even in the case of Plimoth, perhaps the best-known American colony, the written record simply is not enough to tell the complete story and the material record is an important source of supplementary and often novel information.

James Deetz has conducted archaeological investigations of the Plimoth colony and surrounding territory (1969, 1971, 1973, 1977). Perhaps more than anything else, his archaeological research has provided us with what he characterizes as the "texture" of the lives of the colonists (Deetz 1980; Figure 2.1). For example, excavated trash pits at Plimoth dated to the period of the first Thanksgiving have produced some 10,000 bone fragments—and not a single turkey bone (Deetz 1969:43). The most common *faunal* remain recovered by Deetz in these trash pits has been pig bones. So much for the authenticity of our Thanksgiving menus.

Such pits have also shown us changes in lifestyle and mindset—changes the colonists did not write about and perhaps were not even aware of—as their culture evolved in their new surroundings. For example, throughout the seventeenth century and during the first half of the eighteenth century, the ceramic *assemblage* bears witness to a preponderance of large serving bowls. Individual serving plates or dishes are rare. After 1760, plates become quite common in the archaeological assemblage, as do chamber pots. Deetz ascribes this shift to a changing attitude among the inhabitants of Plimoth from a more corporate, communal spirit, where many people ate out of the same bowls and where members of a household shared a chamber pot, to a more individualistic view, where each person had his or her own plate and chamber pot (Deetz 1977:58–59).

At about the same time a break can be seen in the way trash was disposed of by the seventeenth- and eighteenth-century European inhabitants of the New World. Before 1750, as Deetz (1977:125–127) points out, the settlers at places like Plimoth were not particularly assiduous about trash disposal; trash literally surrounds houses in the first half of the seventeenth century. By about 1750, however, things changed drastically. Instead of simply scattering trash, people began to dig pits specifically for trash disposal. Again, Deetz attributes this to a changing pattern of thought among the settlers in the New World as they became more ordered in all aspects of their lives and thinking. (See Chapter 9 for a discussion of the distribution of trash at the Lighthouse village.)

Whatever the precise reason for the changes in the archaeological record of bowls, plates, chamber pots, and trash disposal, the record tells us

Figure 2.1 Through historical archaeology we can study elements of the recent past that often are ignored in the historical record. Even for sites where the historical record has been intensively studied, Plimoth Plantation in Massachusetts, for example, the material record can provide us with unique insights into the lives of the people who lived there. This photograph shows archaeological research at the Allerton site at Plimoth. (Photograph by Ted Avery, courtesy Plimoth Plantation.)

about the settlers in a way that history simply cannot. Indeed, it provides us with a telling insight into their lives. The tangible sense it provides is an important contribution of historical archaeology.

Understanding the Physical World of the Historical Past

Generally speaking, the historical record does not provide us with direct access to the physical world of the past. Record keepers did not often feel compelled to write about environmental surroundings; such things were taken for granted. When they did write about the natural world, they usually did so from the untrained perspective of lay people. Also, as Deagan (1991:106) points out, "A great deal of the American landscape of 1492 is gone, ultimately as a result of forces set in motion by the encounter." Once again, we must turn to the material record for insights into the physical world in which our forebears lived.

Deagan (1991:107) provides the example of research conducted by Lee Ann Newsom of the University of Florida at the En Bas Saline site in Haiti. Here, through archaeological analysis, it has become clear that previous assumptions concerning the degree of deforestation wrought by European colonization were incorrect. In fact the research has shown that a significant level of deforestation occurred pre-colonially in the period A.D. 1200 to A.D. 1500. The native peoples lived in large farming communities and cleared the forest to plant their crops. After the Europeans invaded and the diseases they brought took hold, the native population dropped precipitously, large farming villages virtually disappeared, and reforestation took place. History provides little insight here, whereas analysis of preserved wood remains from late pre-historic native sites and early historical colonial sites provides more accurate and detailed data regarding the nature of the extant plant communities.

Examining Health and Nutrition of the Historical Past

We all recognize that modern medical science is far more advanced than that of even the not too distant past. We ordinarily think of this advancement in terms of our own lives—today infant mortality is low, we live longer, and we can maintain healthy, active lives longer than our ancestors. From the perspective of historical research, there is another aspect to the relatively primitive understanding of human health, disease, and nutrition of our predecessors. The documents of our own recent past relating to health and mortality reflect the lack of medical knowledge even on the part of medical experts.

Consider the cause of death as diagnosed by medical authorities and as recorded in official documents. Today, due to advances in medical diagnostic techniques, cause of death can be accurately assessed in most cases. Future researchers interested in mortality in late twentieth-century America will find records accurately reporting causes of death. Issues of longevity, infectious disease rates, genetic conditions, and nutritional status in the late twentieth century could all be gleaned from such official records.

In the centuries preceding our own, however, records are not so reliable. In the vital records to be discussed in Chapters 5 and 6, we will find recorded the deaths of a number of the players in the Lighthouse drama. For some inhabitants, the cause of death reported in these vital records may well be accurate. For example, the cause of Sophia Choccum's death in 1848 is listed as "childbirth." It was far more common in the past for women to die during childbirth or immediately thereafter because of hemorrhaging or diseases resulting from unsanitary conditions. This cause of death should have been relatively easy to diagnose, so we can place some faith in the record.

However, other causes of death listed in the official records are not so readily interpretable or credible. The cause of death for one individual associated with the Lighthouse village was listed as "constitutional derangement." Such a diagnosis is enigmatic to us, presumably reflecting a more or less generic category of illness. We simply cannot be sure in such an instance what the actual cause of death was.

Questions of overall health, nutrition, and mortality are often difficult to approach through historical documents but can be assessed directly through the examination of human skeletons. Skeletons commonly exhibit features of nutrition, infectious disease, trauma, genetic condition, and cancer, along with evidence concerning immediate cause of death. Examination of these questions through the archaeological record is called *paleopathology*, and a number of informative works have been published that deal with this sort of analysis of the human skeleton (Brothwell 1971; Krogman 1973; Buikstra and Cook 1980; Larsen 1987; Ortner and Putschar 1981; White and Folkens 1991).

An example comes from the work of Gill, Fisher, and Zeimens (1984). While excavating at a small nineteenth-century Plains Indian site near the historic Bordeaux trading post in southeastern Wyoming, the authors detected the burial of a white settler and excavated the body. Although we do not know the individual's name, nor are there any extant records to inform us of his life, we know quite a bit about him from his skeletal remains. (See Chapter 7 for a brief outline of the analysis of human skeletal remains.)

We know he was a white male in his thirties when he died. We also know he was a large, robust man, more than six feet tall. Beyond this, we know that he lived a physically demanding and, in fact, stressful life; though relatively young when he died, his bones show the effects of a lifetime of hard physical labor. Some degenerative bone disease is apparent in the legs and back that is likely the result of, or at least was hastened by, an arduous way of life. Also, perhaps as a result of a physically demanding profession, the individual had suffered a broken ankle and several broken ribs during his life—the latter were in the process of healing when the man died.

His violent death, though it occurred probably more than 120 years ago, can be reconstructed in great detail. The man was shot at least two times. According to Gill et al. (1984:235), he likely was first shot in the upper thigh or hip, shattering his femur. Having been brought down by the first shot, he received the death blow: a gunshot to the head, just above the left eye. The bullet exited the head from the lower, right rear of the skull. As determined from the positioning of the entry and exit wounds, the bullet's trajectory indicates that the gun was pointed down at the victim's head. The authors suggest that because he was over six feet tall, it is possible he was on his knees, perhaps as a result of the bullet wound to his leg, when he was shot in the head.

Thus we have the case of an individual who lived not that long ago but about whom we know nothing historically. The archaeological record, however, can provide us with a great amount of detail concerning his life and, more particularly, his death. As Gill et al. point out, as the body of data grows from such skeletal evidence, we are able to learn about the lives of these pioneers in a way that we simply cannot by reference to the historical record alone.

Larger skeletal samples have been investigated from historical cemeteries in the American South. Ted Rathburn (1987) investigated the remains of 36 slaves at a plantation in South Carolina (the skeletons were being relocated because of a construction project). He found a great deal of evidence that bore witness to the physically arduous lives of these slaves. For example, there was a substantial amount of bone degeneration at the shoulders, elbows, hips, and lower vertebrae, resulting from a lifetime of heavy lifting and nonmechanized agricultural activities such as hoeing (Rathburn 1987:248).

In another study, Angel et al. (1987) and Kelley and Angel (1987) examined skeletons from a free African-American community in Philadelphia, Pennsylvania and from a number of plantation slave communities in the South. Skeletal evidence showed in a very concrete fashion the effects of a lifetime of hard physical labor and inadequate nutrition among both free and enslaved African Americans. In the skeletal series from the plantations, indicators of poor nutrition included *tibial bowing, enamel hypoplasia,* and *lowered skull base height.* Among the free Blacks, tibial bowing and lowered skull base height were apparent. These all are products of poor childhood nutrition.

Documenting the Lives of the Disenfranchised and the Oppressed

We began this chapter by pointing out that history is not exhaustive or all-inclusive and, in fact, most people are left out of the histories of past centuries. Providing a history for common people is one of the major contributions made by historical archaeology. As Deetz puts it, concerning the archaeology of our own historical past:

It provides access to the ways all people, not just a small group of literate people, organized their physical lives. If only the written records,
rich and detailed as they are, are studied, then the conclusions will
reflect on the story of a small minority of deviant, wealthy, white males,
and little else. I do not think we want that for our national history;
therefore, we need archaeologists to find what was left behind by
everybody. . . (1991:6).

In the previous section, we talked about the analysis of slave burials
and how this can expand our comprehension of history. An examination of
plantation life itself represents an obvious instance where historical archaeology can add to an understanding of our own past, providing insights that the
written record simply cannot.

Certainly much was written about life in the antebellum South. Most of
us have read or seen *Gone With the Wind.* But records of life on southern
plantations invariably were written by people who *owned* plantations.
Throughout much of the South before the Civil War, it was illegal to teach
slaves to read or write (Ascher and Fairbanks 1971:3), so we rarely, if ever,
get an impression of life in the South from a perspective other than that of
wealthy white plantation owners. We hardly ever get the perspective of the
dominant population group on these plantations: black slaves.

Although in general they could not speak for themselves in the historical record, black slaves can speak to us through the archaeological record.
As archaeologist Theresa Singleton states, "Excavation of slave sites supplies
details for the ways in which transplanted Africans adapted to New World sit-
uations" (1985:3) (Figure 2.2).

Archaeologist Charles Fairbanks (1976) has made significant contributions to our understanding of life on southern plantations. Fairbanks excavated slave cabins, an overseer's cabin, and the area around the plantation main
house at the Cannon's Point plantation on St. Simons Island, Georgia. He was
able to gain insights into plantation life, showing in a concrete way differences between the lives of slave owners, overseers, and slaves. As Fairbanks
states, "Many of these differences are barely hinted at in the numerous
accounts of southern plantation life" (1976:172).

In our stylized view of plantation life, many of us have come to think
that while the institution of slavery is utterly morally indefensible, at least
slaves were well fed by their owners to keep them healthy as workers.
Fairbanks, however, found that far from being well fed, after a full day of
labor slaves still had to at least supplement the food provided by the plantation owner. In the *middens,* or trash piles, found around the slave cabins and
the overseer's house, Fairbanks identified the remains of great quantities of
opossum and raccoon, small wild game the slaves must have trapped in the
evenings after their labors for the plantation were completed. The midden by
the big house had no such faunal remains. Here Fairbanks recovered the

Figure 2.2   Artifacts from plantation archaeology can uniquely inform us concerning the lives of the largest population segment on such plantations: the slaves, most of whom could not read or write. Here, students excavate a slave house at Middlebury Plantation in South Carolina. (Courtesy Leland Ferguson, Department of Anthropology, University of South Carolina.)

remains of beef, pork, deer, sea bass, and sea trout (1976:172).

Elizabeth Reitz, Tyson Gibbs, and Ted Rathburn (1985) analyzed a large number of archaeological studies of plantation life conducted in South Carolina, Virginia, Georgia, Tennessee, Louisiana, and Florida. They found that in almost every instance, the archaeological record mirrors the findings of Fairbanks as it relates to the faunal assemblage. In all of these southern states, the material record showed that slaves needed to supplement the diet provided by their owners. The hearths, middens, and trash dumps associated with slave living quarters commonly included the remains of animals hunted or scavenged by the slaves: raccoon, deer, opossum, rabbit, turtle, fish, crab, and even alligator.

From the archaeological evidence it is clear that slaves, although a substantial monetary investment, were not well fed by their owners. The skeletal evidence, you will remember, showed precisely this.

Giving a voice to the voiceless of history—the poor, the oppressed, the disenfranchised—is among historical archaeology's most important contributions to anthropology. A recent book, *The Archaeology of Inequality* (McGuire and Paynter 1991), is devoted entirely to this issue, presenting a series of chapters detailing the way that historical archaeology provides a new perspective of history.

A number of monographs focus on the communities of such individuals. Vern Baker (1978) analyzes the ceramics found in the archaeological excavation (conducted by Adelaide and Ripley Bullen [1945]) at the Black Lucy's Garden site, the homestead of freed slave Lucy Foster. Foster lived in a cabin on one acre of land in Andover, Massachusetts from 1815 to 1845 where she died at the age of 88. She likely could not write, and her white neighbors left little in the form of written history describing what life was like in the North for a freed slave. In Lucy Foster's case, archaeology has allowed us to fill in this gap in our historical knowledge. The Bullens and Baker were able to provide a description of her life based largely on the material record.

In another example, Joan Geismar (1982) has written an excellent book on the fascinating community of Skunk Hollow, New Jersey. Skunk Hollow was a sizeable village in the nineteenth century, located on the border between New Jersey and New York and populated by ex-slaves. This community represents a fascinating element in American history: a successful, autonomous community of free blacks. Again, little was written about the residents of Skunk Hollow, and they did not—and largely could not—write about their own lives. Geismar, through her extremely detailed archaeological and documentary analysis of the site and its people, has provided us with a history of their lives that would have otherwise been impossible.

More recently, historical archaeologist Leland Ferguson (1992) has written an invaluable book titled *Uncommon Ground: Archaeology and Early African America, 1650–1800*. One important theme of the book is that European-American culture was not simply grafted onto enslaved Africans as eighteenth- and nineteenth-century accounts would have us believe. Ferguson shows quite clearly from the archaeological record of plantations, that black slaves brought their African cultures with them and that many practices like pottery manufacture and house construction endured. In Ferguson's well-documented view, the cultures of Europe, Africa, and Native America all contributed to the development of American culture. This can be seen most clearly in the material evidence of the archaeological record.

The work of Fairbanks, Baker, Geismar, Ferguson, and others goes a long way to make up for the biases inherent in the historical record. It is my perception that of the six genres of historical archaeology's unique contributions to anthropology, this is the most important: providing a historical voice to the otherwise voiceless. Providing that voice to the inhabitants of the Lighthouse is the most important contribution of this book.

Documenting Illicit or Illegal Behaviors

In our own recent past, people have engaged in activities that they wished to leave no record of. In some cases these behaviors may not have been recorded, or any documentation was kept by people outside the group participating in the activity.

Certainly, illicit, illegal, or just plain embarrassing behavior may get short shrift in the written record. For example, although neither illegal nor illicit, it was not then and is not now common knowledge that during some periods of the Revolutionary War at least some soldiers in the Colonial army were so poorly provisioned and so desperate for food they took to killing and eating their own horses. This fact is recorded nowhere in the historical records of the War of Independence, yet the evidence unearthed by archaeologist David Poirier (1976) in his archaeological investigation of the winter encampment of General Israel Putnam in Redding, Connecticut supports this interpretation. His investigations yielded horse bones exhibiting butchering marks and evidence of burning in the excavated fireplaces.

Illegal activities are perhaps even more problematic. For example, Patricia Etter (1980) has found the remains of opium pipes at several railroad camps near Donner Summit, California. These sites date to the late 1860s, when large numbers of Chinese immigrants were entering the United States. By 1882 more than 130,000 Chinese immigrants were living in the western United States. A common occupation for these immigrants was railway construction. Many brought the custom of opium smoking along with them to America. As Etter points out, although there is little documentation of the habit because it was both illegal and practiced by a minority group, there is a rich archaeological record of the tradition, at least as it was conducted in the railroad construction camps. Recognizing the nature of such illegal activities is another area in which archaeology can make a valuable contribution to our understanding of our own history.

Evaluating and Revising Historical Accounts of Known Events

Although not mentioned by Deagan in her list of the unique contributions of historical archaeology, testing or assessing the veracity of historical accounts of known events is another important contribution. History can almost always provide a far more detailed account of some past event, but it should be underscored that histories are written by human beings with all of their biases, vague memories, and misconceptions, along with their tendency to remember things in a favorable light. An excellent example of this is found in a story presumably so well documented that archaeology could provide little more than artifacts for museum displays: the excavation of the site of the Battle of the Little Big Horn, Custer's Last Stand.

Historical synopsis of the battle.   The Sioux and Northern Cheyenne Indian tribes were a potent military force well into the second half of the nineteenth century. In 1866 they had gone to war to prevent white encroachment into their territory in the northern Plains. Called the Red Cloud War, hostilities ceased in 1868 with the signing of the Fort Laramie treaty. In essence, the Indians had won, with all of South Dakota west of the Missouri River ceded to the Sioux. The federal government was obliged to keep white settlers out of this hard-won territory. In return the Indians promised to live on reservations staked out in this domain. Although many natives agreed, others refused, settling neither for the land provided in the treaty nor for the terms of the agreement; they preferred to live their traditional, nomadic way of life, unrestricted by reservation boundaries or territorial borders. The federal government defined all of these non-reservation-living Indians as "hostiles."

In the same year that the Fort Laramie treaty ended hostilities and confirmed Indian ownership of part of South Dakota, rumors of gold in the heart of this territory—the Black Hills—began to filter east. With these rumors came a swarm of white prospectors. Although these gold seekers were clearly in violation of a federal treaty, the government could not let them be harmed. In an attempt to control the Indian population, the federal government ordered the natives to go to the reservation. The consequence of disobedience in the face of this order was made explicit: war.

It is clear in hindsight that the non-reservation Indians who seemed the largest threat to the safety of the illegal prospectors did not have the necessary time, the requisite weather conditions, or the inclination to respond positively to the order to retreat to the reservation. The U.S. government decided in 1876 to wage a war against these "intransigents." Lt. General Philip Sheridan ordered Commanders Cook and Terry to prepare for what amounted to a search-and-destroy mission against the estimated 800 Indian warriors who had refused to come to the reservation. Under Terry's command was the Seventh Cavalry commanded by the 36-year-old Lt. Colonel George Armstrong Custer. The decision to hunt down what was presumed to be a manageably small group of hostiles was to set in motion a series of events that would lead to what historian Robert Utley characterizes as "the most spectacular triumph of the American Indian in his four-century struggle against the relentlessly advancing European civilization. . ." (1969:10).

Much remains unknown about the battle that is called "Custer's Last Stand." We do know that Major Marcus Reno, on a scouting mission with elements of the Seventh Cavalry, had located a sizable Indian trail that, it was presumed, led to an encampment of Indians who had failed to comply with the government's order to move to the reservation. On June 22, 1876, Lt. Colonel Custer set out with a little fewer than 600 enlisted men, 40 Indian scouts, and 20 civilians toward the presumed location of that hostile Indian camp in what is now Montana, far outside the reservation lands of South Dakota (Utley 1969:25). Commanding a swiftly moving cavalry, Custer was to arrive at the Indian village before the other men under Commander Terry.

Custer's primary concern, as well as that of the U.S. Army, was not the possible number of warriors that would be encountered. (They estimated that there were probably around 800 Indians and certainly not more than 1,000. Even alone, it was thought, Custer's better-trained and better-armed soldiers would be more than a match for them.) The primary apprehension of Custer was that the Indians would become aware of his presence and slip away into the hills where they would be hard to track down. Custer's orders were to keep the Indians in place and to do everything he could to ensure that the Indians stood and fought. It is a supreme irony that in this he was remarkably successful.

So concerned was Custer about the possibility that the Sioux would escape the trap being laid for them, he decided to move more quickly than he had been ordered. He did not bypass the Indian encampment and wait until June 26 to launch a coordinated attack with the other more slowly moving regiments as originally planned. Instead, certain that his presence had been detected by the Indians and afraid that this would precipitate their departure and dispersion, he decided to attack immediately on June 25. He hoped and believed that the men of the Seventh Cavalry could by themselves deliver a mortal blow to a larger but poorly trained and poorly armed force of Indians.

In preparation for battle, Custer divided the men under his command into three battalions: Major Reno was placed in control of 140 men, Captain Benteen was given 125 men, and Custer took about 210. Following Custer's orders, these 475 men began a series of movements intended to surround, attack, and defeat an Indian force believed to be not much more than twice their number. Unfortunately for them, there had been a serious miscalculation. Instead of a maximum of 1,000, there were at least 2,000 and as many as 4,000 Indian warriors in an encampment of more than 10,000 Sioux and Cheyenne men, women, and children.

At about 2:15 P.M. on June 25, Major Reno, moving into position before the battle, encountered a small party of Indian warriors. Reno and his men took chase only to realize too late that they had been drawn into combat with an enormous force of Indians. Hopelessly outnumbered, Reno's battalion retreated, losing in a very short time about one third of its men (probably about 52 soldiers were killed in this initial engagement).

Following Custer's orders, Benteen's battalion had marched to the southeast to prevent any escape of the Indians in that direction. Because Benteen found no such escape in progress, he turned back along the trail. In the process he was met by Custer's trumpeter John Martin, carrying a message from Custer's adjutant Lt. William Cooke. The scrawled note read: "Benteen, Come on. Big Village, be quick, bring packs. P.S. bring pacs [sic]." Benteen and his men responded but were only able to get to the scene of Reno's besiegement and join his battalion. The men under Reno and Benteen became surrounded and cut off from the rest of the Seventh Cavalry.

We know about Reno and Benteen's predicament and actions because although their battalions had been mauled, there were survivors—Reno and Benteen among them. When reinforcements arrived, the enormous Indian encampment scattered and Reno, Benteen, and their men were spared. As Utley points out, however, in the case of Custer and the 210 men under his command, "No man can know with certainty how Custer's battalion met its fate for no member survived . . . [T]he details of the action, together with Custer's intentions and the factors which shaped them, must ever remain a mystery" (1969:31).

This pessimistic view is a bit of an overstatement since there are other sources of information concerning the battle. Although it is true there were no survivors among Custer's men, it is estimated that the Indians lost only about 30 to 150 men in the entire battle (Scott et al. 1989:13). Historians have reconstructed elements of the battle on the basis of interviews with Indian warriors who participated. (See Utley [1969:50-55] and Graham [1953] for transcripts of some of this testimony as well as the testimony of survivors in Reno's and Benteen's battalions.)

Battle of the Little Big Horn: The physical evidence.   Beyond the historical documentation, there is the physical evidence of the battle itself. The battle-field, along with being a national monument, is also an archaeological site.

On June 28, 1876 the survivors in Reno's battalion quickly buried the dead of the Custer battle, often in extremely shallow graves, ostensibly precisely where they had fallen in battle. In 1877 and in 1879 the dead were reburied in deeper, more secure graves. The locations were then marked with wooden crosses. The bodies of the officers and civilians were exhumed and returned to their families for reburial. Custer's remains were removed to West Point for burial. In 1881 all of Custer's soldiers—at least all that could be found—were disinterred and reburied in a mass grave at the location of a granite battlefield memorial, but the crosses which formerly marked their burial sites were left in place. In 1890 these wooden crosses were replaced with permanent marble markers (Figure 2.3).

The positioning of the markers, apparently reflecting the final locations of Custer's men at the climax of the battle, has long been used to reconstruct the final moments of the struggle. Several writers have suggested that the markers, often grouped in pairs, reflect the final strategy of the Seventh Cavalry soldiers. Surrounded and outnumbered, it appears that the soldiers clustered in pairs to better defend themselves. In an official report of the Custer National Monument prepared in 1890, O. J. Sweet proposed that 43 pairs of markers represented the locations of "bunkmates" who bravely fought and died together (as cited in Scott et al. 1989:50).

Although approximately 210 men died with Custer on June 25, the number of markers has fluctuated through the years; today there are 252, and there have been as many as 262 (Scott et al. 1989:51). How can the discrepancy between the number of soldiers who died with Custer and the number of markers be explained? This is a crucial consideration if the location of the markers is used to reconstruct the last moments of the Battle of the Little Big Horn. The mystery has been approached through archaeology.

Archaeological excavations have been conducted at the site on a number of occasions, most recently in 1984 and 1985 (Scott and Fox 1984; Scott et al. 1989). Block excavations were conducted in the vicinity of 37 of the

Figure 2.3   The marble markers at the Little Big Horn battlefield are supposed to represent the actual spots where the bodies of Custer and his men were found on the day following the battle. The area around many of these markers has been excavated in an attempt to better understand how the battle progressed, and how it ended.

252 extant markers. (See Chapter 7.) Eleven of these 37 represented markers immediately adjacent to another—the so-called "paired" markers. The remains of most of the soldiers had been exhumed by 1881, but the archaeologists felt certain the Army's reburial detail could not have recovered 100 percent of the skeletal and archaeological material. What remained, the archaeologists hoped, would provide important information concerning the final moments of Custer's Last Stand.

The hope and expectation were well founded. The excavators discovered human and artifactual remains surrounding most of the marble markers (Figure 2.4). Interestingly, none of the paired markers, however, produced the bones of more than a single soldier. For example, in the excavation around Markers 67 and 68, fragments of human ribs, vertebrae, and skull were found—all from the same person. Also found in this unit were the csteological remains of a horse. Perhaps as Scott et al. suggest (1989:62), the 1881 reburial detail did not have the expertise to distinguish fragmentary horse bones from human bones and assumed that two soldiers had fallen in this spot.

Scott et al. (1989:50) also point out that another scenario explains some of the paired markers. After the battle, each of Custer's soldiers was indeed buried where he fell. The soil was dry and hard and shovels were in short

Figure 2.4   Excavation around one set of the paired markers at the Custer battlefield. The bone lying on the ground in the right side of the photograph is a human femur (thigh bone) recovered during excavation. (Courtesy Douglas Scott.)

supply. Although some effort was made to bury the officers deeply enough so that animals, wind, or rain would not disturb their remains, most enlisted men were covered with only a thin veneer of earth taken from either side of their bodies. Later details may have interpreted the dual depressions left from this process as two shallow graves and marked them as such.

Thus the position of the markers does *not* support an interpretation of pairs of soldiers fighting in tandem against insurmountable odds. More often than not, the markers were placed where individual men of the Seventh Cavalry fell on the battlefield.

The archaeology of the battlefield, therefore, has helped dispel one battle scenario at the same time that it has, in a general sense, validated the significance of the location of the markers. As a result we can today obtain a better understanding of the final moments of the battle; archaeology has provided tangible evidence where the testimony of the participants does not exist.

In the case of the Lighthouse, we find ourselves in a similar situation. As we will see, the inhabitants of the Lighthouse were not literate and so left no written account of their own story. Others, however, have been more than willing to recount the legend of the Lighthouse village. In fact, in Chapter 3 we will focus on the most important rendering of the legend—a

115-page poetic account written nearly 100 years after the site was abandoned. Again, the archaeological record will enable us in a material way to assess the veracity of that and other accounts.

CONCLUSION

Interpreters of aerial photographs refer to "ground truth," the actual conditions on the ground hinted at through remote photography. Here too we can talk about ground truth—the actual conditions viewed on the ground and discernable through archaeological investigation hinted at by the historical record. Archaeology can provide a baseline of ground truth by providing material evidence through which history can be assessed.

There is another ingredient of the material record which is perhaps equally important, although beyond the realm of cool, dispassionate, scientific discourse. Archaeology of any period provides what archaeologist James Deetz (1980) calls cultural "texture." Even where we can read about a people from our own historical past, we would like more—we need more. Our desire for sensory validation is reflected in our clichés: We say that "seeing is believing," something believable is said to have "the ring of truth," an explanation may be said to "just feel right." It is one thing to be able to read about the Puritan settlers of Plimoth, or about nineteenth century Wyoming cowboys, African-American slaves, Chinese immigrants to the West Coast, the men in the Seventh Cavalry, or the inhabitants of the Lighthouse; it is quite another thing to be able to hold an object in your hand that was a part of these people's lives. Perhaps even if historical archaeology could provide us with no distinctive insights, even if it could add nothing new to the historical record, it would be worth doing simply for this—the tangible sense it provides of our own past. This by itself is reason enough for doing historical archaeology, though clearly it provides much more.

Chapter 3

THE LEGEND OF THE LIGHTHOUSE

The tale of the Lighthouse has been repeated for more than a hundred years, passed down across the generations in the northwestern corner of Connecticut. It is a story phrased in rebellion, in race, and in love.

Although it has attained the status of legend, the Lighthouse was a real place where real people lived. Because so much of what we presume to know about the Lighthouse is part of the myth, we should begin by telling the legend of the Lighthouse village and the Lighthouse "tribe."

LEWIS SPRAGUE MILLS: A SOURCE FOR THE LEGEND

There have been a number of attempts to commit the chronicle of the Lighthouse to paper. In 1894 John Gibbins, a Barkhamsted native (Barkhamsted Hollow; *Winsted Herald* 1894), wrote a play based on the Lighthouse story. But certainly, the most detailed and embellished rendering of the Lighthouse legend appears in a 115-page poem written by Lewis Sprague Mills (1952).

Mills, a well-known Connecticut educator, was born in 1874 in the small rural village of Canton Center, located within the incorporated town of Canton, Connecticut. He attended Columbia University in New York City and returned to his home state where he worked for 54 years as a rural school supervisor (Obituaries, *Hartford Times*, March 8, 1965). Mills had an abiding interest in history, especially local history. As a result, he wrote numerous articles about Connecticut's past, a book titled *The State of Connecticut*, as well as the work that is our focus here, *The Legend of the Barkhamsted Light House*.

The form of Mills's book-length poem was taken from the Finnish epic poem *Kalevala*, also the model for Longfellow's *Hiawatha*. As you read the excerpts included here, you will recognize the meter as being the same as in Longfellow's work.

Mills presents the story as a legend, but one rooted in historical truth. Many of the details provided in Mills's account are impossible to verify and are romantic embellishments that Mills either heard from others or invented himself. This is no indictment of Mills. He deserves enormous credit for saving the legend and recording it in his book. Nevertheless, when discussing Mills's account, we should keep in mind the comments of George Utley, a Barkhamsted native also fascinated by the Lighthouse legend. He wrote the introduction to Mills's 1952 edition of the poem, where, regarding the actual facts of the Lighthouse, he states that Mills "romanticized them with the license which we willingly grant to poets." Also remember that Mills titled his book *The* Legend *of the Barkhamsted Light House*. Mills is explicit in a number of places, both in his introductory remarks and in the poem itself, that he had not prepared a work of science or history. His goal, as he himself stated, was to preserve a legend—a legend based on historical truth. In that he certainly succeeded admirably.

THE LEGEND OF THE LIGHTHOUSE: MOLLY BARBER

> Near the winding Tunxis River,
> Where the groaning mills and presses,
> Flow with sweet and luscious cider
> In the sunny days of autumn
> Lingers yet this ancient legend
> Told by fathers to their children
> Gathered round the supper table
> When the candle light is feeble
> And the wind is in the chimney (Mills 1952:6).

Thus does Mills introduce the Lighthouse legend, a story repeated from generation to generation. In poetic format, he tells his version of the story of the Lighthouse:

> Where now grow the birch and alder,
> Hardy maple, oak and walnut,
> Graceful hemlocks, lofty pine trees,
> Spreading up the shady hill-side,
> Hill-side stoney, steep, and rocky,
> Was a ragged group of cabins,

Dwelt in by a people blended,
Partly white and partly Indian,
Partly from the early settlers,
And the vagabonds of travel (p. 9).

How was this lonely wilderness outpost established and peopled?
Mills's rendering of the story begins with Peter Barber and his daughter
Molly, born in 1715. Molly's childhood in a wealthy household is not com-
mented on, but is central to the tale. When she reached marriageable age,
she fell in love with a man, according to Mills, far beneath her station as the
daughter of Peter Barber, "the richest man" (p. 11) living in the Connecticut
River community of Wethersfield, Connecticut (Figure 3.1).

In a theme common to romantic literary works, although Molly had
found her true love, her father was not appropriately impressed by her suitor
and forbade her marriage to him:

Choose a richer man my daughter,
Never shall you wed this fellow,
Born to toil and lowly labor.
Let him find a slave his equal,
Here among the village wenches.
Seek a richer man, my daughter,
From the suitors that surround you (p. 15).

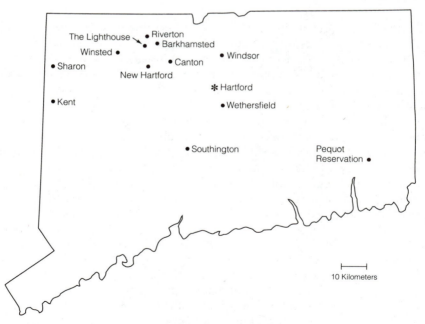

Figure 3.1   A map of Connecticut, indicating the locations of important
places in the Lighthouse legend, including that of the village itself.

Following this romantic literary format and theme, Mills has Molly rebel against her father's command. Instead of running off with her lover as in, for example, *Romeo and Juliet*, the young heroine of our drama presented her father with a threat:

> Cross me now and I will marry
> The man who first may seek my hand,
> Whether white or any color (p. 16).

Taking advantage of poetic license, Mills includes this last line to portend Molly's actions. According to Mills, Peter Barber became obsessed with preventing Molly's marriage to the unsuitable suitor. Apparently, he also became so concerned about her threat to marry whoever might next ask for her hand that he posted a guard around his house to isolate his daughter from contact with the world outside their mansion. Molly, trapped like the fairy-tale Rapunzel in her tower prison, could neither run off with her lover nor carry out her threat to marry anyone else who might ask.

Nevertheless, Peter Barber's protection was incomplete; he made one fateful mistake when he hired a young vagabond to work in the garden at the Barber home.

THE LEGEND OF THE LIGHTHOUSE: JAMES CHAUGHAM

Peter Barber perceived this young man as no threat to the fulfillment of Molly's ultimatum. As headstrong as Molly was adjudged to be by her father, as angry as her father's actions made her, and as serious as her ultimatum may have been, she was not crazy. The man hired to work in the garden was, after all, an Indian of the Narragansett tribe, born on Block Island off the coast of Rhode Island. He was an itinerant worker, having moved to the mainland and traveled up the Connecticut River, learning the ways of the white settlers and doing odd jobs for his subsistence. He may even have been a half-breed with a Spanish mother. Peter Barber probably felt that Molly would never fulfill her threat by marrying a half-breed vagabond.

The young man's name was James Chaugham. He was, by Mills's accounting, a fascinating man who could move easily between the two cultures of the native and the settler. Of his appearance, Mills states:

> Tall and straight and very handsome
> Was this Narragansett suitor,
> Once a savage from the forest
> With a face with paint resplendent,
> And a head-dress gay with plumage
> From the feathered inmates
> Of the forest dense and dusky (p. 20).

SPELLING THE FAMILY NAME

Several different spellings of the Chaugham family name are reflected in the historical record: Chagum, Chogam, Choggum, Chaugum, Chaugorn, Choccum, and so on. The lack of a standard spelling for a family name may seem peculiar to us, but it was common, especially for nonliterate people, in preceding centuries. As will be shown, the Chaughams and the first few generations of their descendants could not write. This means that in every instance where the family name shows up in a document in the eighteenth and nineteenth centuries, a nonfamily member—town clerk, census enumerator, probate administrator—wrote the name phonetically, spelling it as it was heard. In addition, Chaugham is non-English and its pronunciation was likely unfamiliar to those who recorded it in official records or news accounts. An argument can be made to spell the name according to its earliest appearance in the documentary record (Chagum), but I think this would add unnecessary confusion, especially for Connecticut readers of this book who are familiar with the story of the Lighthouse from the Mills poem. The spelling I have used here—Chaugham—is the one most commonly used in twentieth-century publications about the Lighthouse.

Mills describes Chaugham's cultural upbringing in this way:

> On his feet his shoes of deer-skin,
> On his head the plumes of eagles,
> Traveled softly by the rivers
> While his honored father taught him
> How to fish with bow and arrow
> How to shoot the flying squirrel,
> How to trail the wary roebuck,
> How to build a humble dwelling (pp. 21–22).

Mills then details Chaugham's acculturation to the ways of the white settlers along the Connecticut River (Mills calls it the "Central River"):

> Later lived he in a village,
> In a house and not a wigwam,
> "Many moons" among the settlers
> In the hamlet by the river,
> By the mighty Central River,
> Where the big canoes were floating
> On the cove beside the village.
>   Educated too, this Indian,
> In the manner and the customs,
> In the language, and the habits

Of the whiteman's way of living,
Dressed in shirt and coat and trousers,
Seemed he hardly from the forest
But as one with habitation
In a home of gentle culture (p. 22).

Perhaps Peter Barber underestimated the seriousness of Molly's threat. Perhaps Molly saw in James an opportunity to escape the tyrannical rule of her father while punishing him in the only way she could—by eloping with a man who would surely seem even worse than her first choice. Or, perhaps it was love that brought the young white woman and the wandering Narragansett together. This is Mills's belief, and there is no evidence to dispute his claim. Whatever the actual case, James Chaugham became Molly's suitor.

So outlandish was the possibility that Molly would become involved with the Indian, Peter Barber did not become suspicious. Mills, in his romantic rendering, had Chaugham give Molly a rose. They then began to meet regularly in the garden and Molly decided to fulfill her threat and marry Chaugham. The couple soon began to plot their escape from the sumptuous prison constructed by Molly's father.

THE THEME OF THE CAPTIVE

One of the themes of the poem that still fascinates modern readers is the notion of a young, pampered white woman from a well-to-do eighteenth-century New England family abandoning that life and forsaking friends, family, and comfort to be with the man she loves. As Mills puts it:

Hied the maiden to the Redman,
Turned her back on life luxurious,
Left her father's lofty mansion,
By the mighty Central River,
All its ways polite and social,
All the acres broad and fertile,
Of which she was the only heiress;
All her mother's kind caresses,
Smiles and love and kindly counsels,
All her many ardent suitors,
Hoping with this dusky Indian
She might live as spouse and partner (p. 24).

Although Molly left the comfort of white society of her own accord, Mills was following in a long tradition of other literary works produced in North America that presented the theme of a young, "civilized" person forced to live among the "savages." An entire genre of literature, the *Puritan captivity narrative*, was popular in the late seventeenth and early eighteenth centuries. As Sieminski (1990) describes, though based on true stories, these tales of the capture and captivity of whites—often women and/or children—by Indians were powerful metaphors for many Americans. Captivity was viewed initially as a form of "divine testing," and captives' rejection of the Indian ways was seen, as Sieminski states, as tantamount to rejecting the ways of Satan.

As Puritanism waned, however, captivity narratives focused more on celebrating the initiation of civilized whites into the mysterious and somehow envied ways of the uncivilized Indians. This latter perspective allowed Europeans to maintain the precepts of their own cultural upbringing at the same time that it celebrated learning valuable lessons from the more nature-oriented culture of the Indians. This laudatory view of acculturation to Indian ways became a compelling theme in the late eighteenth century.

For example, the *Narrative of the Life of Mrs. Mary Jemison* (Seaver 1918) tells the story of a woman captured in 1755, when she was just 12 years old, by Indians of the Seneca Nation. She was raised by the Seneca, married, bore eight children, and raised them herself. She lived on the Seneca reservation in New York State until she died in 1833. She lived not just among the Seneca but *as* a Seneca, for nearly 80 years. She learned to cook, plant, tend, and harvest corn; to butcher animals; and to preserve meat and prepare hides for clothing.

Initially a captive, Mary Jemison later stayed with the Seneca of her own free will:

> I had been with the Indians four summers and four winters, and had become so far accustomed to their mode of living, habits and disposi-tions, that my anxiety to get away, to be set at liberty, and leave them, had almost subsided (Seaver 1918:46).

Mary Jemison's story, first published in 1840 and reprinted many times, has intrigued people for years. Although her conversion to Indian culture was not consensual, at least not at first, the theme of the narrative is similar in some ways to Mills's rendering of Molly Barber's story.

The captivity narrative moves us even today. One of the most interest-ing characters and the person many are most drawn to in the book and movie *Dances With Wolves* is Stands With Fist, the woman raised by the Lakota Sioux after having been kidnapped by them as a child. Part of the fas-cination of the story of Molly Barber and the reason, in Mills's poem at least, she is the principal character is that we are drawn to the story of a protected, pampered individual—perhaps particularly a woman—who must learn to live the life of a "wild Indian," and who succeeds.

THE EXODUS

In the year 1740, Mills asserts, Molly and James were married, ostensibly by a justice of the peace who was a trusted friend of Molly, but apparently not of

Peter Barber. The couple left Wethersfield and traveled northwest to what is now the town of Canton, Connecticut:

> Secret was their quick departure,
> In the night time stealing westward—
> Molly with her cloak about her,
> Followed Chaugham ever closely,
> O'er the Talcott Mountain speeding,
> Crossing Farmington's broad meadows,
> Turning northward 'gainst the river,
> 'Till they reached an Indian village
> In the foot-hills of the mountains,
> Near the swiftly flowing Tunxis (p. 26).

On a terrace overlooking Cherry Brook, not far north of its confluence with the Farmington (Tunxis) River, the married runaways joined a small group of Indians led by the "sachem," or chief, Tomo. Mills is unclear whether this was a planned, temporary stop in their journey westward, or if the couple intended to live out their lives among the 20 or so wigwams that made up this small village. Whatever the case, Mills states that James and Molly remained for only one "moon"—about a month.

In that month, according to Mills, Molly began to transform, peeling away the layers of civilization she had accumulated during her childhood years. Her metamorphosis included learning the ways of the Indian. In her new existence she:

> Carried water from the river,
> Pounded corn and mended blankets,
> Seemed a simple Indian woman (p. 33).

In the meantime, as the rich city girl became a pioneer woman, her father had not given up hope of finding her and returning her to her home in Wethersfield among her civilized kin. Search parties were on the trail of the couple:

> Slowly through the gloomy forests,
> From the mighty Central River,
> Came the Constable and Sheriff (p. 36).

And, as Mills tells it, they caught up with the couple in the village along Cherry Brook:

> When the sun was high at midday,
> In the valley of the Tunxis,
> Came they to the Indian village (p. 36).

James and Molly were in the village when the searchers entered, but in their month of hiding, Molly's transformation had progressed to such a degree that she was unrecognizable to her pursuers. She was dressed like the other Indian women, her blond curls "greased and blackened," and her pale skin "stained all dark and dusky" (p. 33). Peter Barber's minions left, unaware they had looked their quarry in the eye and not recognized her. They saw just another Indian woman and continued their search, never to encounter Molly or James again.

Although unrecognized this time, James and Molly still feared capture. Perhaps alarmed that they might not be as lucky if more perceptive pursuers were on their trail—even Peter Barber himself—James and Molly knew they needed to move on, farther into the wilderness of western Connecticut beyond Peter Barber's long reach.

With saddened hearts, James and Molly, helped by their friends on Cherry Brook, trekked west:

> When the morning sun was shining,
> Molly Barber and her husband,
> With the aid of Tomo's sannups[1]
> Bearing axes and equipment
> Hastened northward through the forest,
> Ever near the Tunxis River,
> To the side of Ragged Mountain
> In the town of fair Barkhamsted,
> And beside the sparkling river
> Found a place for habitation,
> Builded there a lonely cabin,
> Midst the trees beside the mountain,
> Built a cabin in the Greenwoods,
> Deep within the gloomy shadows.
> First of all the early cabins
> Built within Barkhamsted borders (pp. 40–41).

This was to become a thriving village, a village to be called the Light-house, where James and Molly were to find peace, raise a family, and live out their lives. (See book cover. Looking north along the Farmington River, Ragged Mountain looms in the background. The Lighthouse village was built on the slope of Ragged Mountain.)

And so, in Mills's story, a young white woman, in order to punish a tyrannical father who had prevented her marriage to a man she loved but who was beneath her social and economic station in life, left the safe confines of a wealthy family, married a virtual stranger, abandoned her culture and upbringing, and finally found herself in a crudely built cabin in the

---

[1] An archaic term for married adult Indian men.

wilderness. This would have been a remarkable journey for a young woman of any period, and all the more so in 1740. And yet, according to Mills's poetic rendering, all of the travails and hardships Molly faced could not compare to the wrath of her father:

> Oft she whispered in the darkness,
> "Better face the catamountains,[2]
> Better face the bears and panthers,
> Better hear the wild wolves howling
> Than an angry father shouting" (p. 41).

A NEW LIFE IN THE WILDERNESS

Molly could not go back to her old life now. She had little choice but to adapt. And adapt she did. After nearly a month, the young Molly who had been raised in the environment of wealthy, privileged Europeans was almost gone, replaced by a hardy "Indian" woman, knowledgeable in the ways of nature and ready to live out her life in the wilderness.

Mills lists the names of the Chaugham children, all born and raised in the wilderness community of the Lighthouse village. The children—Samuel, Solomon, Mary, Mercy, Sally, Polly, Elizabeth, and Hannah—were all given English names, but had faces that, in Mills's words, betrayed their Indian heritage.

The children were raised in the cultures of both Europe and Native America. Molly taught her offspring the tenets of Christianity while James taught them Narragansett spiritual beliefs as well as the survival skills needed in the wilderness. The children turned out as an amalgam of European and Native American:

> With a background partly whiteman,
> From the sayings of their mother;
> With a background partly Indian,
> From the sayings of their father,
> Growing up they roamed the valley,
> Traveled often through the township,
> Mingled daily with the natives,
> Meeting many, making friendships (p. 48).

The family thrived as it grew, subsisting on the natural produce of the rich forest and on the crops they planted:

> Oft they hunted through the forest
> For the rabbit and the squirrel.
> Oft they labored by the river

---

[2] Mountain lions.

Building swift canoes for sailing.
Often in the shallow water,
Spearing eels and trout and suckers[3] (p. 55).

The men hunted, Mills states, not with firearms, but with bows and arrows, while in an "ancient mortar" (p. 70) Molly pounded the corn they grew.

One of the children, Sally, died in childhood, and another, Elizabeth, never married. The rest did marry, as their village lost its once nearly absolute isolation and European settlement of the western hills of Connecticut began to expand. Mills lists the names of the spouses of James and Molly's children:

Samuel married Green of Sharon,
Mercy married Isaac Jacklin.
Polly married William Wilson,
Mary Chaugham married Webster,
Hannah married Reuben Barber
(Barber's parents were from Canton),
Solomon and Hayes were married
In the Ragged Mountain cabin (p. 49).

Some of the children stayed in their parents' environs, building cabins of their own on the side of Ragged Mountain. At least initially, Solomon and his wife "Miss Hayes" stayed on, as did Mary and her husband "Old Gum Webster," Polly and her spouse William Wilson, and the unmarried Elizabeth. Mills states that at first, "two of Molly Barber's children dug new cellars on the hill-side" (p. 55). Later in the poem, and presumably, later in time, Mills counts 30 cabins in the village (p. 56), and, eventually, he states there were 32 cabins in the Lighthouse community (p. 90).

In any event, with these marriages came grandchildren, and the village continued to expand:

In the cabins in the village—
Light House children, more descendants,
Children playing on the hill-side,
Children playing by the river,
Children swimming in the river
In the pleasant days of summer (p. 55).

THE "LIGHTHOUSE"

As the years passed, an increasing number of white settlers invaded the once sparsely populated western forest. Commerce between growing towns

---

[3] Thick-lipped freshwater fish.

increased, as did commerce between communities in New York State and Connecticut. Roads, often following aboriginal trails, were built to facilitate trade and travel. In 1772, by Mills's telling, a stagecoach road was built along the Farmington River within sight of James and Molly's village. The road was improved in 1798 and incorporated into the Farmington River Turnpike, a feeder road of the Albany Turnpike that carried travelers between Albany and Hartford. As Mills characterizes it:

> More and more the white man traveled,
> So the road-way by the river
> Was improved for stage coach service
> In the year of sev'nteen hundred—
> Eight and ninety—turnpike road-way
> Past the lonely Light House village (pp. 58–59).

Herein, according to Mills, rests the solution to the enigmatic name — the "Lighthouse"—given to a settlement of Indian, white, and black outcasts in a town some 60 miles from the coast. It was the stagecoach drivers on the old Farmington River Turnpike who named the hamlet. These drivers, journeying from Albany to Hartford, passed through a sparsely populated wilderness. Small, isolated Indian villages lay scattered throughout the forest, but there were no established towns, no landmarks, no signs of civilization on their route until they reached the rural town of New Hartford, Connecticut, some 100 miles from Albany and 25 miles from Hartford (see Figure 3.1). New Hartford had an inn and a tavern, and road-weary travelers from Albany stopped there to rest and refresh themselves before embarking on the final leg of what was a wearisome and difficult trip.

The small outpost of James and Molly was the first sign of settlement and civilization (of a sort) on the road from Albany. When coach drivers, possessing no odometers or accurate maps, saw the light from the hearth fires visible through gaps in the walls of the crudely constructed cabins on the side of Ragged Mountain, they knew they were only a few miles from the inn at New Hartford:

> Passing on the lonely turnpike,
> In the year of eighteen hundred
> And the years that slowly followed,
> Through the dim and fearful shadows,
> Where the mists hung dark and heavy,
> When the great owls hooted sadly,
> Nightly came the stage a-creaking
> On its journey to New Hartford.
> Seeing light within the forest,
> "There's the Light House!" cried the driver,
> "Five more miles to reach New Hartford!"
> Thus was named the ancient village,

Village of Barkhamsted Indians,
On the side of Ragged Mountain,
By the winding Tunxis River (p. 59).

So, in a sense, the Lighthouse village served a function similar to that of
a coastal lighthouse, guiding weary travelers to their "port." We can suggest
that the Lighthouse was aptly named for another reason, one the stagecoach
drivers on the Farmington River Turnpike did not intend. The village itself
was, indeed, a safe harbor for people who could not find one in the larger
society, a settlement where they could live out their lives in peace. The
Lighthouse was like a beacon, directing the landless and disenfranchised outcasts of society to a village that would accept them.

The village flourished, and time wore on. In 1800 James Chaugham
died. He was buried in a community cemetery that contained the remains of
young Sally and would eventually include, according to Mills, 50 of the
Lighthouse people. Some of the gravesites bore no memorial marking their
locations. Others, including that of James, patriarch of the settlement, were
marked with simple, uninscribed, upright fieldstones.

Then too, the young woman who had abandoned her comfortable life
for a lifelong adventure in the wilderness, who had become a great grandmother many times over, and who was the matriarch of this intensely interesting community, also died:

When the autumn moon was yellow
And the forest colors fading;
When the maple leaves were falling,
Floating on the Tunxis waters,
And the birds were southward flying
In the pleasant Indian summer,
Thus 'tis written in the records,
Granny Chaugham's days were over,
All her joys and sorrows ended
For she died in eighteen twenty—
And her age—*one hundred five years* (p. 71).

Describing the funeral of Molly Chaugham, Mills states:

Then they bore her to the graveyard,
Left her there alone in silence,
With a field-stone for a marker.
Molly's life and work were ended.
Burdened by her father's anger,
She had struggled on unbroken,
Hidden in the gloomy forest,
On the side of Ragged Mountain
In the town of fair Barkhamsted (p. 72).

Molly, so it seems, had been the social glue that kept the community together. For perhaps 40 years following her death, decreasing numbers of her descendants inhabited the village, as social forces pulled children, grand-children, and great grandchildren to other communities and other towns.

> After Molly's sad departure,
> To the Land of the Hereafter,
> Dwelt Elizabeth, unmarried,
> And a couple village children,
> Safely in the lonely Chaugham cabin,
> On the side of Ragged Mountain.
> As the years were rolling onward,
> Few the children in the village,
> Scattered were the Light House people,
> Through the State and through the nation,
> Seeking other habitations (p. 74).

With only Elizabeth and a few children remaining, the village continued a slow process of decay until the cabins began to deteriorate. In 1854, Elizabeth died. The final inhabitant of the village, Elizabeth was buried in the Lighthouse graveyard. The remaining descendants of James and Molly had already scattered to the surrounding towns of Colebrook, Winchester, Harwinton, and Woodbury.

THE LEGACY OF THE LIGHTHOUSE

And thus, the legend of the Lighthouse ends. Mills presents a fitting tribute to the founding couple and to all their descendants. Although James and Molly are gone, they left a legacy, Mills asserts, that will never be forgotten:

> On the side of Ragged Mountain,
> In the town of fair Barkhamsted,
> By the rolling Tunxis River
> Generations speeding onward
> In an ever widening circle,
> Carry far the blood of Chaugham
> And his spouse, brave Molly Barber
> Through the ages still they journey,
> Ever more and more descendants,
> From the Ragged Mountain cabin,
> Home of fearless Molly Barber
> And her spouse, the Honest Chaugham (p. 97).

The legend as told by Mills is thus complete. A brave, young, and improbable couple, fighting against the will of European society and the odds imposed by a harsh wilderness, succeeded to an astonishing degree. They did far more than merely survive, they thrived, creating a remarkable village made up of society's discards. They left hundreds of descendants, who today, although they may have forgotten the story of their own ancestors, still carry the blood of James and Molly.

It is a compelling story. Although this is where the legend ends, with the death of James and Molly's daughter Elizabeth and the abandonment of the village, this is where our work truly begins. We need to assess the historicity of the legend. Was there a racially mixed, pioneer outpost established in the western hills of the Farmington Valley by a white woman and her Narragansett Indian husband? Did they have eight children, most of whom married and had children themselves in the village? How did they survive? What was the dynamic of their relationship with the outside world? And what truly happened to the people of the Lighthouse? In our attempt to answer such questions, we can begin by examining the sources of the legend as used by Mills.

Chapter 4

SOURCES OF THE LIGHTHOUSE LEGEND

The Lighthouse legend presented by Lewis Mills is fairly complete. The characters are fleshed out, the drama is detailed, and the tale is internally consistent. The question remains, however, how much, if any of it, is accurate? We can begin to assess the veracity of the Mills account by examining his sources.

We should keep three things in mind throughout this discussion. First, Mills clearly was dedicated to preserving the legend of the Lighthouse. An advertisement for his book that appeared in a local magazine stated that Mills spent 20 years investigating "the greatest of all New England Indian legends" (The Barkhamsted Lighthouse. *Lure of the Litchfield Hills* 1952).

Second, Mills had no intention of writing an objective, dispassionate history of the Lighthouse village. He was preserving a *legendary* account of an actual place. Mills should not be criticized for *not* doing that which he did not intend to do—write an authentic history of the Lighthouse settlement. As Mills knew, the legend was based on kernels of truth, but many of the details necessary for writing a complete, objective, and accurate history of the Lighthouse were unknown—and likely unknowable at the time he wrote his poem.

Third, today we have a much wider array of sources of information than did Mills. It is far easier for us to reconstruct the actual story using the original documents than it would have been for him. Beyond this, Mills was not an archaeologist and so did not have access to the material record—the "ground truth" we talked about in Chapter 2—beyond the Lighthouse story.

MILLS'S SOURCES

Mills based his rendering of the Lighthouse legend on very few sources simply because there were so few available at the time. Recognizing the nature of Mills's intention to keep the legend alive and within the limitations of his access to primary records, what evidence did he use? He provided an explicit list of his references and even included excerpts from some of his major sources in the 1952 publication of the poem.

Mills used only four major sources to reconstruct the main part of the legend, including the story of Molly and James's elopement, their settlement on the slope of Ragged Mountain, and the raising of a family. Those sources were: an article published in the local newspaper, the *Mountain County Herald*, on September 30, 1854; the published version of local historian William Wallace Lee's address presented at the celebration of Barkhamsted's centennial in 1879 (Lee 1881); an article published in the *Connecticut Courant* on January 29, 1900; and an article published in the *Winsted Evening Citizen* on March 3, 1933.

We can now turn our attention to the sources that Mills used, assess their importance, and determine the level of confidence Mills placed in them, as well as the degree to which we can rely on their veracity.

The *Mountain County Herald*, 1854

The *Mountain County Herald* was a small, rural newspaper. It began publication in 1853 in the town of Winsted, Connecticut, a minor industrial hub in the northwestern corner of the state in the nineteenth century. The *Mountain County Herald* became the *Winsted Herald* in 1858 and eventually ceased publication in 1900.

The *Mountain County Herald* piece, published in 1854, though very short, was extremely important to Mills—and still is to us—because it represents an eyewitness description of the Lighthouse village by a reporter who actually visited the occupied site. People, presumably descendants of James and Molly, still lived in the village when the anonymous *Herald* reporter conducted his investigation.

Mills mentions and excerpts the article in an appendix to the 1952 publication of his poem. Although relying to an extent on this newspaper account, Mills maintains a different perspective from that of the reporter about the Lighthouse locality as well as about the inhabitants. Mills's opinion of the Lighthouse is one predicated on admiration, fascination, and respect. On the other hand, to say that the reporter was not terribly impressed by the condition of the inhabitants, nor by their way of life, would be a supreme understatement. Of the environmental context of the site location, the reporter wrote:

The "Light-House" is situated upon the East band [sic] of the Farmington River, in Barkhamsted, some twenty-five miles north-west of the city of Hartford, and a more desolate, rocky and forlorn looking locality it is impossible to conceive.

Having dispensed with the site surroundings, the reporter then characterized the habitation:

It consists of some four or five huts, or shanties, built upon the side-hill, under over-hanging rocks . . . Said huts are built after a style of architecture about half-way between a wood-pile and a log fence, and, surrounded as they are by rocks, and scraggy stunted trees, with no outward signs of comfort within, have an appearance of utter destitution and starving indolence.

Finally, the writer, Mills's primary eyewitness to the occupied Lighthouse village, described the human inhabitants of the settlement. The reporter was no more impressed by the appearance of the people than he was by the scenery or the architecture:

Around these habitations, (for such as they are,) the passer-by will discover from five to twenty half-clad specimens of the *genus homo*, of every possible size, and shade of color—from that of the thick-lipped curly pated African—through the red of the Indian and the yellow of the Mulatto to the white of the Anglo-Saxon race. These colors have been mingled and commingled by the amalgamation of the different races for so many generations that the observer will be much troubled to decide whether they are black, red or white, half bloods, or quarter bloods, or whether they have any distinctive marks of any one race about them.

The writer alleged that the Lighthouse inhabitants were mostly alcoholics, frequenting local taverns where they begged for the money necessary to support their habit.

The writer was mystified, however, that although the people of the Lighthouse clearly lived a miserable and unenviable existence—at least as far as he was concerned—they seemed to be quite happy:

These little bipeds gaze upon the occasional traveler by their home with as much nonchalance as though they were the sons and daughters of the most aristocratic of the land, and they apparently receive as much enjoyment in their wild and uncouth gambols upon the rugged mountains and rocks that surround their isolated habitations, as those who revel in all the luxurious indolence that wealth can furnish.

Apparently the reporter attempted to disabuse the Lighthouse inhabitants of their satisfaction with their way of life. Even though they accepted the charity of local people, the Lighthouse inhabitants seemed to the reporter to be not terribly charitable in accepting advice on how to "better" themselves. Such advice, stated the reporter, they "resent in language not particularly adapted to ears polite." The reporter remained unconvinced concerning the genuine happiness of people living in what he considered squalor.

Much of the article clearly was editorializing, but Mills obviously incorporated some of its objective information into his poem. The *Mountain County Herald* writer mentioned, for example, that some people at the Lighthouse earned at least a portion of their income through the sale of baskets and brooms that they crafted at the village; Mills repeats this in his poem. But, ultimately, the article was anything but a factual accounting of life at the Lighthouse in the waning days of its occupation in the middle of the nineteenth century. For the reporter, the Lighthouse habitation and the condition of the inhabitants became little more than an object lesson, a cautionary tale for those who might despair at the minor problems and setbacks in life:

> Go visit the locality yourself, and after viewing the degradation and wretchedness displayed at the Light-House, go home satisfied with your own condition in life, whatever it may be, as being far better than that of many of the dwellers upon this mundane sphere.

Perhaps Mills viewed the reporter's description of life at the Lighthouse village as fundamentally accurate, but not one that was representative of their society during the time of James and Molly. Because the article was written in a very late period of the Lighthouse's occupation, Mills may have recognized that the reporter was doing little more than sermonizing, unable to admit that the people of the village were happy, and, in fact, vigorous in the defense of the quality of their life.

Fortunately, Mills did not take the reporter's perspective too seriously, nor did he allow the clearly biased opinion of the *Mountain County Herald* writer to color his own perspective. If he had, it is unlikely that he would have written his poem, or that its story would be so compelling.

William Wallace Lee's Centennial Address

It is clear that Mills derived much of the verifiable content of his version of the legend—that is, the entire framework for the story—from the short discussion William Wallace Lee devoted to the Lighthouse in his address presented at the Barkhamsted centennial celebration in 1879. In the introduction to his poem, Mills states, "The poem here given follows, in the main, the story of the Light House as given by William Wallace Lee." Lee's remarks were published in the centennial celebration volume he compiled in 1881 (Lee 1881).

Lee, a machinist by training and a historian by avocation, was born in Barkhamsted in 1828. He moved to Meriden, Connecticut in 1862, where he served as a representative to the state legislature in 1885 and 1886. Lee was socially and politically active; as his biographer J. A. Spalding states: "Mr. Lee has never knowingly missed an opportunity for recording his vote in favor of equal rights, temperance, and strong morals" (Spalding 1891:241).

Interested in Connecticut's history in general and Barkhamsted's in particular, Lee organized the centennial celebration, invited the guests, and prepared the keynote address. In that address, Lee presented in great detail the history of his home town and an examination of the Lighthouse legend. The basis for his description of the Lighthouse history included three primary sources: the journal of Jesse Ives, an interview with a woman Lee identified as "the widow of Joseph Elwell Sr.," and conversations with "Uncle" James Eggleston.

The journal of Jesse Ives.   John Ives and his son, also named John, moved to Barkhamsted from North Haven, Connecticut in 1772 (Lee 1881:39). Jesse (1781–1861) was the son of the younger John Ives (Hart 1883). Jesse Ives became a prominent citizen of Riverton, serving as postmaster from 1827 to 1835.

Ives became the first proprietor of the Ives Hotel, which still stands as the Riverton Inn and continues to operate as a country inn some 180 years after opening. Ives purchased the property on which the Riverton Inn was located in the early nineteenth century (in 1805 [Adams 1968:9; Roberts 1968:19] or perhaps in 1815 [McCormick 1975:151]). Either using a dwelling already on the property or constructing a new building (it is uncertain which), Ives opened the inn less than two miles from the Lighthouse site.

Lee stated that he "copied almost verbatim from the journal which was kept by Jesse Ives, wherein he kept whatever he deemed worthy of being recorded" (Lee 1881:39). Lee had a great deal of trust in Ives's account because Ives and the Lighthouse inhabitants were close neighbors, at least by early nineteenth-century standards. Remember, however, that Ives was born in 1781; it is likely, therefore, that he didn't begin his journal until the turn of the nineteenth century, some 60 years after the Lighthouse village was founded. So, although Ives may have had substantial contact with village inhabitants in the nineteenth century, he was born too late to have witnessed firsthand the establishment and early years of the village.

Interview with Mrs. Joseph Elwell Sr.   The second of Lee's sources was the widow of Joseph Elwell Sr. Mrs. Elwell, by her own claim, was an eyewitness to life in the Lighthouse and a direct descendant of James and Molly. Lee identified her as "a daughter of Chaugham's third child" (1881:38) but does not provide a first name. Through documents we have examined and that are discussed in Chapter 6, we found her first name to be "Polly" and that she was a daughter of a Mr. William Wilson and his wife Polly Chaugham Wilson, who was, in turn, a daughter of James and Molly. The "widow of Joseph Elwell," therefore, was a married granddaughter of James and Molly

Chaugham. Lee interviewed Mrs. Elwell in the spring of 1866 when, by his reckoning, she was 84 years old. Mrs. Elwell died shortly after her interview with Lee.

Conversations with "Uncle" James Eggleston.

Lee's final source was "Uncle" James Eggleston, who was a child in Barkhamsted at the end of the eighteenth century. According to Lee, Eggleston worked on the construction of the Farmington River Turnpike, which passed by the Chaugham residence. It is from Eggleston that Lee derived the very story that Mills presents about the naming of the Lighthouse village:

> As the stage drivers were coming from the north, especially in the short days, they would readily recognize Chaugham's place by the light that shone through the crevices in his log-house, and it was the only place that could be so recognized in the thick woods that lined the road, and knowing then the distance to the end of the route, fell into the habit of saying, "Well; we are only five miles from port. There is the Lighthouse" (Lee 1881:41).

Lee's synthesis of the Lighthouse story.

The brief synopsis presented by Lee in his centennial address—it takes little more than a single page of the speech—provided most of the facts of the story that Mills poeticizes into 115 pages. We can summarize Lee's version in a single paragraph.

James Chaugham was a Narragansett Indian culturally, but was probably of mixed biological ancestry. He was born and raised on Block Island, left the island to travel up the Connecticut River where he became acclimated to the ways of the white European settlers of the river. He traveled to Wethersfield where he met Molly Barber, whose father recently had prevented her marriage to a man he considered unsuitable. To punish her father, Molly had threatened to marry the next man, white or black, who asked for her hand. James asked, Molly assented, and together they absconded to the western hills of the Farmington Valley. Here, the couple raised eight children (Lee 1881:38–39).

Lee enumerated and named the Chaugham progeny and their spouses as told him by Mrs. Elwell: son Samuel and his wife, Miss Green of Sharon, Connecticut; daughter Mercy and her husband, Isaac Jacklin; daughter Polly and her husband, William Wilson; daughter Mary and her husband, "——— Lawrence" (no first name is given); daughter Hannah and her husband, Reuben Barber; son Solomon and his wife, Miss Hayes; daughter Elizabeth, unmarried; and daughter Sally, who died young.

According to Mrs. Elwell in her interview and Jesse Ives in his journal, James died in 1800, and Molly died in 1820 at 105 years of age. The same sources place Elizabeth's death in 1854, at the age of 80 years.

Compare this synopsis with the general story told by Mills in his poem. It is clear that his rendering is an embellished version of the facts Lee presented based on interviews with Mrs. Polly Elwell and James Eggleston, and a reading of Jesse Ives's journal. The only apparent contradiction is reflected in the name of daughter Mary Chaugham's husband. If you will remember our discussion of this part of the story from Chapter 3, Mills maintains that Mary married "Gum" Webster. Lee, as just mentioned, provided the name "——— Lawrence." As we will see in Chapter 6, Lee was correct and it is uncertain precisely how Mills confused the relationship of the Chaughams and the Websters.

Connecticut Courant Article

The third major source used by Mills was an article that appeared in the *Connecticut Courant*, now called the *Hartford Courant*, on January 29, 1900, several decades after the village was abandoned.

Part of the article is little more than a simple recapitulation of Lee's centennial address. But a minor new wrinkle is added to the story, one that Mills ignores. The reporter asserted that James Chaugham might not have been Narragansett at all. Because the history of no other town along the Connecticut River told a story of an itinerant Narragansett traveling north to Wethersfield, the reporter suggested that Chaugham was a local, Connecticut-born Indian, "the head man of the last remnant of a tribe of Indians who lived along the Farmington or Tunxis River. . . ." As we will see, "Chaugham" is, in fact, a Narragansett name and the *Courant* reporter was almost certainly wrong.

The second part of the article described an interview with Sol Webster and his wife Mary, a couple who, the reporter asserts, were "the only survivors of the tribe." Sol Webster, as you will remember from Chapter 1, was the father of the "nearly white" daughter whose birth was recorded in the Barkhamsted vital records of May 14, 1858. Webster and his wife were listed there as residing at "Barkhamsted Light House."

In any event, Sol and Mary were interviewed at the end of their lives; in fact, it was later stated in the *Winsted Evening Citizen* of March 3, 1933 that Sol died the day after he was persuaded to leave his sickbed for a photograph to accompany the *Courant's* article (Figure 4.1).

The reporter may have hoped that Sol and Mary Webster, as people somehow connected to the Lighthouse story, could provide some insights, perhaps by adding details to Polly Elwell's story or by correcting misapprehensions about the founding of the village. Unfortunately, Sol and Mary added little additional information about the Lighthouse or its people. As the reporter admitted, "Both are lineal descendants of Chaugham's daughters but do not seem to be able to untangle their genealogies."

In terms of specific data, Sol Webster told the *Courant* reporter that there were 32 families in the Lighthouse village. This number almost certainly is the source for Mills's assertion that there were 30 or 32 cabins on the Ragged Mountain hillside (Mills 1952:56, 106). Webster also said that there

Figure 4.1   Photograph of Sol and Mary Webster that accompanied a January 29, 1900 article about the Lighthouse that appeared in the *Connecticut Courant*. In 1858 the Websters were listed in Barkhamsted's official records as residing at the "Barkhamsted Light House" (see Figure 1.2).

were 200 graves in the Lighthouse cemetery; as the reporter discovered when he visited the site, far fewer than that number were marked, and those that were had been identified with plain fieldstone markers that bore no inscriptions.

The rest of the interview, unfortunately, does little to inspire our confidence in the accuracy of Sol Webster's memories. According to the reporter, "Old Sol" told him that: "Changham [*sic*] was an Indian who came from England with Columbus when he discovered America."

With this in mind, it may be deduced that Sol and Mary Webster remembered little about the village, its founders, or their kinship with them. What little they did profess to remember is suspect, at best. The interview provided little, ultimately, that would have been of use to Mills in his researching of the story for his poem.

Winsted Evening Citizen Article

The *Evening Citizen* article represents the fourth and final major source of information for Mills. As might be expected for a piece written in 1933, this article simply repeated Lee's account of the story as it appeared in his centennial address. The writer, however, provided a detailed enumeration of the descendants of James and Molly. The family names, listed by Mills in his poem, of the people who married into the subsequent generations of descendants of James and Molly—Adams, Hobson, Doty, and Cochran—were given in the *Evening Citizen* article. The lives of some of the descendants of James and Molly were discussed in this article as well. We will be examining the Chaugham lineage in detail in Chapter 6. It is sufficient to say at this point that Mills used this article to trace the descendants of the Lighthouse founders.

SOURCES NOT CITED BY MILLS

Other published accounts of the Lighthouse story existed that Mills may have consulted, but did not cite. He was certainly aware of some of these other publications, but apparently felt little need to discuss them. Some of those are fundamentally derivative of Lee's version, but at least one presents some new and interesting information.

Lee's 1868 Article

There was another article by William Wallace Lee, published in 1868 in the *Winsted Herald,* where he told what is essentially the same story as the one he related in his Barkhamsted centennial address. In fact, this article was Lee's first published version of the story he heard from "Chaugham's last surviving grandchild, who died last fall, more than ninety years old." This must be Polly Wilson Elwell, the widow of Joseph Elwell, daughter of William Wilson and Polly Chaugham, and granddaughter of James and Molly.

In this article Lee admitted that "much concerning the Light House is involved in obscurity and much that is known is traditionary" (Lee 1868:2). But he rejected the assumption that the entire story was merely a "creation of fancy," intended as some sort of a morality tale.

Lee dated the founding of the village to "something more than one hundred years ago," establishing the inception of the village in 1768 or earlier. Lee related essentially the same tale as that previously presented for the founding of the village, but added some details not contained in the published version of his centennial address. He identified the actual "Light House" here, not as the entire village but as the large cabin constructed by William Wilson, Polly Chaugham's husband, about whom, Lee asserts, "nothing authentic is known." It was the light from this particular cabin, Lee stated, that could be seen from more than one-half mile away and that gave the entire village its name.

Later in the article, Lee mentioned the names of Stephen and Joseph

Elwell, two white brothers from Southington, Connecticut, who moved to Barkhamsted and married into the Chaugham family. Although new blood was occasionally infused into the family, Lee despaired that there had been an unfortunate amount of intermarriage among the Lighthouse people: "Wilson's posterity have married and inter-married until there is now scarce a person of average intelligence among them."

Finally, Lee reported that the village had been abandoned and all that was left were some cellar holes and 50 or so "plain unlettered" gravestones, "hardly distinguishable among the pines." Apparently in the few years preceding Lee's writing of this article, the descendants of James and Molly sold off all their land on Ragged Mountain and "dispersed in various directions."

Eyewitness Account of J. E. Mason

Of even greater interest are two articles by J. E. Mason of New Haven, published consecutively in the June 23 and June 30, 1855 editions of the *Mountain County Herald*. (They originally appeared in another newspaper, the *New Haven Journal.*) Mills was aware of Mason's account. He even quoted from it, without attribution, in the preface to *The Legend of the Barkhamsted Lighthouse*. Mills, however, makes no further reference to Mason's articles, and ignores some interesting information Mason added to the history of the site. It seems likely that Mills simply did not put much faith in Mason's articles because of important discrepancies in the story related by Mason and the one accepted by Lee.

Mason hoped to illuminate what, even in 1855, was the "legend" of the Barkhamsted Lighthouse:

> The millionaire in his mansion, with more money than brains, the
> laborer in his cottage, with more children than dollars, have all heard
> of Barkhamsted Light House, and considered whether it was a *real* or
> an *ideal* structure (Mason 1855, June 23).

Mason traveled by train from New Haven to New Hartford in 1855 or thereabouts, where he rented a carriage and traveled to what was then called Hitchcocksville, now Riverton. There he met Jesse Ives, 74 years old, and stayed overnight at his inn. Mason's story of the history of the Lighthouse that appeared in the June 23 article is, by his own telling, largely based on the reminiscences of Jesse Ives.

As related by Mason in the article of June 23, James "Changam," a Narragansett Indian from "Rhode Island," traveled to Barkhamsted in 1779 with his white wife. (You'll recall that Lee's version, accepted by Mills, tells that James Chaugham, a Narragansett from Block Island—off the coast of Rhode Island and considered part of that state—arrived in Barkhamsted before 1768.) As in other versions of the legend, James and his wife (unnamed in Mason's article) had married in opposition to her father's wishes and fled to Barkhamsted. They built a house—Mason calls it a "wigwam"—in 1779 and lived there until 1790, when James died. There were two sons and six daughters, "whose dusky features and straight black hair showed Narragansett blood."

One of the daughters, Polly, married William Wilson, a white man. They settled nearby and raised 12 children. Wilson built an expansive log home to accommodate his large family, and it was this individual structure, Mason maintained, that was called the "Lighthouse" by drivers on the old coach road. This is the earliest published account explaining the name now associated with the settlement.

In the second article, Mason described his visit to the village itself. He mentioned seeing the ruins of what he presumed to be William Wilson's large log home—that is, what Mason called the "Lighthouse." Chaugham's descendants were still living in a cluster of "wigwams" about one-half mile south of Wilson's cellar hole.

When Mason entered the village, he knocked on the door covering of one of the structures and was attacked by two large dogs. He was saved by a large Indian man, whom Mason does not name, and saw many children in the wigwam. The man seemed unwilling to speak to Mason, who, in trying to fend off the dogs, had accidentally struck one of the children. Later, Mason found a more talkative adult, a woman who was none other than Polly Elwell, the same woman Lee interviewed in 1867, more than 10 years later.

At the time, Polly was 67 years old but, according to Mason, in robust health and appearing much younger. (This age does not correspond to information provided by Lee, who said that Polly Elwell died in 1867 at either 84 or 90 years old.) She told Mason that she was a granddaughter of James Chaugham and had married Joseph Elwell, a white man, and with him had 14 children.

Mason also met one of Polly's daughters and her 14 children—all of whom, according to Mason, were under 14 years of age. Some Lighthouse families were quite prolific: James and Molly had 8 children; their daughter Polly Wilson had 12; as just mentioned, Polly's daughter Polly Elwell bore 14 children; and Polly Elwell's niece, Mary Webster, had 14 children. Not all of these children, however, survived to adulthood (see Chapter 6).

Having met Polly's grandchildren, Mason described their dress. On their heads, some wore the pelts of animals; Mason jokingly wondered whether some of those were actually still alive. Of their clothing he stated:

> Their dress was of a singular fabric. It consisted of a coat, hat, waist-coat, all made from the same kind of cloth. This kind of cloth was manufactured before any now in use among mankind. . . .

Eventually, Polly took Mason to view the cemetery and showed him the graves of James and his descendants. She informed him, in Mason's accounting, that only one "foreigner" was buried in the cemetery. When Mason professed ignorance of Polly's meaning, she told him, "He was a foreigner—like you." When Mason disputed this characterization, claiming lineal descent from the Puritans at Plymouth, it became clear that Polly equated "foreigner" with white European: "We were Americans when you foreigners came here," Polly told Mason.

If there was only one white person buried in the Lighthouse cemetery in 1855, it almost certainly would have been William Wilson, the white man who married Polly Chaugham and who was, in turn, Polly Elwell's father. It is an interesting point that Polly considered everyone else in the cemetery to be Indian though most were of mixed blood and, as we will see in Chapter 6, many of James and Molly's descendants were categorized as "white" on official documents.

Polly ends her interview with Mason with the following words:

> We Narragansetts, once great, now poor. Pale faces got our corn and hunting grounds—killed us with bad liquor—and the Great Spirit takes us to white man's heaven. Narragansetts all gone—me last one.

Mason's articles are extremely important because they provide us with the report of an interview with Jesse Ives and, even more significantly, with another eyewitness account of the village while it was still occupied.

It is also helpful to have another published version of an interview with Polly Elwell. With the exception of her age, the information she provided to Mason conforms with that she gave Lee more than 10 years later. What is most telling, however, can be derived from her attitude. Although James Chaugham was almost certainly at least one-half Narragansett, there has always been an undercurrent of doubt among those who have investigated the story about whether the people at the Lighthouse could really be considered "Indians." I think Polly could have been no more explicit about it; the people of the village itself, regardless of the European or African admixture that had certainly occurred, viewed themselves as Narragansett. At least that area of skepticism surrounding the legend can be dismissed.

Edmund Smiley's *Short History of Riverton*

One final example of a relevant piece not cited by Mills, although certainly known to him, is the privately published *Short History of Riverton, Connecticut* written by Edmund Smiley in 1934 (republished in Wheeler and Hilton 1975). Smiley, a Barkhamsted native and prominent local lawyer, recounted what is basically Lee's story: James Chaugham, a Narragansett Indian from Block Island, moved to Wethersfield where he met and married Molly Barber. The couple fled to the slope of Ragged Mountain in Barkhamsted where they established a habitation and raised a large family.

The only new information added by Smiley is minor; it concerns the pronunciation of Chaugham's name. Smiley claimed that, instead of a two-syllable pronunciation, it should read more like "Shawm" or "Shawn" (1934:5).

Looking at the various transliterations of the family name as recorded in official documents (for example, "Choggum," "Chogam," and "Chuggum" as written in the deeds, vital records, and federal censuses), it is obvious that Smiley was simply wrong.

This brings us to the single most important aspect of the Smiley publication. Although Smiley does not mention it in his list of sources of information for his publication, at least one living resident of Barkhamsted maintains that Smiley borrowed the only existing copy of Jesse Ives's journal to use in his research (Douglas Roberts, 1990, personal communication). The journal has not been seen since—it has been missing for close to 60 years. According to Roberts, Smiley died before returning the journal. All of Smiley's possessions, including his many books, were divided among his heirs. Apparently, the journal was among those books, some of which were destroyed by heirs who did not want them.

We may never know precisely what happened to the journal. Its disappearance and possible destruction is sad indeed, but not tragic if we remember that J. E. Mason interviewed Ives in 1855. In Mason's article we have some insight, in an indirect way to be sure, about what probably was written in the missing Ives journal. Ives told Mason that a Narragansett Indian from Rhode Island named Changam moved with his unnamed white wife to Barkhamsted in 1779. Compare this to Lee and Mills, who maintain that the Narragansett was named Chaugham (or some version of that name), that he came from Block Island (a part of Rhode Island), and that he arrived in Barkhamsted before 1768, possibly as early as 1740. In Chapter 6, we will assess which version—Mason's or Lee's—is more accurate.

CONCLUSION

The Legend of the Barkhamsted Light House was not simply based on the imagination of Lewis Sprague Mills. Neither was it the product of an intensive investigation of original documents, nor of the material record of the archaeological site that remains of the Lighthouse village. Instead, it was based on the very few extant summaries dealing with the village that were available to Mills. He used historian William Wallace Lee's Barkhamsted centennial celebration address to provide the framework for his poetic version of the story. Lee based his telling on three sources: the journal of Jesse Ives, an interview with one of James and Molly's granddaughters—Polly Wilson Elwell—and, to a lesser degree, conversations with James Eggleston.

For the rest of the story as told in his poem, Mills relied to a small degree on three newspaper articles and possibly some other publications. It would be wrong, however, to ignore the fact that to flesh out the story of the Lighthouse, Mills relied primarily on his own imagination.

Chapter 5

DIGGING IN THE DOCUMENTS:
Sources

Science is rarely a neat, linear enterprise. We cannot expect to discover things in an order convenient to our understanding of our research subject. Only sporadically in our data collecting are we fortunate enough to observe causes before we observe their effects, to comprehend simple relationships before more complex ones present themselves, or, in a historical investigation, to find our facts in an order that reflects their actual chronological occurrence.

In most archaeological investigations, the *law of superposition* in *stratigraphic analysis* (Chapter 7) puts archaeologists in the interesting, if unenviable, position of discovering our chronologies in reverse order. The first layers we peel back in the soil are the most recently laid down. As we dig deeper into the ground, we sequentially expose our story—but backwards.

Documentary research often proceeds in a like fashion. It is not unusual to begin with the more obvious, more accessible, and more recent records, using these to trace our way back to the older, *primary documents*.

Our documentary analysis of the Lighthouse village has been no exception to this. As you have seen in Chapters 3 and 4, we gradually have been peeling back the strata of the Lighthouse legend. Like separating the layers of an onion—or like excavating the stratigraphic layers of sediment that may encapsulate an archaeological site—we have sliced back through levels of information. Beginning with an account of Mills's 1952 poem in Chapter 3, we pared back to the nineteenth-century sources of that poem in Chapter 4, and then, going further still, stripped back to the sources of *those* sources. We

began by examining the most accessible, most recent sources of the legend—
in a chronological sense, those furthest removed from the period of occupation
of the Lighthouse—and then proceeded to trace the story back to sources clos-
er in time to the village and its people.

At this point we still have not yet reached the basal layer in the soil—we
are not yet at the heart of the onion. Most of the sources discussed so far, with
the exception of the eyewitness reports of the occupied village published in
the *Mountain County Herald* in the 1850s, have been, at best, secondary. Even
the two *Herald* articles date to more than 100 years after legendary accounts
say the village was first occupied by the newly married James Chaugham and
Molly Barber.

The secondary sources are even more problematic in reconstructing a
verifiable history of the Lighthouse settlement, because these all have relied on
intermediary sources for the history of the village and those who lived there.
The secondary sources have been easy to find, but, as a result of their being so
far removed from the time of the Lighthouse, their value is limited or, at least,
questionable. So, the investigation of primary sources—our digging in the
documents—becomes a crucial part of the research.

AN INTRODUCTION TO THE PRIMARY RECORD

Here it will be useful to describe the primary documents, records kept on all
people, including those who lived in the Lighthouse village. Such records can
provide tangible documentation of the existence of individual people.
Referring specifically to the investigation of probate documents but applying
equally to other primary documents, Benes and Benes characterize analysis of
the primary record as "browsing through an almost endless succession of
semantic attics—each as precisely dated and sited as a well-focused archaeological excavation" (1989:5).

We all leave a documentary paper trail. One need only be born, marry,
have children, or die to be included in the primary documentary record.
Governmental and institutional bureaucracies on a formal level, and families
on an informal level, have been producing, maintaining, and preserving these
paper trails for a good many years. These records, in a sense certifying our
existence and documenting our lives, can be divided into three general categories with a variety of document types within each. Following Rubincam
(1960), we can partition these as follows:

   I. Family Records:

      A. Bibles
      B. Correspondence
      C. Diaries
      D. Diplomas

II. Institutional Records:

    A. Church records

    B. Educational records

    C. Newspapers, including articles, birth and marriage notices, and obituaries

III. Public Records:

    A. Census records

    B. Federal mortality schedules

    C. Military records

    D. Vital records

    E. Court and probate records

    F. Tax lists

    G. Land records

    H. Cemetery records

We now can discuss each of these as sources of information in *genealogical research*. What follows is not an exhaustive or all-inclusive discussion of genealogical research methodology, but is an outline and brief discussion of the types of data available in a project like the one that is the focus of this book. We will concentrate on the particulars of the record in Connecticut. (See Abbe 1984 and Jacobus 1960 for detailed discussions of the Connecticut record.)

Although record keeping varies throughout the country, one can usually find the kinds of data discussed in this chapter in state libraries (copies of the federal census and microfilmed vital, land, and probate records), the libraries of state historical societies (the federal census and microfilmed vital, land, and probate records), large university libraries (varied sources), as well as county repositories (probate records are housed in county courts in most states) and town halls (original vital and land records, microfilmed probate records). The location of church records varies; microfilmed copies often are available in state libraries as well as state and local historical societies.

A number of institutions have enormous genealogical collections open to researchers. Among the most important and useful of these are the New England Genealogical Society in Boston, Massachusetts; the New York Public Library in New York City; the Library of Congress and the Library of the National Society of the Daughters of the American Revolution, both in Washington, D.C.; the Newberry Library in Chicago, Illinois; and the Los Angeles Public Library. It also should be pointed out that the Church of Jesus Christ of Latter-day Saints (the Mormons) has made an enormous effort to collect, preserve, and bring together, from many parts of the world, historical documents related to genealogy. The Mormons have provided to local governments and libraries microfilm copies of many of the documents they have examined in those areas. Much of this material is made available by the church at their Genealogical Society Library in Salt Lake City, Utah.

Many helpful guides exist for those interested in pursuing their own genealogical studies. For a short but useful directory of the kinds of documentary data available to the historian or genealogist, see Miller (1969). For an introduction to such research describing the various sources of information, see Crandall (1986). For a more detailed discussion of primary document accessibility, the location of local and national documentary repositories, as well as the practices of the various states regarding such documents, see Greenwood (1973). For a general discourse on the vicissitudes of genealogical research, see Rubincam (1960) and Wright and Pratt (1967). For a humorous but informative discussion of genealogical research, see Galeener-Moore (1987; a book appropriately titled *Collecting Dead Relatives*).

Galeener-Moore describes her book as a discussion of the "problems and pitfalls of this fascinating, laborious, and expensive way to waste your time" (1987:vii). Such sarcasm may seem, at times, accurate, but I think you will see that in examining the primary record as it relates to the people of the Lighthouse village, we are in no way wasting our time. Following our introduction to the primary documents, we will present and assess in Chapter 6 the contribution they made to our unraveling of the legend of the Lighthouse.

FAMILY RECORDS

The first set of documents to be discussed we call family records. These records represent the informal documentation kept by a family about itself. In this category are family Bibles, personal correspondence, diaries, and diplomas.

Family Bibles

Each town in Connecticut maintained a digest representing a legally mandated, running account of births, deaths, and marriages. (See the discussion of vital records under "Public Records" in this chapter.) Families also often kept their own records of births, deaths, and marriages, commonly recording them in a Bible handed down from generation to generation. Today many people interested in their own family genealogy rely on the listings provided in such family Bibles. Of course the existence of such a genealogy depends on the family having been literate.

Many families have not kept these informal family records up to date, or they have disposed of them or packed them away in attics or basements where they slowly but inexorably deteriorate. In Connecticut the State Library has attempted to collect and copy many family Bible records. Some 25,000 records, a tiny fraction of these documents, have been preserved in this project.

The records kept in family Bibles, as well as the great majority of the kinds of records being discussed here and examined in this project, are handwritten. The combination of changes in English written characters and in the

English lexicon in the past few hundred years, as well as just plain awful penmanship, can make the task of "translation" of such written records extremely difficult. It takes patience and practice. Harriet Stryker-Rodda's (1986) pamphlet, *Understanding Colonial Handwriting,* can be of some help here, but there is no better teacher than experience.

Personal Correspondence

Another valuable source of information about a family's genealogy is personal correspondence—letters written to or from members of a family. It is common even today for relatives separated by distance or time to write an occasional letter detailing a family's activities, listing births, deaths, marriages, accomplishments, and so on. Of course the existence of correspondence depends on the family, or at least some members of the family, being literate. Beyond this, where public records often are preserved as a matter of law and institutional records are maintained as a matter of practice, the preservation of family correspondence is largely serendipitous. How many of us possess letters written by our grandparents, much less the correspondence of even older generations in our lineage? In the specific case of the Lighthouse, as we will see in Chapter 6, none of the inhabitants appear to have been literate, so family correspondence cannot be of use to us.

Diaries

Along with personal correspondence to other members of a family or to friends, some people write what amount to letters to themselves. Diaries often contain information concerning day-to-day occurrences; such data can be helpful in genealogical and historical research. The existence of a diary demands a certain level of literacy, and preservation of the diary is largely a matter of luck.

The Lighthouse people, as just stated, were not literate and so did not maintain diaries, but we have already spoken of the importance of the journal of Jesse Ives, proprietor of an inn in Riverton, in investigating the Lighthouse settlement. Unfortunately, as already pointed out, this potentially important source of information disappeared sometime in the 1930s.

Diplomas

Families often keep diplomas or certificates of gradeschool matriculation. These usually list the recipient's name, date of graduation, and information pertinent to the award. The long-term survival of a diploma is a matter of chance; as in the case of family correspondence, how many of us can find our own diplomas, much less those of even our immediate forebears? In many cases, however, those who have attended school are listed in the official records of their institution. Such records will be discussed separately in the next section.

INSTITUTIONAL RECORDS

During the course of their lives, individuals interact with institutions such as churches, schools, and newspapers. Most institutions keep records on the people who join or with whom they have contact or dealings.

Church Records

Varying by denomination and practice, churches traditionally kept track of the most important events in people's lives: birth, baptism, confirmation, marriage, and death, along with administrative records of admissions, disciplinary actions, and dismissals from the church. These records often are redundant with those of a town's vital records but can provide information that never made it into the town archives. Also, churches with attached cemeteries, a common pattern in colonial New England, kept lists of people buried in the church graveyard. In some cases, the caretakers of church cemeteries kept a record book that included the location of each grave, the date of burial, the name of the purchaser of the plot, and an account of payment for upkeep. Church cemetery records provide evidence of a person's presence in a community as well as the date of his or her death.

Many church records have been microfilmed and are commonly available in town or state libraries. For example, in 1930 the Connecticut State Library requested that churches send them their records of births, deaths, and marriages; more than 600 churches did so (Abbe 1984:122). The state published an annotated list of the available Connecticut church vital records (*A Guide to the Vital Statistics in Church Records of Connecticut, 1942*).

Educational Records

Nearly every public school in the United States kept a register of the names of attendees. Many of these registers have been destroyed, but some have survived. In Connecticut, surviving registers are housed in the State Library and in the collections of the Connecticut Historical Society.

Newspaper Articles and Obituaries

Newspaper articles can be firsthand accounts, like those about the Lighthouse published in the *Mountain County Herald* in the middle of the nineteenth century. The unnamed reporter and J. E. Mason actually visited the community and wrote about life in the village. Articles written by reporters who were eyewitnesses of an event or place can be invaluable in historical research. But, as should be readily apparent from the very different perspectives of the reporters who visited the Lighthouse, firsthand newspaper accounts are not necessarily objective or free of bias or preconceptions.

Also, many newspaper articles do not represent firsthand reports but are based on interviews with eyewitnesses. This can introduce an additional level of uncertainty because reporters overlay their perspective or angle onto those of the people being interviewed.

Beyond feature articles or stories, newspapers do provide primary, contemporary records of individuals, because they commonly report deaths. Obituaries can be elaborate, with detailed information about the individual, or they can be quite short, merely death notices listing little more than the name of the deceased, the date of death, age at death, and place of residence. Many newspapers also list births and marriages.

The problem with newspaper obituaries as well as birth and marriage notices is that if you do not know the precise date of the event or of its appearance in a newspaper, such notices can be difficult to find. When indexed by name, the information is substantially easier to track down. During the Depression, a WPA (Works Project Administration) project in Connecticut was dedicated to copying and indexing all death and marriage notices appearing in state newspapers, dating from the earliest settlement to the Civil War period. A card catalog in the State Library, alphabetized by name, makes this part of the research quite simple.

PUBLIC RECORDS

Our final major category is public records, the official documents kept by various levels of government on the lives of individuals. Here are included the census, mortality schedules, and military, vital, probate, tax, land, and cemetery records.

The Census

The United States government conducted its last official accounting of the population of the nation in 1990. Such census taking—in other words, official head counting—is far from being a new idea. The 1990 census marked the twenty-first decennial of the U.S. federal census, the first one having been carried out in 1790.

Censuses were taken more than 5,000 years ago in the Middle East (Halacy 1980), and we know that the ancient Babylonians, Egyptians, Chinese, Peruvians, Greeks, and Romans, at one time or another engaged in census taking. European nations were relatively late in getting involved with population counting. The first national census in Europe was conducted by Sweden in 1749. After that, the Spanish in 1798, the French in 1801, the British in 1801, the Italians in 1861, and the Russians in 1897 conducted their first national censuses (Bureau of the Census 1909).

Censuses in the British colonies.   Although the British did not formally measure the size of their own population until the nineteenth century, they were
interested in the population of their colonies long before this. A primary initial
concern, as Wells (1975) indicates, was an assessment of the military strength
of individual colonies. Colonies were economic investments—expensive ones
at that—and a colony too small to adequately defend itself from indigenous
people or competing colonial powers might become an economic liability. In
the seventeenth century, the British had just wrested control of Jamaica from
the Spanish, and there was great concern about Indian attacks on their colony
in Virginia. The British, therefore, needed to know the population size and,
hence, the strength, of individual colonies. Moreover, as Bickford points out,

> The dominant economic theory of the colonial period, Mercantilism,
> asserted that population meant power, so periodic efforts were made to
> determine the extent of colonial population (1979:35).

Therefore, population enumeration became an important tool for imperial
powers in economic decision making in the seventeenth century.

The British made a number of general attempts before 1670 to encourage
enumerations in the American colonies and after 1670 increased their efforts.
Between 1670 and 1702, almost all of the colonial governors received instructions regarding population enumeration from the *Council for Foreign
Plantations,* the governing body in Great Britain in charge of the colonies.
Each governor was enjoined to measure the population of men, women, children, masters, servants, free men, indentured servants, slaves, and the number
in the militia (Wells 1975:13).

Unfortunately for the council, not all colonies responded to these instructions. At the same time, the bureaucratic level above the Council for Foreign
Plantations, the *Privy Council,* had many items on its agenda, and counting
colonial population was not paramount.

With the establishment of the *British Board of Trade* in 1696, this
changed. This additional level of authority consisted of a cohort of bureaucrats
whose sole focus was the colonies. The Board of Trade sent out letters to all
colonial governors in 1721, 1731, 1755, and 1773 (Wells 1975:17) requesting
that enumerations be conducted. Their instructions were general; the board
merely wished to know the number of inhabitants, the amount of increase or
decrease since the previous count, and reasons postulated for the change in
population.

Altogether in the years preceding the American Revolution, some 39 censuses were conducted in the 13 colonies (Halacy 1980). The three pre-
Revolution censuses in Connecticut were noted by the government of the
colony in the record of transactions of the general assembly. They were later
published in a series of volumes called *The Public Records of the Colony of
Connecticut,* as compiled by Charles Hoadley in 1880. These censuses were little more than statistical compilations. Names of individuals or of families were
not recorded, so these census data provide only summary statistical information.

The federal census.   On February 22, 1790 the Congress of the United States of America passed a bill directing that an enumeration be conducted of the population of the new country. Of importance to us in this study, Indians were quite explicitly *not* to be included. The purpose of this census was to determine for each state its federal tax burden as well as the number of representatives it should have in the House of Representatives of the Congress:

> Representatives and direct taxes shall be apportioned among the several states which may be included within this union, according to their respective Numbers, which shall be determined by adding to the whole Number of free Persons, including those bound to Service for a Term of Years, and excluding Indians not taxed, three-fifths of all other persons (Article 1, Section 2, U.S. Constitution).

Because Indians were not to be taxed and could not vote, they were not to be counted. Also, here we see the institution of the notorious "three-fifths" rule, where black slaves were, for purposes of representation and taxation, each counted as only three fifths of a human being.

To keep the number of representatives to the Congress as well as the tax burden an accurate and current reflection of each state's population, the census was to be conducted every 10 years. The amount of detail recorded in each of these decennial censuses changed over time. The first census recorded the names of only the heads of households. The rest of the people were counted and categorized by sex, age, and color as follows: all free white males under 16, all free white males over 16, all white females, all free blacks, and all slaves. Unfortunately these non-household heads went unnamed in the 1790 census.

Subsequent censuses added categories. In 1800 through 1840, only the names of household heads were recorded, but the age and sex breakdowns were more detailed. The enumerator sheets included columns for the number of people in each household in the following categories: males under the age of 10, males between 10 and 16, males between 16 and 26, males between 26 and 45, males over 45; females under 10, females between 10 and 16, females between 16 and 26, females between 26 and 45, females over 45; all other free persons except Indians not taxed; and slaves. The column labeled "all other free persons except Indians not taxed" provides an accounting of all non-white, non-Indian, free individuals (males and females).

It was not until 1850 that the census began recording the names of all individuals in a household: males and females, young and old. In 1850 and thereafter, censuses also recorded the actual ages, occupations, and birthplaces of individuals.

Census records represent an official document of the federal government, but one cannot assume, even for our most recent census of 1990, that they are entirely accurate. Especially in early years, the enumerators—the people actually going to each household and collecting the required information—were not well trained, and levels of skill, motivation, and commitment varied greatly. People not home when the enumerator was in the area might be missed entirely, or information of questionable accuracy was sometimes solicited from a neighbor. Beyond this is the problem that enumerators were recompensed according to the number of individuals or families they recorded. Thus there was a temptation to overcount. It is fairly common to see the same family, with some variation in the details recorded, show up more than once in a census taker's collected data.

Census indexes are available in most cases for all census records for each state. There are a few exceptions, however: The records for some states for the 1790 census were destroyed during the War of 1812, and the 1890 census records were largely consumed by a fire in 1921 (Crandall 1986:167).

The indexes for the surviving censuses usually are alphabetically arranged by last name and sometimes summarize the data recorded in the census records themselves. The indexes also provide the page number for each particular census record for each individual on a microfilm record of the census it pertains to.

Because census records contain personal information, they are closed by law to public inspection for 72 years after their collection. Census data prior to 1930 are part of the public record and can be inspected by anyone; they often are available in state libraries or historical societies. Census records from 1930 to the present are private and generally cannot be examined by the public.

Federal Mortality Schedules

Federal mortality schedules were a short-lived statistical record of deaths kept in conjunction with the federal census. Mortality schedules were taken in 1850, 1860, 1870, and 1880. They are records of the names of individuals who died before June 30 within the census year. Each deceased person is listed by his or her name, age, sex, color, legal status (free or slave), marital status (unmarried, married with surviving spouse, widowed), occupation, month of death, length of illness, and cause of death.

Because they record only those deaths that occurred in the census years listed, the mortality schedules are of limited value to us, but they are worth a look and can provide valuable information.

Military Records

Military records, including *service records* and *benefits records*, are maintained by the federal government. Service records minimally list the names of individuals who served in the wars conducted by the United States: the Revolutionary War, the War of 1812, the Mexican War, the Civil War, the Spanish-American War, World Wars I and II, the Korean and Vietnam conflicts, and many other smaller skirmishes, including the Indian Wars of 1818–1858. Because there was no independent American government at the inception of the War of

Independence, record keeping initially was spotty, but thereafter the records improve.

Service records ordinarily include the names of the soldiers, their rank, their state, their military organization or unit, and sometimes their date of enlistment in and separation from the armed forces. Many of the original service records are maintained by the Adjutant General's Office in Washington, D.C. These records have been abstracted and are available at the National Archives, also in Washington, D.C. The federal government publishes a useful directory for these documents, *Guide to Genealogical Records in the National Archives* (1982).

For military service before the Revolutionary War and for those colonists who remained loyal to the British and fought against the Revolutionary forces—the so-called Loyalists—military records were kept by the British. Copies of some of these records are available in the United States, for example at the New York Public Library in New York City. Also, the New Jersey State Library has records of lands confiscated after the Revolutionary War from Loyalists in that state.

Military records are often difficult to use because there is no comprehensive name index. One needs to know where and when the person served and whether he or she was an enlisted soldier or an officer—and these are often the very pieces of information one is searching such records for in the first place. In many cases, however, states, historical societies, and even individual researchers have compiled the names of soldiers from their states who served in the armed forces. In the case of Connecticut, a number of publications list the names of citizens of the state who served in various wars, for example, *Rolls of Connecticut Men in the French and Indian War* and *Rolls and Lists of Connecticut Men in the War of the Revolution,* both published in the Collections of the Connecticut Historical Society. In the case of Barkhamsted, the situation is made even easier. William Wallace Lee, whose contribution to our knowledge of the Lighthouse legend we discussed in Chapter 4, compiled a list of the men of Barkhamsted who served in battle from the War of Independence to the Civil War (Lee 1897).

Veterans benefits records include information on two types of pensions, death or disability pensions and service pensions, as well as another kind of benefit—bounty lands.

Death or disability pensions were given to invalid veterans or to the widows and orphans of those killed in service. Service pensions were awarded to surviving aged veterans or their widows if the soldier had served more than a certain minimum amount of time in the armed forces. Bounty land benefits included free land promised to soldiers as an inducement to enlist.

Records of the benefit recipients are preserved in the National Archives. Greenwood lists the published sources and physical repositories of all service and benefits records from the Revolutionary War (1973:417–430), as well as the more detailed records of the post–Revolutionary War period. These records include files of disability, death and burial records, enlistments, prisoner-of-war lists, and draft records (1973:444–466).

Vital Records

In most other countries, basic demographic data including lists of births, deaths, and marriages are collected by the national government. This has not been the case in the United States. As Greenwood (1973) points out, the U.S. Constitution does not specifically delegate the responsibility for such record keeping. As a result, this assignment evolved over a period of time into a local governmental responsibility.

But states in this country did not maintain such records until fairly recently. Massachusetts was the first state to mandate the recording of births and deaths and the filing of birth and death certificates at the state level, and this was not passed into law until 1841. Less than 100 years ago, in 1897, Connecticut mandated such statewide record keeping (Crandall 1986:66). Until this very late period, the states did to their local municipalities what the federal government had done to them vis-à-vis vital record keeping; they simply passed the task on. It therefore fell to the counties or towns of individual states in the United States to maintain what are called the vital records.

In the Virginia colony in 1632 and in the Massachusetts Bay colony in 1639, the colonial government instructed local officials to keep an official record of births, deaths, and marriages (Crandall 1986:65). By 1640 the Court of Election of the Colony of Connecticut ordered that individual towns keep a record of marriages that took place within their borders. In 1644 it was decreed that town clerks should also register births that occurred in their towns, and by 1650 deaths were included in the record-keeping tasks of the town clerk (Abbe 1984:120).

Compared to the federal census where population is counted at a given interval, a town's vital records are a running account of population statistics. Although there can be some short delay in official record keeping, a town's births, deaths, and marriages were, and are, recorded contemporaneously with their occurrence.

A listing of births in a town's vital records ordinarily included birth date, child's name, sex, color or race, names and race of the parents, and sometimes the ages and place of residence of the parents and the number of other children they had. Marriage listings in a town's vital records commonly included the names of the couple, their place of birth and residence, the date of the nuptials, the name of the attending religious or legal official who performed the ceremony, and occasionally the names of the couple's parents. Death records cited the name of the deceased, date of death, cause of death, place of residence, and sometimes parents' names.

The amount of information ultimately recorded regarding birth, marriage, and death varied in different towns and in different states. Some town clerks were scrupulous in keeping the records up to date; others were lax in record keeping. Sometimes people simply did not inform town or county clerks of a birth, death, or marriage. Merely because a child was born, a couple married, or a person died was no guarantee that the occurrence would show up in the vital records, although legally it should have.

It is also the case that the quality of a town's vital records changed through time, and not always for the better. Generally, records in Connecticut are good between about 1660 and 1776—before the Revolution (Abbe 1984:120; Jacobus 1960:127). As a rule, town clerks closely followed the edicts of the colonial government. After the Revolution, however, things became somewhat confused; it was not always clear who should be keeping records. Town vital records, therefore, vary greatly in quality for some time after 1776. Ordinarily the quality of a Connecticut town's vital records declined after the Revolution and did not improve dramatically until almost the second half of the nineteenth century. It was not until 1848 that the state directed each town to keep an official record of births, deaths, and marriages.

In some towns, especially smaller communities early in their existence, the actual vital record book was arranged by family name. Town clerks would begin a fresh page in the records for each newly married couple, listing the date of their marriage and other information considered important. Following this, town clerks listed the births of the couple's children and, ultimately, the deaths of the original couple. As their children grew up and married, a new page, or at least a new part of another page, would be started for them.

As towns grew in population, this approach to record keeping became cumbersome. Most town clerks abandoned a family-by-family arrangement of the vital records for a straightforward chronological framework. The vital records books then were divided into three sections: births, deaths, and marriages. Information was recorded chronologically within each section. Charts were drawn up with columns for specific data categories, such as: date, names, race, place of residence, and so on (see Figure 1.2).

Vital records vary in how easily they can be used. Many vital record books were indexed by name, but older indexes vary in their inclusiveness. Often one must go through the records page by page, looking for names connected to the research being conducted. This can be frustrating and tiresome. In Connecticut, Lucius Barbour, whose title was Examiner of Public Records, copied and indexed the vital records of each of the state's towns from the period of earliest settlement to 1850. His index (called, appropriately, the *Barbour Index*), is alphabetized by name; although imperfect, this makes tracking down an individual in the state much easier than it might have otherwise been. His index is housed in a card catalogue in the Connecticut State Library. A microfilm version is available at the Connecticut Historical Society.

A town's vital records are a direct, contemporary, public document of a town's demography. These statistics can provide—and have provided for us— key clues to our unraveling of the Lighthouse story.

Court Records and Probate

Court records are official documents of court activities that list the names of jurors, plaintiffs, and defendants, among others. If an individual served as a juror, was sued, sued someone, was arrested, or was the victim of a crime, his or her name should appear in the court records.

Early in Connecticut's history, local, minor legal disputes were handled by a justice of the peace. A local justice of the peace in all likelihood kept a log of his proceedings. Many such logs were destroyed, but the Connecticut State Library has collected and preserved many.

Of greater general importance is *probate*. Not all people are called to jury duty, and fewer still are criminals or the victims of crimes, few sue or are sued, but we all die. Probate records are those legal memoranda relating to the disposition of the estate of a deceased person. Probate documents commonly include:

1. A last will and testament. The *will* technically is the legal statement by which an individual disposes of his or her *real estate* (property including land and houses), and the *testament* is the legal statement by which an individual disposes of his or her personal property.
2. A *petition for probate*. This is the official request that the will and testament be probated or proved; in other words, read and acted upon by the authorities.
3. A petition for a *letter of administration*. When there is no will (when the person is said to have died intestate), the courts maintain records of the disposition of the deceased's estate.
4. An inventory and appraisal of both the real estate and personal estate of the deceased.

Each state has its own particular practices regarding probate. In most of the United States, probate is handled on the county level. In the colony of Connecticut in 1666 each of the original four counties had its own joint County and Probate Court (Jacobus 1960:131). It was the job of the Probate Court to adjudicate the decisions of the recently deceased about the disposition of property—in other words to read the will, verify its authenticity, and ensure that its provisions were carried out and that various laws regarding inheritance were enforced. As the colony grew, the four original probate courts could no longer handle the crush of cases. Beginning in 1719 these courts divided and divided again until there now are some 130 probate districts in the state (Abbe 1984:125).

Probate records are, by law, preserved. In Connecticut they are microfilmed and filed alphabetically by the name of the deceased by probate court district. Probate documents are extremely valuable in determining the economic status of an individual. They also are useful in the reconstruction of family histories, because the names of heirs often appear in the documents.

Tax Records

Local tax records ordinarily include documentation of real estate property taxes and personal property taxes (usually including taxes on livestock and slaves).

In Connecticut such records were kept by individual towns in what were called "rate books." Each year the names of household heads were recorded, along with the extent of their real estate holdings and the amount of tax owed. These rate books are of some value in naming individuals and providing a relative measure of their wealth, at least in reference to their land holdings. Unfortunately many of the rate books have been lost. The Connecticut State Library maintains a collection of some rate books, and the Connecticut Historical Society has a listing of the rate books still in the possession of individual Connecticut towns.

Land Records

Another class of legal, public records maintained by towns are land documents. Such records represent official verification of land transactions. Land records, commonly kept on standardized forms with specific information filled in by the town clerk, confirm the name of the *grantor* or land seller, the name of the *grantee* or land purchaser, a description of the location and dimensions of the property being transferred, its acreage, the amount paid by the grantee to the grantor for the land, and the date of the transaction. Such records were signed by grantors—or marked by those unable to write their names—officially and legally transferring land title to the grantee "and his/her heirs and assigns forever."

The keeping of such records has remained very much the same in Connecticut towns since their founding. One can still walk into a town clerk's office and see shelves filled with land record books. Those documenting such transactions for the 1990s are not so different from those of the 1690s. Towns have long taxed individuals on the basis of their lands—acreage, use, presence of structures—and so need to keep track of ownership. Alphabetized grantor and grantee indexes often make the search for individuals involved in real estate transactions relatively easy, although these are not always perfect.

Land records thus provide us with evidence of the presence of individuals in a town, either as grantors or grantees. Also in locating property and recording the existence of structures, land records sometimes allow us to situate the people whose names appear on the documents. Such records have proven to be invaluable in our documentary investigation of the Lighthouse.

Cemetery Records

Cemetery records kept by churches were mentioned in the section of this chapter concentrating on institutional records. It was usual for towns also to keep a running list of the people buried in cemeteries within the town's borders. Such records commonly are housed in town clerk offices and list the name of the deceased, the date of his or her death or funeral or both, and the name of the cemetery. During the depression, as part of the same WPA project mentioned in relation to the indexing of state newspaper death notices, Connecticut initiated a program to record over one million gravestone inscriptions from more than 2,000 state graveyards (Abbe 1984:123). This catalogue makes it relatively easy to track down individuals buried in an established cemetery where markers were erected on their grave. The gravestone itself is a written document, often telling something about the person buried beneath it. Tombstones usually include the name of the deceased, the date of death, and the person's age at death. They may also list the names of spouses, children, and parents, and they may further describe the person's life. As such, these monuments can provide information not otherwise readily available.

CONCLUSION

The preceding chapter was not intended as an exhaustive set of instructions for conducting documentary research even in just the state of Connecticut, much less in the rest of the United States. Documentary materials vary in their availability and location in different states, and not every potential source of historical information has been described here. But, in this brief foray into the primary documentary record, we have discussed a fairly substantial array of sources of information. A great deal of unevenness exists in the utility of each of the data sets, but there is much to be learned in their investigation by the historian, genealogist, and anthropologist.

The primary record is a tool for illuminating the lives of past people in an explicitly personal way. The primary record provides what amounts to a library of personal details, information considered marginalia about people whose existence might otherwise have been ignored. But in these compendia of personal trivia, a genuine history emerges of people who were not the subject of historical narratives, people who lived unremarkable lives. They may not have been heros or scholars, but they were born, baptized, attended school, married, purchased land, fought as soldiers, had children, and, ultimately, died. Although their individual lives were not mentioned by the history writers, in various, myriad venues they were counted, named, listed, and recorded. In being so accounted for, they have attained at least a small measure of immortality. The people of the Lighthouse, perhaps representing the least of the least, have been immortalized in the primary documentary record in this manner. Our next task is to conduct a documentary excavation in the strata laid down by the record keepers of eighteenth- and nineteenth-century Connecticut.

Chapter 6

DIGGING IN THE DOCUMENTS:
The People of the Lighthouse

"Through a glass, darkly." The phrase comes from the *New Testament* (1 Cor. 13:12) where it is used to describe our narrow human perceptions. Our cognizance of the universe and of ourselves is clouded, our comprehension limited. It is the same when we try to gaze back across the centuries in search of the people of the Lighthouse. Try as we might by examining the records discussed in Chapter 5, we still have not been able to identify precisely who all of these fascinating people were, nor have we been able to trace their entire personal histories. Often we glimpse only their shadows, espy little more than their ephemeral images. Indeed, we seem to view the Lighthouse inhabitants, as the Bible phrases it, "through a glass, darkly." When we are lucky, the glass clears, the distortion dissipates, and we can learn much from the primary historical record.

FIRST ENCOUNTER

The last chapter began with a commentary on the degree of serendipity involved in a historical investigation—how we do not typically discover our data in an order that reflects their historical sequence. We often begin with documents far removed from the time of interest and work back to those primary records contemporary with the focus of our study. Even within the context of these primary documentary sources, an investigation does not necessarily proceed along a neatly linear, chronological pathway. In fact the first primary record we found in investigating the Lighthouse was not related to the marriage of James and Molly, or the founding of the village, or the birth of any of their children. The first record we came upon was an obituary for a Mrs. Mary Chogum. Her name appears in a list of recent deaths in Barkhamsted in the March 31, 1818, edition of the *Connecticut Courant* newspaper. The short obituary gives no particulars except Mrs. Chogum's age at death: 100 years.

At first I did not know what to make of the newspaper death notice. My initial confusion is understandable and stems, in part, from the nature of such research. At the time I found the obituary, I thought I knew that James Chaugham, a Narragansett Indian, had married a white woman named Molly Barber; I thought I knew that she was born in 1715 or thereabouts and was from Wethersfield, Connecticut; I thought I knew that James and Molly established their wilderness home in 1740; and I thought I knew that one of their daughters was named Mary. All of this knowledge, remember, was based on readily accessible and relatively recent sources—the top layers in our documentary stratigraphy. So, when I found the obituary of a Mary Chogum, I assumed she was James and Molly's daughter Mary, listed in Mills's poem as the wife of "Gum" Webster. I had no idea why she was listed in the obituary under the name Chogum, which would have been her maiden name. A little math presented yet another inconvenient puzzle; if daughter Mary was 100 years old at her death in 1818, she was only three years younger than her mother was supposed to be!

This was impossible, so I knew I must have something wrong. Who was this Mary Chogum who died in Barkhamsted in 1818? A very rare name like Chogum in a northwestern Connecticut town in the early nineteenth century almost certainly had to be related to the story, but how? As you will see in this chapter, a little digging in the Barkhamsted town deeds and reference to an ordinary baby name book—the kind prospective parents use today to find names for their soon-to-be-born children—gave us the answer.

ANONYMOUS CENSUS RECORDS

As stated in the previous chapter, the British made a number of attempts to estimate the population of their colonies in America. Greene and Harrington (1932) provide a synopsis for such population estimates. For Connecticut the first population calculation was produced in 1636 when there were some 800 people in the colony (Greene and Harrington 1932:47). By 1709 there were more than 4,000 inhabitants and by 1749 the numbers had grown to more than 70,000 (1932:49). Such estimates, although of historical interest, are of limited value here as none provides us with individual or family names or a geographical breakdown of the colonial population. They were merely estimates of total population within the colony.

Connecticut's 1756 Census

The first actual census of Connecticut's population, where enumerators went out and counted heads at the behest of the British Board of Trade, was conducted in 1756. Again, no family names were given, as the limited goal of the census was simply a statistical compilation of population size. In the 1756 census the total population of Connecticut was given as 130,612. A breakdown by race was also provided: 126,976 whites, 3,019 "Negroes," and 617 Indians.

Further, a breakdown of the total population by each town within the state was included in the 1756 census report to the Board of Trade (Table 6.1). A racial breakdown for each town also was provided. The town of Barkhamsted is listed with a population of 18, all of whom were, according to the census, white. One nineteenth-century wag disputes the count, claiming that most of these 18 were either Indians or trespassers (Jones 1881). In nearby New Hartford, a town sometimes included with Barkhamsted in various official records, the population is given as 260, again with no Indians officially recorded.

We cannot make too much of these statistics beyond a general impression of the relative size of the towns. The censuses were, in large part, informally conducted, and local enumerators were not necessarily consistent in how they counted—or in *who* they counted. Because no Indians are recorded for Barkhamsted in 1756 may mean that, despite the claim of the legend, James

Table 6.1   1756 Census, Litchfield County, Connecticut

Town	Whites	Negroes	Indians
Barkhamsted	18	—	—
Canaan	1,100	—	—
Colebrook	—	—	—
Cornwall	500	—	—
Goshen	612	—	—
Hartland	12	—	—
Harwinton	250	—	—
Kent	1,000	—	—
Litchfield	1,366	—	—
New Hartford	260	—	—
New Milford	1,121	16	—
Norfolk	84	—	—
Salisbury	1,100	—	—
Sharon	1,198	7	—
Torrington	250	—	—
Winchester	24	—	—
Woodbury	2,880	31	—

Chaugham had not yet migrated to the town. Or, it might mean he intentionally was not counted because he was "only" an Indian. Or, because he was of possibly mixed ancestry, he may have been included among the 18 white inhabitants. Or, in a large and largely unpopulated town in the wilderness, it is not inconceivable that he and his family were uncounted because no one was aware of their existence.

Connecticut's 1762 Census

Another census ordered by the Connecticut General Assembly in October 1761 was completed in a relatively short time and reported to the General Assembly in the following year. In the *Public Records of the Colony of Connecticut*, only general population statistics were provided: 141,000 whites, 4,590 blacks, and 930 Indians, a "considerable part whereof dwell in English families, and the rest in small tribes in various parts of the colony" (Hoadley 1880:630).

No further breakdown by town is provided in the *Public Records* and nothing further was known of the 1762 census until Connecticut historian Christopher Bickford came into possession of a copy of the original census records (Table 6.2) in 1979 (Bickford 1979:36–38). Although 68 Connecticut towns are listed and figures provided for their populations of whites, blacks, and Indians, for reasons yet unclear Barkhamsted does not appear at all. The

Table 6.2	1762 Census, Litchfield County, Connecticut		
Town	*Whites*	*Blacks*	*Indians*
Barkhamsted	—	—	—
Canaan	1,084	42	—
Colebrook	—	—	—
Cornwall	553	9	—
Goshen	719	3	—
Hartland	—	—	—
Harwinton	585	3	—
Kent	1,298	6	127
Litchfield	1,514	12	—
New Hartford	655	18	—
New Milford	1,708	23	—
Norfolk	367	—	—
Salisbury	1,220	20	—
Sharon	1,386	21	—
Torrington	513	—	—
Winchester	—	—	—
Woodbury	3,514	53	—

population may have been still so small that Barkhamsted's residents were counted in with its larger neighbor, New Hartford. New Hartford's population was given as 673, with 655 whites and 18 blacks (Bickford 1979:37).

Connecticut's 1774 Census

The census of 1774 was ordered by the General Assembly in its session of October 1773 and published in the record of that assembly in the following year (Hoadley 1880). Although the purpose was statistical and neither individual nor family names were recorded, the 1774 census is far more detailed than the two previous censuses, with an accounting given of the population for each town broken down by sex, race, marital status, and age. For whites, age was categorized as under 10 years old, between 10 and 20, and between 20 and 70; for blacks and Indians, age was categorized as under 20 and over 20. (See Table 6.3.)

RACE AND THE PRE-REVOLUTION CENSUSES

There is an important point to be made about racial designations in the censuses and how they may be interpreted. Wells states that Indians commonly were ignored in these colonial censuses:

> As persons who were not clearly part of the British empire, they were of little interest to London, and hence they were counted only rarely (Wells 1975:39).

But in some cases the Board of Trade was explicit in requiring that Indians be included in enumerations. As Bickford (1979:49) states, the instructions from the board to the governor of Connecticut dated July 15, 1755, were clear; there was to be an accounting of the population of white, black, *and Indian* inhabitants of the state.

Evidence indicates that, at least sometimes, Native Americans and African Americans were counted together as a single group and categorized as "Negro" or black. As Wells (1975:90–91) points out, a sharp increase in the statewide percentage of blacks in the 1762 census over the 1756 census (3.2 percent from 2.3 percent), may be an indication of at least some portion of the Indian population being counted as black. In the 1774 Connecticut census (Table 6.3), "Negroes" and "Indians" were counted separately, but in the summary statistics, they were combined into the single category "Black" to distinguish them as a group from those labeled "White."

From the perspective of census takers in the eighteenth century, intermarriage between Indian and black and between Indian and white may have confused the situation further. That the percentage of the total black population declined in the 1774 census (to 2.6 percent) may mean that Indians and blacks were once again distinguished in the enumeration.

Table 6.3		1774 Census, Litchfield County, Connecticut		
Town	*Whites*	*Negroes*	*Indians*	*Total "Black"*
Barkhamsted	250	—	—	—
Canaan	1,573	62	—	62
Colebrook	150	—	—	—
Cornwall	957	10	7	17
Goshen	1,098	13	—	13
Hartland	500	—	—	—
Harwinton	1,015	—	3	3
Kent	1,922	12	62	74
Litchfield	2,509	37	8	45
New Hartford	985	3	13	16
New Milford	2,742	34	—	34
Norfolk	966	3	—	3
Salisbury	1,936	9	35	44
Sharon	1,986	1	25	26
Torrington	843	2	—	2
Winchester	327	12	—	12
Woodbury	5,224	80	9	89

After having disappeared in the 1762 census, Barkhamsted appears again here, its population at 250. Unfortunately it is the only town in all of Connecticut with no breakdown whatsoever for its population. We have no idea how many of the 250 were males, how many were females, what their ages were, or how many people in town, if any, were identified as "Indian" either by themselves or by the census takers. The 1774 census, therefore, although showing us the increase in Barkhamsted's population since the 1756 census, is of limited help in our effort to track the Indian population of the Lighthouse.

Interestingly, for the nearby town of New Hartford, a detailed population breakdown is provided. In 1774 there were 985 whites in town, 3 "Negroes," and 13 "Indians." The "Negro" and "Indian" counts were then combined in the summary category "Black." Four of the Indians were males under 20 years of age, three were females under 20, one was a male over 20, and five were females over 20.

It is tempting to consider the possibility that some, or even all, of these 13 Indians were living at the Lighthouse. It is possible that as a result of the imprecision in town boundaries in the eighteenth century, the Lighthouse may have been considered, at least by some, to be part of New Hartford. As we shall see in our discussion of the town land records, in at least two transactions, James Chaugham's place of residence is listed as "New Hartford." Although Barkhamsted is counted as a town in both the 1756 and 1774 censuses, it was not formally incorporated until 1779, adding to the confusion of the census takers.

All of this would be readily solvable had the census takers recorded family names, and had these lists been preserved. Unfortunately there are no such lists for most of the colonial censuses. These colonial counts were little more than statistical tabulations. The British Board of Trade requested fairly general information about population, and most colonies provided counts only. As a result, while it may be tempting to view the Indians of New Hartford as inhabitants of the Lighthouse village, we cannot come to any definite conclusion.

THE PRIMARY RECORD OF THE LIGHTHOUSE PEOPLE

The glass through which we view the Lighthouse inhabitants is clouded. But when we begin to investigate the vital records, church documents, and land records of individual towns, the glass into the past clears and we begin to see more concrete images.

James Chaugham

The legend states that James Chaugham was from Block Island. A version of the Chaugham name shows up on that island—there is even a body of water there called Chagum Pond. Beyond this the name appears twice in the official records of Block Island. First, in a court account dated October 9, 1711, local resident John Dodge "brought up an Indian Man by warrant to the Cunstable . . . for stealing a canoe and running away." The Indian, apparently already an indentured servant, was punished by being fined 50 shillings and assessed a six-month extension of his contracted servitude. The Indian man's name was recorded as Samuel Chagum.

Also in the Block Island records is the last will and testament of a Samuel Sands. In the will, dated December 11, 1713, Sands provides instructions for his funeral and disposes of his real and personal property. Sands was married and he and his wife Elizabeth had five daughters: Sybell, Marcy, Sarah, Ann, and Mary. The first three daughters were married and lived off-island with their families. To them Sands bequeathed sums of money totaling a few hundred pounds, 10 sheep, and a cow, as well as personal belongings including a "great looking glass" (a large mirror), a silver tankard, some silver spoons, and a variety of other possessions that Sands obviously wished his married daughters to remember him by. To his wife he left a quarterly payment of £10 to help her live out her life in comfort on the family farm. To his unmarried daughters, Ann and Mary, he left money and some treasured personal effects, and he instructed that each be allowed to live on the family farm on Block Island until they married. Daughter Mary, moreover, was given by her father "an Indian boy named James the son of Priscilla" and the money necessary to raise the boy until he reached the age of seven years.

This information is intriguing indeed. Although no last name is provided for the boy, we are faced with the following string of coincidences: Of the relatively small number of Narragansett Indians on Block Island in the early eighteenth century, there was an Indian man named Samuel Chagum and a young Indian boy named James who was younger than seven years old in 1713. This would have made him around 30 by 1740 when James Chaugham met 25-year-old Molly Barber and about 80 on the death of James Chaugham in 1790 or thereabouts.

Thus in our search for the roots of James Chaugham, we have found an Indian boy named James of the right age on the right island, and the Chaugham family name appears during the same period for an Indian on the island. Could the boy James have been related to Samuel Chagum—a nephew or even a son? Is the young Indian boy bequeathed to Mary Sands by her dying father to raise until his seventh birthday the very James Chaugham who married Molly Barber? The limited data currently available do not contradict that interpretation, but there simply is not enough information to confirm this possibility with any degree of certainty.

Molly Barber

As the daughter of a prominent and wealthy man living in one of Connecticut's first and most thoroughly historically documented towns, Molly should be the easier actor to trace in this eighteenth-century drama. This has turned out not to be the case. We begin with a vexing point of confusion: her given name. I started this chapter by telling you of my puzzlement at finding the obituary for a Mrs. Mary Chogum. Who was this person? The only Mary Chaugham I knew of was one of James and Molly's daughters. This added to the confusion because that Mary was too young to have been the woman in the obituary, and she was supposed to have been a married woman whose last name, or so Mills stated, would have been Webster.

The answer to this minor mystery was really quite simple. Here is where the baby name book came in handy. *Molly,* it turns out, has long been a common nickname for *Mary.* Molly Barber's given name actually was Mary Barber. As will be shown, this is born out in the official land records: Out of eight land transaction documents bearing her name, the woman explicitly referred to as the wife or widow of James Chaugham is six times listed as Mary Chaugham and twice listed as Molly Chaugham. It is common for people who have a nickname or familiar name to use their more formal, given name on legal documents, and this seems to have been precisely what Molly Chaugham often, although not always, did. Thus the obituary I had initially located in my investigation of the primary documents was, in fact, that of Molly Chaugham, wife of James. Without knowing it at the time, I had found Molly—albeit at the end of her life—almost immediately in my investigation of the primary record.

The legend states that Molly was from Wethersfield, Connecticut. That town's vital records have been intensively examined and published (Adams

1859), and in our research the original records have been very closely scrutinized. If there had been a Mary/Molly Barber (or Barker or Baker) in Wethersfield in the 1710s, 1720s, 1730s, or 1740s, she should have been in those vital records. But there is no Molly Barber; in fact there are no Barbers at all in Wethersfield at the appropriate time. In all likelihood this means that, despite the assertion of the legend, Molly could not have been from a well-established family in Wethersfield.

This finding led me to make an educated guess. All of the information I was working on concerning Molly Barber could be traced to her aged granddaughter Polly Elwell when she was interviewed by William Wallace Lee in the late 1860s (Lee 1868, 1881). How many of us today can state with assuredness the name of the town a grandparent came from? How many could answer that question some 50 years after that grandparent had died? Perhaps Polly had simply gotten it wrong.

But where else might Molly have been from and where else could she be found? There was one rather obvious place to begin looking. Another old Connecticut town on the Connecticut River about 12 miles north of Wethersfield is Windsor, a sensible place to continue the search for Molly. The lands of Barkhamsted had been given to the "proprietors," the tax-paying land owners, of Windsor, not Wethersfield. Beginning in 1732 and lasting well into the second half of the eighteenth century, the lands of Barkhamsted were mapped, surveyed, and distributed free to any land owners in Windsor willing to pay the real estate taxes on the property (Wheeler and Hilton 1975). One hundred eight of Windsor's proprietors took up the offer. A young woman growing up in Windsor would almost certainly have heard of the western lands available in Barkhamsted, and she would have been aware that it was essentially an uninhabited wilderness—a good place to hide. The Farmington River, beside the Lighthouse village, flows right through Windsor where it serves as a tributary to the Connecticut River. Paddling upstream from Windsor along the Farmington brings you, in fewer than 50 miles, to the doorstep of the Lighthouse village. (See Figure 3.1.) Windsor was a logical place to begin our expanded search for the real home of Molly Barber.

We quickly discovered that not one but two Mary Barbers lived in Windsor at about the right time (Stiles 1892:51). The first Mary was born on March 24, 1714, to Joseph Barber and Mary Loomis Barber. The second Mary was born on August 6, 1712 or 1713, to Nathaniel Barber and Mary Filley Barber. Which, if either, was our Molly?

After a careful—and disappointing—investigation of the Windsor vital records, it turned out that neither was the woman we were looking for. Neither one had a father named Peter as the legend would have us believe, and both were married and had children in Windsor. The timing of their marriages and of the births of their children made it certain that neither could have been married to James Chaugham.

Still unable to trace the origins of Molly Barber, we watched the glass once again darken and our images of the past fade.

The Late Eighteenth Century: 1770–1783

To this point we have been able to speak only of probabilities or likelihoods. We have been aiming our investigative light at fleeting shadows and phantoms. When we reach into the latter half of the eighteenth century, however, the shadows become concrete beings, the phantoms come into sharper focus.

The indisputable paper trail left by the Lighthouse people and preserved in the primary documentary record began in 1770, 30 years after the legend tells us the settlement was established in Barkhamsted. In the land records, not of Barkhamsted but of the adjacent town of New Hartford, Connecticut, it was recorded that on December 11, 1770, Noadiah Hooker sold a small parcel of land (the acreage was not specified) to a gentleman by the name of "James Chaughom" for £5, 10 shillings. Less than a year later, also in New Hartford, was a report of the sale of another parcel of land, this time 40 acres, by a "Cornelius Indian" of Farmington, Connecticut to "James Chaughom, an Indian" for £15. In May of 1775 it was further recorded that James Chaughom purchased from Asher Hinmon another 20 acres in New Hartford. This land adjoined that already purchased by James and cost him £8. So, by 1775 an Indian man by the name of James Chaughom owned more than 60 acres of land in the town of New Hartford, Connecticut. Clearly in these land records we have found James, patriarch of the Lighthouse village.

The family name, now spelled "Chogam," first appeared in the Barkhamsted land records on March 3, 1779, when Abraham Kellogg of New Hartford sold to James Chogam, for £21, 70 acres that "lyeth at a place called Ragged Mountain." According to the deed, the land was bounded on the north by the property of Nathan Gillet, Sr., and on the south by the tract of James McJarrew—the original Windsor grantees of those tracts. As can be seen from the map of the original land distribution (Figure 6.1), the tract purchased by James, therefore, was the lot (lot III–91) originally given to Samuel Moore of Windsor in the third phase of Barkhamsted land distribution (Figure 6.2).

Soon thereafter, in 1782, another sale is recorded, this time of 49 acres by Samuel Hall Williams of Branford, Connecticut to "Samuel Choggum" for £9, "being and lying most of it on Ragged Mountain, so-called." This property, the deed specifies, was a segment of the lot (lot III–92) originally given to Nathan

---

KEY EVENTS: 1770–1783

- James Chaugham buys 60+ acres in New Hartford.
- James Chaugham buys 70 acres on Ragged Mountain in Barkhamsted, establishing ownership of the land on which the Lighthouse village is located.
- Samuel Chaugham buys 49 additional acres on Ragged Mountain in Barkhamsted.

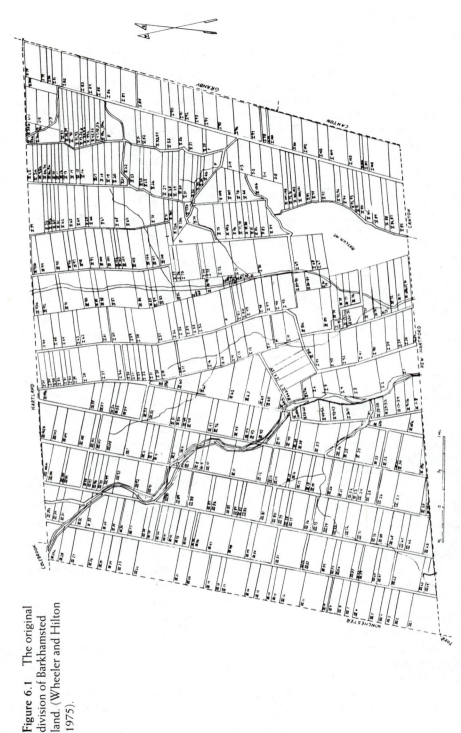

Figure 6.1 The original division of Barkhamsted land. (Wheeler and Hilton 1975).

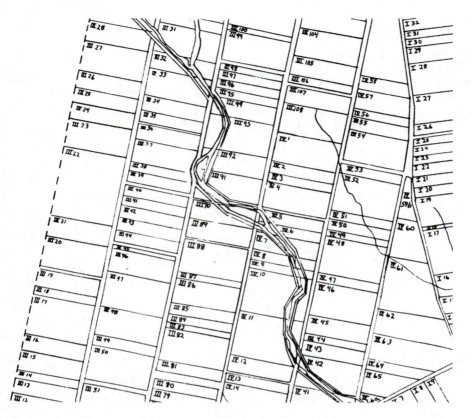

Figure 6.2   The original distribution of the land on Ragged Mountain.
Tract designations are used in the text to indicate lands bought and sold by
Lighthouse residents (Wheeler and Hilton 1975).

Gillet, Sr., of Windsor. (See Figure 6.3.) This is the tract mentioned in the 1779
transaction as being immediately north of the lot purchased by James
Chaugham. Both lots purchased by the Chaughams, the deeds indicate, are on
Ragged Mountain, the location of the Lighthouse village as indicated by various
secondary and tertiary historical sources. Also remember that according to
those same sources Samuel Choggum is one of James and Molly's two sons.

The 1779 and 1782 land purchases have been noted by historians tracking the history of the Lighthouse village. For example, John Warner Barber in
his *Connecticut Historical Collections* (1838) cited these dates as evidence that
the Lighthouse settlement was not established until this relatively late period;
that is, some 40 years after the legend says James and Molly were married. He
based this inference on the reasonable assumption that the Chaughams would
not have lived in an area until they had legally purchased land there.

This assumption, however, may be faulty. The 1779 and 1782 dates likely
do not represent the founding of the village but something else that is equally
interesting. The land within the boundaries of the town of Barkhamsted was

---

LAND DEALS ON RAGGED MOUNTAIN

The sequence of land ownership on Ragged Mountain becomes quite complex. Although I have not been able to trace every acre on the mountain, I can account for most of the land purchased by the Chaugham family, traded amongst themselves and in-laws, and then, ultimately, sold off to outsiders. Figure 6.3 depicts the chronology of land transactions related to the Lighthouse village. If you have trouble following the family itself, jump ahead to the kinship diagram shown in Figure 6.5.

---

given to 108 proprietors of the town of Windsor, Connecticut beginning in 1732 (Wheeler and Hilton 1975). The lands cost them nothing; they merely agreed to pay the real estate taxes associated with their parcels. The Windsor proprietors set about the task of dividing the land (commonly into lots of 50 acres, but there were variously sized tracts), as well as surveying, mapping, and distributing these lots soon thereafter (see Figure 6.1). The task was done in five separate phases and took several decades. The lands surrounding Ragged Mountain were not distributed until the third division, which took place in 1760 (see Figure 6.2).

Most of the Windsor proprietors who opted to accept the land offer apparently had no intention of removing to Barkhamsted; some likely never even visited their property. Today Barkhamsted still is a rural town with a small population; it was rightfully perceived as a wilderness in the eighteenth century. The purpose for most of those willing to take on the tax burden of these lands was simply investment. The hope was that Barkhamsted might grow and the lands increase in value. Most of the lands were soon sold by the original owners, and then sold again and again. As seen here, James and Samuel Chaugham did not purchase their two lots totaling 119 acres from the original Windsor grantees but from subsequent owners.

The question remains: What do the 1779 and 1782 purchases signify? Do these represent the real dates for the establishment of the Lighthouse village, with James, Molly, and their children moving there from their property in New Hartford or from someplace else? That is possible, but there is another reasonable explanation that conforms to the legend as well as to the fact that there is no evidence to support any other habitation. It is plausible that sometime after the Ragged Mountain parcels were divided up in 1760 and before the 1779 and 1782 land transactions, the owners with legal title to the tracts on the west side of Ragged Mountain, namely Abraham Kellogg and Samuel Hall Williams, became aware of a small problem: On what ostensibly was their property existed a thriving village of a few decades old, consisting of at least a few dozen individuals. Because James and Molly had an adult son purchasing land in 1782, they must have been together for some time before that, and we have no evidence they had lived anywhere else. And in the 1782 deed, Samuel Chaugham's place of residence is listed as "Berkhamsted." It seems reasonable to suggest that James and Samuel simply were ensuring *legal* title to their

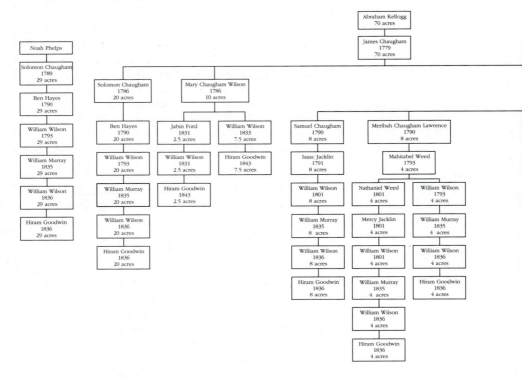

Figure 6.3   Chart summarizing the buying, amalgamation, and sale of land on Ragged Mountain by the residents of the Lighthouse village.

homes by purchasing in 1779 and 1782 the very land on which their small village already stood. The land purchases in New Hartford in 1770 and 1775 may have represented an attempt by James to hedge his bets, uncertain that his family would be able to stay on the Ragged Mountain land.

Whatever the significance of the New Hartford purchases, it is clear that at least as early as the late 1770s the family lived in the village established on the side of Ragged Mountain in Barkhamsted.

Summary: 1770–1783

Whatever the significance of the New Hartford purchases, it is clear from the land records that the Chaughams were present in northwestern Connecticut at least by this period. By no later than the late 1770s, the family owned much of the property on which the Lighthouse community was located, although it seems likely that their presence on Ragged Mountain predates their purchase of the land.

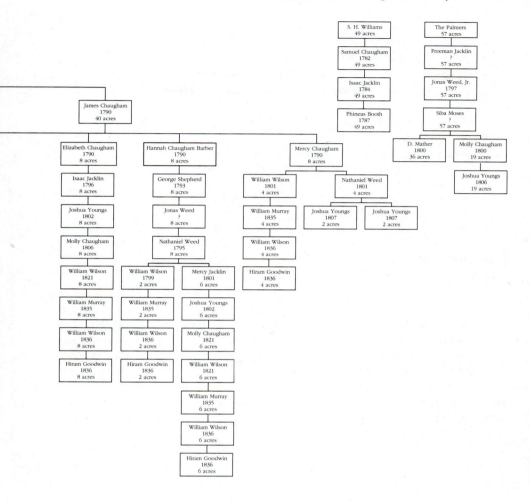

The Late Eighteenth Century: 1783–1800

In the final decade and a half or so of the eighteenth century, the Chaughams and their descendants were busy with land dealings. Beginning in 1784 a surprisingly large number of land transactions involving the inhabitants took place. On November 5, 1784, Samuel Chaugham sold the 49-acre lot (lot III–92) he purchased from Samuel Hall Williams to an Isaac Jacklin for £12, a profit of £3 on the Ragged Mountain parcel bought just two years earlier. But Samuel had not sold his land in the heart of the Lighthouse community to a stranger. As noted in the records of the West Hartland Second Congregational Church, on January 22, 1785, Isaac Jacklin and James and Molly's daughter Mercy Chaugham, both of Barkhamsted, were married. Jacklin held on to this property until January 1787 when he sold it to Phineas Booth.

KEY EVENTS: 1783–1800

- Samuel Chaugham sells his land to free black Isaac Jacklin.
- Isaac Jacklin marries James and Molly's daughter Mercy.
- James Chaugham divides part of his landholdings among his wife and his children Mary and Solomon.
- James Chaugham dies around 1790 and his remaining property is distributed to his children.
- Several of the children—Solomon, Samuel, Hannah, Meribah, and Elizabeth—sell their portions of their late father's estate and strike out on their own.
- Molly relinquishes all rights to any of her late husband's lands and moves to Sharon, Connecticut.
- Son-in-law William Wilson, married to James and Molly's daughter Polly, and son-in-law Isaac Jacklin, married to their daughter Mercy, obtain most of the Ragged Mountain property.

Jacklin was an interesting and important character. He was described as having been a "servant of Secretary Wyllys of Hartford from whom he ran away before the Revolutionary War, and took refuge in the Ragged Mountain Region of Barkhamsted" (Boyd 1873:230). George Wyllys, Jr., served as Secretary of State in Connecticut in the middle years of the eighteenth century. Later census records identify the Jacklin family as being black; his father's name was Freeman, a common name given to freed slaves. There was a Freeman Jacklin born on November 25, 1716, in New London, Connecticut. Freeman's father, Robert Jacklin, had been a slave owned by Dr. Peter Tappan of Newbury, Massachusetts. Robert Jacklin was emancipated by Tappan on October 15, 1711, apparently moved to New London where Freeman was born, and then to Dutchess County, New York on the Connecticut border. It seems likely that Isaac was the grandson of the freed slave Robert Jacklin.

The family's land base grew again on August 25, 1786, when Solomon Chaugham purchased from Joseph Shepard, Jr., for £3, 5⅘ acres on the other side of the Farmington River, about two miles from the Lighthouse village. This was a portion of lot IV–20 originally taken by Thomas Sadd of Windsor (see Figure 6.1).

The land deals continued on September 20, 1786, when James sold 10 of his 70 Ragged Mountain acres for "the consideration of ten pounds lawful money received of Mary Willson of said Barkhamsted and for the consideration of the love, good will, and affection which I have and do bear towards her the said Mary of Barkhamsted aforesaid."

The section sold was the southern portion of James's lot III–91, as seen in Figure 6.2. Who was "Mary Willson" to whom James bears such love and affection? She represents another curious case of name confusion. Mary Willson turns out to be a married daughter of James and Molly, but not the daughter Mary named in the legend as derived from Polly Elwell. This particular puzzle can be solved with documents to be discussed later in this chapter.

On the same day as this transaction, James sold to his son Solomon the northern 20 acres of lot III–91 for £20. This left James with 40 acres of the original 70 he purchased from Abraham Kellogg.

A short time later, on September 10, 1787, James (specified in the deed as "an Indian") sold to Samuel Lawrence (also specified as "an Indian") the 20-acre lot in New Hartford purchased from Asher Hinmon for £8 in 1775. Then on June 13, 1788, James Chaugum (again specified in the land record as "an Indian") "for the love and good will I have to my wife Mary Chaugum," gave Mary the 40 acres in New Hartford that he purchased from Cornelius Indian for £15 in 1771. James seemed to be selling off or giving away much of his land, but, as we can see, he was keeping it in the family.

More land was added to the village on November 11, 1789, when Solomon purchased from Noah Phelps 29 additional acres on Ragged Mountain. The land, a rocky hillside valuable only for its timber, cost Solomon just £5. According to the deed, this land represented the rest of the original land grant given Nathan Gillet, Sr. (lot III–92), 49 acres of which Sol's brother Samuel purchased in 1782 and then sold to Isaac Jacklin, his brother-in-law-to-be, in 1784. At this point the family—James and Molly, their sons, daughters, and son-in-law—owned a combined total of 138 contiguous acres on Ragged Mountain. This was to be the most land they would ever own on the mountain.

The Death of James Chaugham

It was sometime around the beginning of the final decade of the eighteenth century that James Chaugham, patriarch of the village, died. James may have been ill toward the end of his life or he simply may have been advanced in years. If the Indian boy James on Block Island was, in fact, James Chaugham, he would have been about 80 years old in 1790. Age or infirmity may explain why James disposed of so much of his land to his family in the late 1780s. It seems reasonable to assume that James was providing a land base for both his wife and his children before he died and his property distributed through probate. Such land transferals were fairly common in New England and elsewhere. In an eighteenth-century Connecticut sample, more than half of the adult sons whose fathers owned real estate received land from them before their fathers' deaths (Ditz 1986), giving them a land base early in life that would allow them to marry and provide for a family of their own. Many people do much the same thing today in an attempt to avoid the costs, delays, and legal entanglements of the probate process.

There is further documentary evidence of James's death by 1790. As we discussed in Chapter 5, the first federal census was conducted in that year, and the 1790 census records for Connecticut still exist. Although there is no breakdown by town for the northwestern part of the state, there are records for Litchfield County, the location of Barkhamsted. The original written records are rough and the transcription is not precise, but it is almost certainly the case that the "Mary Chaugorn" listed as a family head is, indeed, Mary Chaugham. The last document bearing James Chaugham's mark is dated June 3, 1788. Because only the names of household heads were listed in the 1790 census, this may indicate that sometime after June 3, 1788, and by the time the census was taken in 1790, James had already passed away. Alternatively, it is possible that since Indians were not counted in the census and as James was an Indian, his existence was unrecorded and Molly, being white, was listed as the household head.

In any event, on November 17, 1790, his father James dead or very near death, Solomon sold to Benajah Hays of Granby, Connecticut all of the land he personally owned in Barkhamsted. Included in this transaction was his small lot about two miles from the village itself, the 20 acres he had purchased from his father that was a part of lot III–91, along with the 29 acres of lot III–92 he bought from Noah Phelps. It is likely that Solomon was about to leave the village and strike out on his own. But why would Sol have sold land right in the middle of the village to an outsider? It is possible that Hays was already part of the family. According to James and Molly's granddaughter Polly Elwell when she was interviewed by William Wallace Lee in 1869 (Chapter 4), Solomon Chaugham married a woman named "Miss Hayes." There is a possibility that Miss Hayes may have been the daughter of Ben Hays of Granby, although, maddeningly, there are no records to confirm this. On March 6, 1793, Hays sold the land he bought from Sol to William Wilson for £25; at this point, Hays was cited as living in Herkimer, New York. In the 1810 census records for New York State, there is a Benajah T. Hayes listed as a household head in Steuben County, New York. William Wilson, as mentioned in the legend and as will be shown, is another son-in-law of James and Molly.

The other son, Samuel, also left the village around this time. In a land transaction dated February 2, 1791, it was recorded that "Samuel Choggum of Sharon, Connecticut," a town on the border with New York State and about 25 miles west of Barkhamsted, sold to his brother-in-law Isaac Jacklin "all my right, title, interest, and estate that I have or ought to have in and unto all the real estate of Mr. James Chaugum late of said Barkhamsted deceased, it being one fifth part of said estate and already divided among the heirs by their own mutual agreement." As James had sold off all but 40 acres of his Barkhamsted lands, a one-fifth part would have been about eight acres.

Next, James and Molly's daughter Hannah, who married a man named "Reubin Barber" (they are referred to as husband and wife in the land transaction document), sold "all the lands that fell to me by heirship out of my father's estate" to a George Shepherd on October 18, 1793. Hannah's portion of the estate is located precisely in this document. There were two sections; the first "lyeth between Samuel Chaugum's right and Mercy Jacklin's right" and the second is "plow land" located "between Meribah Lawrence's right and the proprietor's highway." Shepherd almost immediately sold this land to Jonas Weed who ultimately gave it to his son Nathaniel on September 11, 1795.

It turns out that the Weeds were neighbors of the Chaughams, living less than one mile south of the Lighthouse village on the Farmington River Turnpike. Jonas, Sr. had come to town in 1777, apparently fleeing Danbury (or, perhaps, Stamford, where the vital records have several listings for Jonas Weed) during the Revolutionary War when he was suspected of harboring Tory sympathies (Lee 1881, 1897). Jonas and his wife Mahitabel had two sons: Jonas, Jr., and Nathaniel. Jonas Weed, Sr., is buried in a family plot next to the turnpike (now East River Road) about a mile south of the Lighthouse village.

The next important land document to surface clears up a number of other elements of the legend. On December 16, 1793, the "Meribah Lawrence" just mentioned in Hannah's land sale sold to William Wilson for £2 the western portion of the "land that my father James Chaugham owned at his death . . . that fell to me in said division." This lot is described as lying "between the rights of Mercy Jacklin and Hannah Barber." The document bears the marks of Meribah Lawrence and her husband Samuel Lawrence. On the same day, Meribah sold the eastern portion of her lot to Mahitabel Weed, wife of Jonas Weed, Sr., for £4. Mahitabel and Jonas gave this additional section of land on Ragged Mountain to their son Nathaniel on April 2, 1801.

Who are Meribah and Samuel Lawrence? Polly Elwell in her interview with William Wallace Lee (Chapter 4) mentioned no daughter named Meribah—and that name turns up in no version of the legend that I am aware of—but Polly did state that her grandparents James and Molly had a daughter Mary (this would have been Polly's aunt) who married a man named "———— Lawrence." Meribah Lawrence must be that Mary; perhaps Mary was the name she used ordinarily, and her given name, used only on official documents, was the more formal Meribah. Her husband Samuel Lawrence has already turned up in this chapter. He was identified as "an Indian" in a land document recording his purchase from James Chaugham—who now can be identified as his father-in-law—of 20 acres in New Hartford. Finally, the "William Wilson" who purchased the land from Meribah and who bought the land that Ben Hays bought from Solomon Chaugham turns out to be the husband of another of James and Molly's daughters, Polly. Little is known about Wilson beyond the fact that he served in the Revolutionary War (Lee 1897).

Note that the document recording Meribah Lawrence's land sale specifies that the land the children inherited was property "James Chaugham owned at his death." That James had not disposed of this property before his death and also the language of the sale of Samuel's one-fifth portion, describing the land as having been "divided among the heirs by their own mutual agreement," indicates that James died intestate—without a will expressing his desire as to how his estate would be distributed among his heirs.

In 1794, at least four years after James's death, a number of land transactions took place in rapid succession. On February 6 the widowed Mary Chaugham sold her 40 acres in New Hartford to Asher Hinmin. This was the land James purchased from Cornelius Indian in 1771 and formally transferred to Molly in 1788. Hinmin (spelled "Hinmon" on the document) previously had

NAME CONFUSION

Remember in the Mills account (Chapter 3), James and Molly had a daughter named "Mary" who married "Old Gum Webster." This is one point where Mills was certainly wrong. Montgomery ("Gum") Webster turns up later in our story. His son Sol, as we will see, married into the Chaugham lineage and was the individual interviewed for the January 1900 *Connecticut Courant* article about the Lighthouse, discussed in Chapter 4.

Here is an instance where substantial confusion results from the differences between people's given names, formal names, and the names they were called by members of their family. James and Molly's daughter Polly who married William Wilson had a different given name, as indicated in official documents. Although her sister Meribah may have been called Mary (or perhaps on this point Polly Elwell was wrong), the given name of Polly Elwell's mother actually was Mary, though she too was called Polly. The wife of William Wilson is always referred to as the daughter of James Chaugham and is sometimes reported as Mary and sometimes as Polly. That they are, in fact, the same person and William Wilson was not just married twice is attested to by the following sequence: In a 1786 document, Wilson's wife is listed as Mary; in 1822 she is Polly; and then in documents dated 1831 and 1833 she is Mary again. Polly is another common nickname for Mary and this explains the confusion, in part. Thus the "Mary Willson" to whom James sold 10 acres of his Ragged Mountain land in 1786 for £10, love, good will, and affection was his married daughter Mary Chaugham Wilson. That was her legal name, but everyone called her Polly.

The confusion over given names, formal names, and informal nicknames has proliferated but can be cleared up. Molly Barber, whose given name was Mary, had a daughter whose given name was Meribah, but apparently was called Mary (at least according to an elderly niece of hers, years after her aunt had died). Molly had another daughter whose given name was Mary but who was called Polly, another common nickname for Mary! To complete the circle, as we will see in the census records to be discussed, Polly and William Wilson had at least two children: a son—William, Jr.—and a daughter—also named Polly. The daughter Polly married Joseph Elwell and is the Polly Elwell we mentioned previously as the important source of information for J. E. Mason in his 1855 *Mountain County Herald* article and for William Wallace Lee in his 1879 Barkhamsted Centennial address.

sold another 20-acre lot in New Hartford to James Chaugham—the lot James sold to his son-in-law (or son-in-law-to-be) Samuel Lawrence.

The day after Molly sold her New Hartford land, she signed a fascinating document formally relinquishing any right she might have had to James's Barkhamsted land for a payment of £15 from his heirs; that is, her own children. Finally on March 19, 1794, Molly Chaugham (in one of the two official documents where her nickname Molly was used) bought 22.5 acres on Spruce Mountain in Sharon, Connecticut for £17.

A WOMAN'S PLACE AND DOWER RIGHT

What transpired in the 1790s after James's death reflects a family's attempt to formalize and legalize decisions made upon his death without the benefit of a legally binding, formal expression of his desires in the form of a will.

Before James's death, he disposed of much of his land to his wife and his son Solomon. As noted, providing land to a son was a common practice of fathers, enabling sons to support families of their own.

That Molly also received land from James before his death is understandable. Before 1723 in Connecticut, married women could not own land themselves. A married couple was legally considered to be a single entity, called a "unity of persons." As Cott (1977:5) states:

> A married woman had no legal existence apart from her husband's: she could not sue, contract, or even execute a will on her own; her person, estate, and wages became her husband's when she took his name.

The husband thus had all of the power in the "unity of persons" that was a marriage and had complete control over even those lands his wife possessed before their marriage, land she would have inherited from or been given by her father. In 1723 in Connecticut things changed somewhat with the passage of a law, An Act Preventing the Sales of the Real Estate of Heiresses Without Their Consent (Salmon 1986). After passage of this law, husbands no longer held absolute power, merely managerial rights, over land owned by their wives before their marriage. In effect this meant that a husband still could control the lands. He could, for example, decide how the lands would be used, lease the property, farm it, leave it as a woodlot, and so on, but he could not *sell* the land without his wife's consent. If his wife died, the lands would be inherited by their children. If there were no children, ownership of the wife's lands reverted to her family.

The rather tenuous grip women had over land they owned before marriage explains why fathers often were loathe to provide their unmarried daughters with any land at all. As Ditz (1986:66) points out, even into the 1770s, while some 85 percent of sons whose fathers owned real estate inherited land from them, only a little more than 40 percent of daughters were given land by their fathers, who feared that such lands would be lost to the family.

All of this must be understood from an eighteenth-century perspective. It was considered natural that women should be dependent on men for the duration of their lives; as children they were dependent on their fathers and as wives they were dependent on their husbands. Married women were supposed to be dependent and the law ensured that they were dependent on their husbands. At the same time, men were expected to be providers for their wives and children. Just as law made women dependent on men, the law induced men to support their families.

(continued)

Although this was considered to be the natural order of things in the eighteenth and nineteenth centuries, it did create a significant problem. Fathers and husbands could die, leaving women—sometimes with children—without a man to provide for their needs. Some men did not plan adequately for the needs of their families if they, the men, died. A woman with adult children might become impoverished if her husband left all of his property to the children and left no provision for his widow. If a man were to dispose of all the family's real estate before his death—as was his right—his wife and their children would have no way to provide for themselves and might become destitute upon his death. As Salmon (1986:184) points out, "In many communities, widows and single women alone constituted the largest segment of recipients of poor relief."

This dilemma led most states to enact legislation establishing what was called *dower right*. Certainly the dower right can be considered paternalistic. In one sense it kept women dependent on their husbands, even after their husbands died. Salmon goes so far as to characterize the dower right as mandating "the enforced dependency of widows" (1986:183). Its enactment can be explained in part by the self-interest of a community that didn't want the expense of taking care of widows whose husbands had not provided for them. Recognizing that the law itself made women dependent, it was consistent to have a protection like dower right to ensure that a woman would be able to support herself and her children upon her husband's death when there was no man on whom she could depend.

Specifically the dower right gave a widow the right to use one third (or one half if there were no children) of her deceased husband's lands to support herself. In many cases dower right superseded the wording of a will and included not just the lands the husband owned upon his death but any of the land the couple owned any time during their marriage.

The implications were significant. A man could not cut his wife out of his will—her dower right would supplant that document. A man might foolishly sell off all his real estate before his death, but in some states (Connecticut was one of these) a widow still could assert her dower right to that property, land now owned by others.

This made selling land difficult. After all, who would wish to make an investment in real estate if a widow could legally claim a use right of one third to one half of the property for the duration of her life?

The dower right led to the practice of requiring women to sign land sale documents involving their husbands, thereby acknowledging their acceptance of the sales and renouncing their dower right. Some states, Connecticut included, went so far as to demand a private hearing or interview conducted by a justice of the peace with a woman to make sure she understood the rights she was giving up and to ensure that she had not been coerced by her husband into placing her signature on the document. All of this provided women with a measure of power over the family real estate holdings. Dower right served as a powerful inducement to husbands not to sell land their wives didn't want sold.

Probate, Dower Right, and the Estate of James Chaugham

What happened before and after James's death is understandable within the context of inheritance and dower right. Although a will was and is an important way for a person to ensure that his or her wishes are carried out, many people (both then and now) neglect to have a will legally drawn up. By law all estates should go through probate where either the will is read and the wishes of the deceased are carried out or, in the absence of a will, an administrator is appointed who will decide how the estate should be distributed. Regardless of law, however, Ditz (1986:40) estimates between 40 percent and 70 percent of all estates were not probated in the eighteenth and nineteenth centuries. Benes and Benes (1989:11) suggest that in some communities less than one quarter of male property owners went through probate. In these cases families did what they could to informally dispose of property without the state imposing its will. The Chaughams seem to have attempted to do precisely this.

Remember, it is recorded in the land sale dated February 2, 1791, that upon his death the land that James owned had been distributed to the heirs through "mutual agreement." It seems that in their informal division of the land, however, they had not reckoned with the dower right provision of Connecticut probate law. Technically and legally, the widow Molly had a right to one third of those 40 acres. And remember, on February 7, 1794, the day after she sold her 40 acres in New Hartford, Molly signed a document relinquishing, for the payment of £15, "to the heirs of James Chaugum and their heirs and assigns forever all the right, title, interest that I ever had or ought to have in or to the estate of said James Chaugum." Thus Molly was giving up her dower right or any other right the state might have declared her to have over her husband's lands as a result of the lack of a will and the fact that the estate had not gone through a legal probate.

This clarifies why Molly, now without any land of her own, on March 19, 1794, purchased 22.5 acres on Spruce Mountain in Sharon, Connecticut. Sharon, you will recall, is recorded as the town of residence of Molly's son Samuel as of February 1791.

The Family after James

These transactions present us with many insights into the family after James's death, but also leave us with many questions. Was Molly's removal to Sharon of her own volition or was she pushed off the Barkhamsted lands by her children? Was Samuel Chaugham's removal to Sharon part of a breakup of the family? Did Samuel and Meribah Lawrence follow Molly out to Sharon after selling their New Hartford land? It is impossible to tell. We do know that by October 31, 1796 Molly's unmarried daughter, Elizabeth, had also moved to Sharon. On that date she sold her one-fifth portion of her father's estate that she inherited upon his death to her brother-in-law, Isaac Jacklin. (She is referred to as "Elizabeth Chaugham, of Sharon" in the document.)

In this record, the final one fifth of James's estate is now accounted for. Mercy Jacklin held on to her portion, and we have now documented the sale of their one-fifth parcels by Samuel (to Isaac Jacklin), Hannah (to George Shepherd who sold it to Jonas Weed who gave it to his son Nathaniel), Meribah (who divided her land between William Wilson and Mahitabel Weed; the latter gave her land to her son Nathaniel who, in 1799, sold two acres of that lot to William Wilson for $12), and now Elizabeth (selling to Jacklin). (See Figure 6.3.) Note that two of James Chaugham's living children were not given any land in the distribution of the estate after his death: Solomon and Polly (whose given name was Mary). Solomon, as we have already seen, owned a considerable amount of acreage in Barkhamsted, most of it on Ragged Mountain, but sold all of it in 1790. He disappears from the historical record at this point. He likely moved away and had no need of land in Barkhamsted. Polly (who was married to William Wilson) already owned 10 acres on Ragged Mountain sold to her by her father in 1786.

Summary: 1783–1800

By the final decade of the eighteenth century, dramatic changes had transpired on Ragged Mountain. James had died and his widow Molly had relinquished right to any of his land in Barkhamsted. Molly purchased property in Sharon and moved there (later when she sold the land her residence was listed in the land transferral as that town). Solomon had sold all of his land and was gone. Samuel had sold his land and was living in Sharon, as was his unmarried sister Elizabeth. The Lighthouse village land was owned by two sons-in-law, William Wilson and Isaac Jacklin, and a neighboring family, the Weeds. The Lighthouse village, it would seem, largely had passed to the next generation.

Ragged Mountain: 1800–1820

On March 14, 1799, Molly sold her 22.5-acre lot in Sharon for $180. After having owned that lot and perhaps living there for five years with her unmarried daughter and one of her sons and his family, Molly once again established a land base in Barkhamsted. On April 8, 1800, Molly purchased one third of a 57-acre lot (about 19 acres) in town from Siba Moses for $50; Daniel Mather bought the other two thirds of the lot. The parcel contained portions of the original lots IV–5 and –6 (see Figure 6.2) and is, not coincidentally, immediately south of the Lighthouse nucleus on James's original land (lot III–91).

To make matters even more interesting, the grantor of the lot, Siba Moses, had purchased the land from Jonas Weed, Jr., who in turn bought it in 1797 from none other than Isaac Jacklin! Isaac Jacklin had been given or had inherited the land from his own father, Freeman Jacklin, who purchased the lot from Joel, Jonathan, and John Palmer of Windsor in 1794. Isaac's father,

---

KEY EVENTS: 1800–1820

- Molly returns to Barkhamsted, purchasing land near the village.
- Issac and Mercy Jacklin sell off their land holdings to William Wilson and move to the nearby community of Winsted.
- Molly trades off her land near the village for acreage within the original land purchase on Ragged Mountain.
- Joseph Elwell marries James and Molly's granddaughter Polly Wilson.
- Molly dies in 1818.

Freeman Jacklin, whose residence was listed in the land sale as Barkhamsted, purchased land near his son's in-laws. There is no record of his being in town before 1794, but he certainly could have been. Remember, there was a Jacklin family with a son named Freeman living in Dutchess County, New York just over the border from Connecticut. Perhaps Freeman Jacklin's presence in Barkhamsted was the reason Isaac moved to town in the 1780s, where he met and married Mercy Chaugham. It is equally possible that the elder Jacklin moved to the Lighthouse after his son's marriage to Mercy Chaugham in 1785.

According to the records of the 1800 census, "Mary Chaugum" was the head of a household in Barkhamsted. Remember, these records do not name other members of a household, they only record them according to age and sex categories. The household included one free white woman more than 45 years old (certainly this is Molly) and three "other free persons except Indians not taxed." This catchall category, as described in Chapter 5, includes free blacks and people of mixed race. The census taker recorded Molly as white, but those in her household—this may have included the unmarried Elizabeth—were recognized as being of mixed race.

The 1800 census also records William Wilson as the head of a family in Barkhamsted. His household is inventoried as follows: one free white male 16–26, one free white male 26–45, one free white female greater than 45, and six other free persons except Indians not taxed. Wilson was certainly the free white male 26–45, and the six other "free persons" likely include his mixed-race wife and their children.

The census records also indicate that at least one branch of the family had moved, if only temporarily, to New York State. Samuel Chogham and a Benjamin Chogham are both listed as household heads in Dutchess County, New York, the county directly west of Sharon, Connecticut. Samuel is recorded as being the head of a household consisting of two males 10–16 years of age, one male 26–45 (this would be Samuel himself), one female under 10, one female 16–26, and one female 26–45 (Samuel's wife). Bejamin's family contained one male under 10, one male 16–26 (this would be Benjamin), one female under 10, and one female 16–26 (Benjamin's wife). Based on his age (26–45), this Samuel listed in the New York census of 1800 must have been James and Molly's son—the same Samuel who purchased land in Barkhamsted in 1782. Benjamin, then, was almost certainly Samuel's adult son.

On Ragged Mountain on April 2, 1801, three separate land deals were made. Nathaniel Weed sold for $22 to Hannah's sister "Marcey" Jacklin the six acres that can be traced back to Hannah (remember, he had already sold two acres of this eight-acre lot to William Wilson in 1799). Weed next sold the Jacklins the lot he bought from Meribah Lawrence in 1793; this was a part of the lot Meribah inherited from her father. Again on the same day, for $24 the Jacklins sold Weed a portion of the original lot laid out to Mercy upon her father's death. In essence the Weeds and the Jacklins played a game of real estate musical chairs, probably trying to spatially consolidate their holdings on the mountain (see Figure 6.3).

Then on October 2, 1801, Isaac and "Massy" Jacklin sold three parcels of land for $60 to William Wilson. These parcels included the rest of the lot Mercy inherited from her father along with "said land I, Isaac Jacklin purchased of James Chougum's heirs." Based on subsequent land sales by the Jacklins, the latter was almost certainly the land Isaac bought from Samuel Chaugham in 1791 and may have included the portion of Meribah's lot that Weed sold him in April.

On June 10, 1802, Isaac and Mercy Jacklin sold more of their property on Ragged Mountain to Joshua Youngs and described it as being most of the two lots that "fell to Elizabeth Chaugham, one of the heirs of said James Chaugum . . . and of Hannah Barber, the wife of Reubin Barber, one of the heirs of James Chaugum." Youngs was a Farmington, Connecticut resident who purchased land in Barkhamsted in 1800 about a mile south of the Lighthouse on the other (west) side of the Farmington River (lot IV–11; see Figure 6.1). There he built a sawmill and wood shop, creating a small mill community called "Youngsdale" (Wheeler and Hilton 1975). His purchase of land on Ragged Mountain reflects a pattern of land acquisition he followed until his death in about 1820.

The June 10, 1801, document specified that those two lots—the two one-fifth portions of James Chaugham's estate—totaled roughly 14 acres. That is about what we previously determined: James owned 40 acres when he died and the land was then divided into five sections, probably of about eight acres each. Since two acres of Hannah's lot had already been sold to William Wilson, the two lots—Elizabeth's eight acres and what remained of Hannah's six acres—together would have equaled about 14 acres.

Isaac and Mercy's household is not listed in the 1800 census for Barkhamsted or anywhere else. As stated previously, the early censuses simply are not that accurate. The Jacklins most probably were still living in Barkhamsted when they began selling off their land on Ragged Mountain.

In another interesting sequence of land exchanges, on March 19, 1806, Molly transferred ownership of her 19 acres (the lands she purchased in 1800) just south of the Lighthouse to Joshua Youngs "for divers good causes and consideration thereunto moving; especially for other lands this day deeded to me and received to my full satisfaction of Joshua Youngs of Farmington." The land Youngs traded for Molly's 19 acres was none other than the 14 acres on Ragged Mountain he purchased from Isaac Jacklin just four years previously.

This land, remember, contained most of the parcels doled out to Hannah and Elizabeth on their father's death. It seems that through a rather circuitous route, and with the cooperation of Joshua Youngs, Molly re-established her ownership of at least a portion of the land that her husband James purchased initially in 1779 and to which she relinquished any title or claim in 1794.

It is unclear precisely why the land transactions on the mountain in the early nineteenth century were indirect, circuitous, and complex. Why, if Molly wished to return to the Lighthouse, did she not simply buy land from one of her sons-in-law, especially since one of them, Isaac Jacklin, was selling off his property on Ragged Mountain? Why was it necessary first to buy land near the village, land her son-in-law Isaac Jacklin had owned but had sold to someone else? Why was it necessary for Molly to wait until that same son-in-law sold land within the village to an outsider and then, in effect, to trade another parcel of land for that land?

It is tempting to suggest that there were problems within the family, problems that may have precipitated Molly's initial departure to buy land in Sharon but that then brought her back to the community she helped establish with her husband. One should not read too much into the sequence of events, but it is possible that all was not right between Molly and her daughter and son-in-law, Mercy and Isaac Jacklin. One version of the legend adds the ironic twist that James and Molly, whose interracial marriage shocked polite society, opposed their daughter Mercy's marriage to a man of African descent. We do not know if this is true or if it played a role in the relationship between the Jacklins and Molly. In any event, by the time the transactions were complete, Molly once again owned some of the village land and Mercy and Isaac had left the Lighthouse.

With the exception of a single land sale, we enter a period of relative quiet on the mountain and within the family. In 1806 Samuel Choggam apparently moved back to Connecticut and purchased land of his own: 5-plus acres in Kent, the town immediately south of Sharon.

On April 1, 1808, Meribah's husband Samuel Lawrence died in New Hartford. As recorded by the New Hartford Congregational Church, he was between 40 and 50 years old when he died. Widowed and apparently childless, Meribah disappeared from the official records. Samuel had sold off his New Hartford land in February 1794. Meribah may have returned to the Lighthouse to live out her life, or she may have remained in New Hartford. This branch of the Chaugham line seems to end here as there is no record of any children born to the Lawrences.

On June 24 and 25, 1807, Nathaniel Weed sold whatever acreage he still owned near the Lighthouse village to Joshua Youngs. The June 24 document describes the land as "lying on the east branch of the west river lying on the island that was formerly owned by James Chaugum's heirs . . . ." The price was $5. The southern half of the island referred to here constituted the western section of lot III–91, James's original parcel on Ragged Mountain (see Figure 6.2). On the next day Weed sold to Youngs for $40 "all the land I own lying near Mary Chaugham except the land I before this date [i.e., the day before] quit claimed to said Joshua Youngs lying on the island." It is likely that Youngs was purchasing land where he might possibly construct another mill, taking advantage of the power offered by the Farmington River.

By the 1810 census Samuel Chogam and his household are listed in Kent. The family contained three people, all in the catchall "all other free persons" category. Interestingly, Benjamin Chogam, who first appeared in the 1800 census in New York State, now shows up in Kent, Connecticut. According to the census, Benjamin was now the head of a family of 10 people, all recorded as non-white, non-Indian "other free persons." This clearly reflects recognition on the part of the census taker of the mixed ancestry of this line of the Chaughams.

This same census helps us track down the Jacklin line of the family. After selling off their property on Ragged Mountain in Barkhamsted, Isaac, Mercy, and their children moved to Winchester, the town immediately west of Barkhamsted. Winsted, located within the town, was a small industrial hub in northwestern Connecticut and home to three of the newspapers that ran articles about the Lighthouse in the mid-nineteenth and early twentieth centuries, as discussed in Chapter 4. According to the 1810 census the Jacklin family, with Isaac as its head, consisted of 14 people, all of whom were categorized as non-white, non-Indian free persons. Isaac, as a free black, his wife of mixed white and Native American ancestry, and their children would have been included in this category.

In the May 1, 1817, records of the Barkhamsted First Congregational Church the death of a baby is noted. Its age is given as "three hours." The parents listed in this tragic death are Joseph and "Wife" Elwell. Joseph Elwell was born in 1774, one of six children of Joshua and Abigail Elwell, residents of Barkhamsted. He married Polly Wilson, daughter of William Wilson and Polly (Mary) Chaugham, James and Molly's daughter. The dead infant, therefore, was the child of the Polly Elwell who has been such an important source of information about the Lighthouse village where she lived her life; she was the great grandchild of James and Molly Chaugham.

Then, there is another listing in the family records of the Barkhamsted First Congregational Church. According to those records, on February 6, 1818, the remarkable person whose improbable transformation from a wealthy young woman to an independent pioneer—and whose life in the Connecticut wilderness inspired such admiration among so many, including this author—died. "Mrs. Choggum" passed away on February 6, 1818, at William Wilson's house at the age of 104 years. This matches reasonably closely the description provided by Mills as cited in Chapter 3:

> Thus 'tis written in the records,
> Granny Chaugham's days were over,
> All her joys and sorrows ended
> For she died in eighteen twenty—
> And her age—*one hundred five years* (Mills 1952:71).

Molly's passing did not go unnoticed in Connecticut newspapers. In rapid succession in March 1818, the *Connecticut Courant* (see the discussion at the beginning of this chapter), the *Connecticut Mirror*, the *Connecticut Herald*, and the *Hartford Times* each carried her death notice. And in each case, her age is given as 100 years. It is clear that even in the second decade of the nineteenth century, Molly Barber Chaugham was deemed to be important and newsworthy.

Unlike the estate left by James, Molly's estate did go through the legal process of probate. The records still exist and are dated to 1821, three years after her death. According to the probate documents, not surprisingly, Molly did not die a wealthy woman (Figure 6.4). All she owned in personal property was an iron kettle whose value was assessed by Drayton Jones, the probate administrator, at $1.25, a small kettle worth $.50, and an old chest of drawers whose estimated value also was $.50. Her land made up the bulk of the value of Molly's estate. Remember, in 1806 she had purchased 14 acres on Ragged Mountain from Joshua Youngs that we could trace back to her daughters Elizabeth and Hannah. In probate these 14 acres were listed and appraised at $10 per acre—for a total value of $140. The final total value of her estate was $142.25.

Unfortunately for Molly's heirs, her probate also indicates that she died owing the town of Barkhamsted $284.97, probably in back taxes and legal fees. Drayton Jones was instructed by the court of probate to raise the money needed to pay off that debt. Following those instructions, on January 18, 1822, title to Molly's 14-acre estate was transferred to the town of Barkhamsted for its

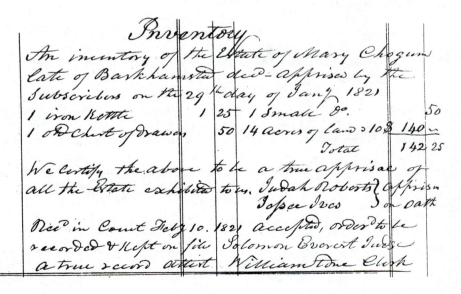

Figure 6.4 The probate listing for Mrs. Mary Chogum, dating to 1821, three years after her death. The total value of her estate is given as $142.25.

appraised value of $10 per acre, covering $140 of her debt. In a rather curious deal on the same day, Barkhamsted turned around and sold the land to none other than Molly's son-in-law, William Wilson, for the "fire-sale" price of $100—a $40 loss for the town in a single day! Certainly the town had no abiding desire to possess land on Ragged Mountain. It merely wished to cut its losses—and they were paper losses anyway—and collect what it could on Molly's debt.

Summary: 1800–1820

By the 1820s more fundamental changes had transpired at the Lighthouse. James and Molly's son-in-law and daughter, Isaac and Mercy Jacklin, had sold all of their Barkhamsted lands and were gone. Molly had died. Another daughter and son-in-law of James and Molly, Polly and William Wilson, owned the land on which the village stood; by 1820 they controlled about 89 acres on the mountain (see Figure 6.3). Although James and Molly were dead and all of their children with the exception of Polly had left the mountain, the Lighthouse itself was to continue for some time as a haven for the disenfranchised. James and Molly's grandchildren and even their great grandchildren from William and Polly continued to live in the village and raise families of their own.

The Final Decades of the Lighthouse Community: 1820–1860

Molly died in 1818, so her name does not appear in the 1820 census. Interestingly, another woman named "Chogum" shows up as the head of a household: the "Widow Chogum" in Kent. She is most likely the widow of James and Molly's son Samuel who had moved to Kent in 1791 (although she may have been the widow of Benjamin Chaugham). This same census continues to list Isaac Jacklin as a household head in Winchester, Connecticut, along with another family headed by a John Jacklin. John is a son of Isaac and Mercy (he is listed as a son in Isaac's will), old enough to have started his own family. Back in Barkhamsted, William Wilson and now his son William Wilson, Jr., are listed as household heads. Joseph Elwell also is listed as a household head in Barkhamsted. It is the Wilsons and the Elwells, the family of James and Molly's daughter Polly, who now constitute the core of the Lighthouse village.

The western branch of the family was active and, on October 26, 1829, a woman living in Kent named Susan "Chocum" married Amos Northrup. On January 12, 1834, a man also residing in Kent named Solomon "Choccum" married a woman named Sophia Bills. As we know that James and Molly's son Samuel had lived in Kent since 1806, it seems likely that Susan and Solomon were his children or, conceivably, his grandchildren; Benjamin might have been their father. No children are listed in the Kent vital records as having been born to the couple, and Samuel's son's wife, Sophia, died in childbirth on March 3, 1848, at the age of 35.

KEY EVENTS: 1820–1860
• William Wilson sells all of the Ragged Mountain property to William Murray, who then returns it to Wilson. • William Wilson sells all of the Ragged Mountain property to Hiram Goodwin, who allows the Lighthouse community to remain on the land. • Solomon Webster marries James and Molly's great granddaughter Mary Wilson. • The Elwell and the Webster families of James and Molly's descendants constitute the core of the village's population. • The village is abandoned by about 1860.

Things changed very little on Ragged Mountain until the 1830s. In the federal census of 1830, no Chaughams at all are listed for Connecticut: Isaac Jacklin, now in the over-55 category, continues to be listed as a household head in Winchester, and all 10 people recorded as living under his roof are classified as "free colored persons."

Also in the 1830 census William Wilson, Joseph Elwell, and Stephen Elwell are listed as family heads in Barkhamsted. "Gomery Webster" is listed for the first time as a family head in Barkhamsted. As we will see, this is "Old Gum Webster," incorrectly cited in Mills's poetic rendering of the legend as the husband of James and Molly's daughter Mary. As shown previously, he was not married to Mary (Meribah) Chaugham or to Polly (Mary) Chaugham, but, as will be shown, did become connected to the family through the marriage of his son Solomon.

The one piece of land on the mountain that had remained intact was the 10-acre lot James Chaugham deeded to his married daughter Polly (Mary) Wilson in 1786. This changed on January 22, 1831, when her son William Wilson, Jr., sold one quarter of that lot to Jabin Ford. It would seem that Polly (Mary) had given a portion of that land to her son. Interestingly, however, on November 1, 1833, William Wilson, Sr., bought back this parcel of land that his son had sold in 1831.

On November 6, 1830, Joseph and Polly Elwell sold to Rufus Holmes of Colebrook a "dwelling house standing on the Farmington River Turnpike" that they owned near William Wilson's house. On March 25, 1833, the Elwells mortgaged 2.5 more acres on the mountain to Bela Squire to pay off a debt. Squire owned a tavern on the Farmington River Turnpike about a mile south of the Lighthouse and, according to the deed, had lent Joseph $25. If the money was paid back within two years, the land would revert to the Elwells. The acreage was described as part of the 10-acre lot Polly inherited from "Mary Wilson, deceased, late wife of William Wilson." Here we see William Wilson's wife and Polly Elwell's mother named as "Mary," although Polly Elwell told William Wallace Lee quite explicitly that her mother's name was Polly, further supporting the contention that "Mary Willson" and "Polly Wilson" were the same person. Thus, of the 10 acres she purchased from her father in 1786, 2.5 went to her son who sold them (but which were bought back by his father) and at least 2.5 acres went to her daughter and son-in-law, who used this property to finance a loan. The Elwells seem to have paid off the debt, since 10 years later, on April 8, 1843, they sold the entire 10-acre lot for $50 to Hiram Goodwin. On that same day and for the same price, Goodwin sold the Elwells a parcel of a little more than an acre within the Lighthouse property. As will be shown, Goodwin purchased all of the Lighthouse land in 1836. On September 6 of the same year, the Elwells sold that small lot with a dwelling house to T. B. Graham.

William Wilson and his family were also engaged in land transactions in the 1830s. Jabin Ford, who purchased land from William Wilson, Jr., and his sister apparently were designated by the town to dispose of excess town land to private land owners. In this capacity on September 24, 1832, the Fords sold to William Wilson "and Harriet Wilson, wife of William Wilson, Jr.," a narrow strip of land that bordered the elder Wilson's land and that had been set aside for a highway in the original land distribution in the early eighteenth century.

Isaac Jacklin died in Winchester on May 13, 1835, at the estimated age of 90 years. Jacklin's estate was probated; he had written a formal will on March 25, 1830, and amended it (technically, he wrote a codicil, or addition to it) on March 18, 1835. Jacklin instructed that upon his death all his debts be paid off and that the estate he left be used to provide for his wife "Mercy Jacklin." He also left small amounts of money to his son John Jacklin and his family as well as to his married daughters Hannah Jacklin Cowles, Sally Jacklin Elwell, and Rhoda Jacklin Collins. It is unclear which Elwell son Sally Jacklin married. All of this, however, was superseded by the fact that Jacklin died insolvent; his debts could not be paid off by his estate. Mercy Jacklin died in 1842 at the estimated age of 85 years.

The Sale of the Lighthouse

On October 26, 1835, William Wilson, Sr., who by marriage and through purchases made of other Chaugham family members, owned virtually all the village's land on Ragged Mountain, sold "all of the land I own in Barkhamsted"—approximated at 80 acres—and a dwelling house on Ragged Mountain to William Murray of Colebrook, Connecticut for $900. A condition to the deed stipulated:

> The said William Murray in consideration of this deed of conveyance
> has undertaken and agreed to support and provide for the said William
> Wilson and his wife Maryann Wilson during their natural lives proper
> food and clothing, fuel and house room in sickness and health and also
> to give them a decent Christian burial at their decease and provide all
> and singular for the said Wilson and his wife those things which are
> proper for them and persons in their circumstances. Now if the said
> Murray shall fulfil in every respect as is here written then this deed is to

be good but if he shall fail in their particulars then this deed is to be void and of no effect or virtue in law.

We know that William Wilson's wife Polly (Mary) had died by 1833; she is referred to as "the late Mary Wilson" in a land document dated to that year. William Wilson and Maryann, a woman who apparently is his second wife, were by this time rather elderly. Although William had a living adult son and daughter, apparently he felt the need for additional assurance of being provided for in his old age. By adding this stipulation to the land deal, he seems to have guaranteed a comfortable end to his and his second wife's lives. Thus it would seem that we have come to an end of ownership of the Lighthouse village by descendants of James and Molly.

Nonetheless, and seemingly inexplicably, on July 18, 1836, William Murray sold the property—all 80 acres of it—back to the Wilsons for the extraordinary price of $15, a loss to him of $885 in fewer than nine months! Could the Wilsons simply not bear to part with the Lighthouse lands? Was William Murray an extraordinary philanthropist? Did Murray fail to live up to the stipulation of the deed? We simply do not know. It is possible that Wilson was using the land as collateral and had been able to pay back most or all of the loan, but this was not mentioned in the document.

In any event, on December 3, 1836, the Wilsons sold the property again, to Hiram Goodwin for $655; although it is described as being precisely the same property sold to Murray, the estimated acreage has swollen to 120 acres. This time there is no stipulation that the grantee is obliged to care for the grantors in their dotage.

Judge Hiram Goodwin had moved to Barkhamsted from New Hartford in 1830 (Wheeler and Hilton 1975). An important local personage, he served two years as the town's representative to the state legislature and served two terms in the state senate, along with being the local probate court judge. His name commonly turns up on probate documents.

It seems that Judge Goodwin allowed the residents of the village to stay on the land. Writing two years after Goodwin purchased all of the Lighthouse lands on Ragged Mountain, nineteenth-century historian John Warner Barber (1838) noted in his book, *Connecticut Historical Collections*, that 20 or 30 people continued to inhabit the Lighthouse village.

Meanwhile in June of 1837 back in Kent, Connecticut, Samuel Chaugham's son Solomon used his 3/4 of an acre of land with a house—land he likely inherited from his father Samuel who had purchased a little more than 5 acres in Kent in 1806 and who died before the 1820 census—as collateral to borrow money to pay off a debt to a man named, quite coincidentally, Lewis Mills (his middle initial is "M," our Chapter 3 poet's is "S"). According to the land document, Solomon could retain ownership of the land when he paid off the $200 debt. He did so, but then in February of 1839 he used the same land as collateral again to pay off a $100 debt to Harvey Smith. This debt was not repaid in a timely fashion, Samuel lost the land, and he was never mentioned in the documents again.

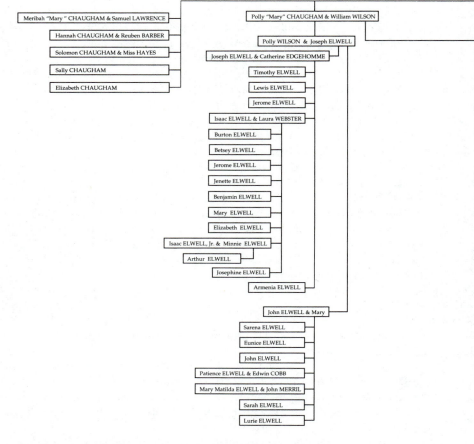

Figure 6.5   Genealogy diagram of the descendants of James and Molly.

The Elwell family was busy in the 1840s marrying and having children. James and Molly's granddaughter Polly married Joseph Elwell. There were probably several children and we know of two: Joseph, Jr. and John. Joseph, Jr. married Catherine Edgehomme on September 12, 1842. John married a woman named Mary. John and Mary, both of whom are designated "Mohegan" in the Barkhamsted vital records, had children in 1849 and 1855. John's occupation is listed as "basketmaker" and "laborer." Joseph, Jr. and Catherine are recorded as having children in 1850 and 1855. He is listed as a farmer and both are designated as "white." Remember, Joseph, Jr. and John Elwell both were great grandsons of James and Molly Chaugham. The kinship diagram presented in Figure 6.5 should help you follow this discussion of the Chaughams' descendants.

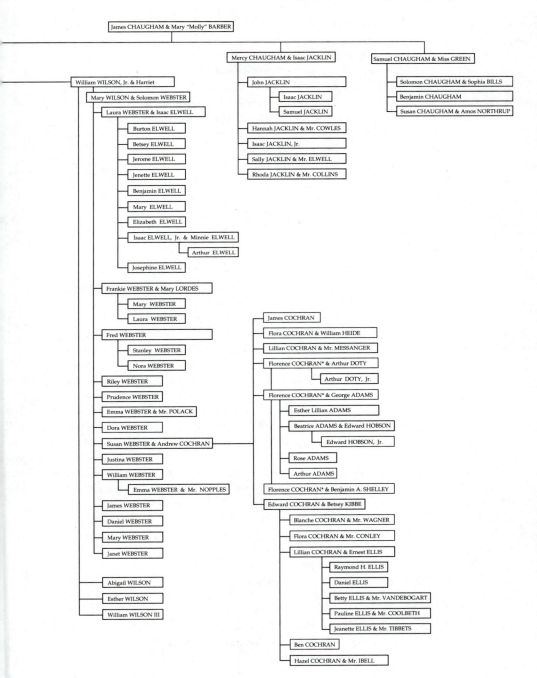

The primary documentary record of the Webster family clears up the confusion present in the January 1900 *Connecticut Courant* article (see Chapter 4). Montgumery (or Gomery, or Gum) Webster and his wife Sibel moved from Southington, Connecticut to Barkhamsted sometime before 1830; "Gomery" Webster is listed as a household head in the 1830 census. Gum Webster, his wife, and their children are variously designated in the Barkhamsted vital records as "Mohegan" (an Indian tribal name from the southeastern part of Connecticut), "Indian," "Creole" (here meaning of mixed race), or simply, "Mixed." A child was born to the 46-year-old Gum Webster (labeled "Creole" in the first Barkhamsted vital record reflecting his presence in town) and his wife (no name is given but she is labeled a "Mohegan") in May 1848. Although their child was born in Barkhamsted their place of residence is given as Southington, Connecticut, and Gum's occupation is listed as "basketmaker." The child died on May 20 after only three weeks of life; in the death record the child's name is listed as "Henry."

Gum, now designated "Mohegan," and his wife, called "Creole" (the vital records have switched their racial categories as recorded in 1848) and named in the records as "Sibel," on June 15, 1849, had another child in Barkhamsted (now listed as their residence) and named him Stephen. Then, on October 11, 1850, a man named Solomon Webster married a woman named Mary Wilson. We know precisely who Solomon Webster and Mary Wilson were because in the 1850 census, at long last, the names of *all* family members were recorded, not just household heads. Sol is the adult son of Gum Webster and this Mary Wilson is the daughter of William Wilson, Jr., and Harriet Wilson, making her a great granddaughter of James and Molly. Sol and Mary Webster are none other than the couple interviewed by the *Connecticut Courant* in January 1900. (See Chapter 4, Figure 4.1.) In that interview, Sol claimed to have been a descendant of James Chaugham, but it really was only his wife who could legitimately make that claim.

The 1850 census, along with reporting the presence of a 35-year-old laborer named John Chogam in Kent (living with the Pratt family and almost certainly the son of one of Samuel Chaugham's grandsons), also lists the names of the Gum Webster family: Montgomery (48 years old and a laborer), Sybil (46), Solomon (22, a laborer), Minerva (16), Henrietta (12), William (10), Prudence (5), and Samuel (11 months).

William Wilson, Sr., is not listed in the 1850 census; his death that year is noted in the Barkhamsted vital records. In this same census, his son William Wilson, Jr.'s family is listed: William (55 and a laborer), Harriet (47), Esther (23), Mary (17), Abigail (12), and William (10). The census must have been taken sometime prior to Sol and Mary's marriage in October because it lists them as living with their respective parents. Joseph and Polly Elwell also show up in this census. Their family is listed as follows: Joseph (67 years old and a basketmaker), Polly (53), Joseph, Jr. (35, a basketmaker), Catherine (38), Isaac (6), Timothy (5), Lewis (2), and Jerome (8 months). Notice that two generations of Elwells lived in the same census household; Joseph, Jr. and his wife

Figure 6.6   Photograph taken toward the end of the nineteenth century of John Elwell and his daughter Lurie. The house in the background is not on Ragged Mountain but in the Nepaug area of Canton, Connecticut, where the Elwells lived after leaving the Lighthouse. This area is now under the Nepaug Reservoir (New Hartford Historical Society. New Hartford, Conn.).

Catherine and their children lived with Joseph, Jr.'s parents. Joseph and Polly's other son, John, lived in his own household: John, a 35-year-old basketmaker (precisely the same age as his brother Joseph, Jr., but that means little) lived with his wife Mary (31) and their children Sarina (12), Eunice (10), John (8), Patience (5), and Mary (10 months). John lived into the early twentieth century and had his photograph taken along with one of his daughters, Lurie (Figure 6.6). Ten-month-old Mary Elwell, born in 1849 or 1850, lived into her late seventies, dying in 1929 in the town of Burlington, Connecticut. Older people in town still remember her telling them she was the last of the "Lighthouse tribe." Figure 6.7 is a photograph of "Old Til" (her middle name was "Matilda").

Soon after their marriage, Sol and Mary began having children, as reflected by the Barkhamsted vital records. On July 30, 1851, Mary (Wilson) Webster gave birth to a girl. The death of Mary's father, William Wilson, Jr., is listed in 1855; he was 56. Then on May 14, 1858, Sol and Mary had the child whose record I discussed in Chapter 1. This child, a girl, is listed in the vital records as being "nearly white," reflecting her mixed racial ancestry, and her parents' place of residence is given as "Barkhamsted Lighthouse" (see Figure 1.2). Thus we know in this very direct and formal way that Sol Webster, a man likely of Mohegan Indian ancestry, and his wife Mary Webster, great granddaughter of James and Molly Chaugham, were living and having children at the village established by Mary's ancestors, the village called in various renderings of the

Figure 6.7   Photograph taken in the early years of the twentieth century of Mary Matilda ("Til") Elwell Merril, one of John Elwell's daughters. According to residents of northwestern Connecticut who knew her, "Til," who died in 1929, maintained that she was the "last of the Lighthouse tribe" (New Hartford Historical Society. New Hartford, Conn.).

legend, "The Lighthouse." There can be no doubt that "The Lighthouse" was the real name of a real place. Although the ownership of the lands on which the Lighthouse village is located had largely passed into the hands of Judge Hiram Goodwin, the settlement continued to exist, if, perhaps, in an attenuated form. It seems that Goodwin owned the land and allowed the descendants of James and Molly to continue living there.

Summary: 1820–1860

We can follow the life histories of many of the players in the Lighthouse drama during this period. Of primary significance, we have seen how William Wilson, who had gained ownership of the Ragged Mountain hillside during the previous period, sold it off to Hiram Goodwin. Goodwin now owned the property but the Wilson and Elwell families continued to live at the Lighthouse, making up the core of the community.

After the Lighthouse Was Abandoned

Sol and Mary continued having children: a girl in 1858, another in 1859, and again in 1861, 1866, 1867, 1869, and 1870. The child born in 1869 is listed in a note in the Barkhamsted vital records as the couple's twelfth! Reflecting the tragically high infant mortality rate of the time, however, not all of these children survived. Sol's young brother, Henry, died at the age of three weeks in 1848, and the girls born to Sol and Mary in 1861 and 1870 died at four and three months, respectively. By the 1860 census, Sol (now 30 years old) and Mary (28) are listed in their own household with their children Laura (9), Frankie (6), Fred (4), Riley (3), and Prudence (1). As reflected in the land records, the Websters purchased their own land in the 1860s and appear to have moved away from the village itself. The same holds true for Joseph Elwell, Jr. In this way, with various of James and Molly's descendants going their own way in the 1860s, the Lighthouse village seems to have been abandoned.

School Records

As mentioned in Chapter 5, one source of information about the inhabitants of a community are school registers wherein the names of children attending a community school are tallied. Many eighteenth- and nineteenth-century school registers have disappeared, but there are two existing Barkhamsted student lists for the period in question: the registers for 1858 and 1865 where children are listed under their fathers' names.

As the registers in the mid-nineteenth century document, children born into Lighthouse families attended public school. The school register of the 9th School District for 1858 indicates that John Elwell's children, John, Jr., Patience, Mary, and Sarah, attended school in "Hitchcoxville" (usually written Hitchcocksville, today called Riverton). John Elwell's brother Joseph, Jr. had three children at the same school: Timothy, Lewis, and Jerome. Also for 1858 "Saul" (Sol) Webster's children William, Prudence, Laura, Franklin, and Frederick are listed for that same school. In the 1865 register, Jerome, Lewis, Laura, Franklin, and Frederick attended, as well as another child of Joseph Elwell, Armenia, who went to the 9th School District. By this time two of John Elwell's children, Sarah and Matilda, attended school in the 2nd School District. Between 1858 and 1865 we can see that some of the Lighthouse children grew up and no longer attended school, and that siblings too young in 1858 were in school by 1865.

These few school records that have been fortuitously preserved account for children from four to sixteen years of age. The records indicate how the children of the Lighthouse were becoming incorporated into the larger European-American society.

LIFE GOES ON

Life continued to play out its dramas both large and small among the descendants of James and Molly. In an interesting turn, on December 5, 1865, Isaac Elwell, Joseph, Jr.'s son and a great great grandson of James and Molly, married the daughter of Sol and Mary Webster, Laura Webster, who also was, in turn, a great great grandchild of James and Molly! Isaac and Laura began having children in 1868. In the birth records, Isaac's occupation is listed as "vagabond." The marriages of two of John Elwell's daughters, Patience and Mary Matilda also are recorded in the 1860s.

Time passed, and some of the people we have come to know died. Joseph Elwell, Jr., died in 1865. Polly Elwell, whose testimony about her family and her life at the Lighthouse village has been of such great importance, died on September 1, 1867, soon after William Wallace Lee interviewed her (Lee 1868; see Chapter 4). Her age in the vital records was given as 96, but the 1850 census recorded her age as 53. This would have made her only 70 in 1867.

By the 1870 and 1880 censuses the descendants of James and Molly were still living in Barkhamsted, marrying and having children. In 1870 Sol and Mary are listed with their children Franklin, Frederic, Susan, Riley, Janet, and Mary. Their daughter Laura Webster Elwell is listed with her husband Isaac and their children Burton and Betsey. Isaac's mother Catherine is listed as living in the same household with her 19-year-old son Jerome. According to probate records, Catherine Elwell, whose husband Joseph, Jr. died in 1865, was declared insane in 1866 and died in 1870. Toward the end of her life, she and two of her children lived at Sol and Mary Webster's house, where the court-appointed administrator of her estate paid the Websters $1 per week for her care. The court also paid the Websters $1 out of the deceased Catherine's estate to hire a horse and carriage to bring her son Isaac Elwell and his family to his mother's funeral.

By 1880 in the census Sol and Mary, now in their 50s, lived with their married son Frank and his daughter Mary (four years old), along with their other children Riley, Justina, Emma, Daniel, and Dora. Isaac and Laura Elwell lived in Torrington, Connecticut with their children Burton, Jenette, Josephine,

Benjamin, Mary, Elizabeth, and Isaac. The census data, along with information gleaned from church and town vital records, allows us to construct a partial kinship diagram for the descendants of James and Molly (see Figure 6.5).

More of the people we have encountered at the Lighthouse passed away: Gum Webster died August 16, 1883, at 89 years. His son Sol Webster died in 1900, soon after he was interviewed in the *Connecticut Courant,* and his wife Mary died in 1901 at 82 years. With their deaths, the last of those who actually lived out a portion of their lives in the village were gone.

CONCLUSION

We now come to the end of our discussion of the documentary records relating to the Lighthouse village. We traced the purchase of the land on which the village was located, we saw the records of family marriages, the births of James and Molly's grandchildren, the deaths of the founding couple, and the richly detailed documentary account of the lives of village residents into the middle of the nineteenth century. In a sense we have met the people of the Lighthouse through the records of eighteenth- and nineteenth-century Connecticut. We know their names and the names of their spouses and children. We know something of their economic lives, their land purchases, even their trades. And we know some of their personal tragedies, particularly the deaths of many of their infants.

But valuable as the official record has been, it is not enough. These records may list key time posts in the lives of the Lighthouse people, but they do not tell of the fabric of their lives. About the everyday struggle for survival of a group of poor outcasts in northwestern Connecticut, the documentary record is largely silent. To comprehend the character of their existence, we must go where they lived out their lives. There, we hope, we can recapture the essence of their society by recovering the material things that were a part of their lives. In other words, we must now focus on the archaeology of the Lighthouse site.

KEY EVENTS: SUMMARY

1770–1783

- James Chaugham buys 60+ acres in New Hartford.
- James Chaugham buys 70 acres on Ragged Mountain in Barkhamsted, establishing ownership of the land on which the Lighthouse village is located.
- Samuel Chaugham buys 49 additional acres on Ragged Mountain in Barkhamsted.

(continued)

1783–1800

- Samuel Chaugham sells his land to Isaac Jacklin, a free black.
- Isaac Jacklin marries James and Molly's daughter Mercy.
- James Chaugham divides part of his land holdings among his wife and his children Mary and Solomon.
- James Chaugham dies around 1790 and his remaining property is distributed to his children.
- Several of James's children—Solomon, Samuel, Hannah, Meribah, and Elizabeth—sell their portions of their late father's estate and strike out on their own.
- Molly relinquishes all rights to any of her late husband's lands and moves to Sharon, Connecticut.
- Son-in-law William Wilson, married to James and Molly's daughter Polly, and son-in-law Isaac Jacklin, married to their daughter Mercy, obtain most of the Ragged Mountain property.

1800–1820

- Molly returns to Barkhamsted, purchasing land near the village.
- Issac and Mercy Jacklin sell their land holdings to William Wilson and move to the nearby community of Winsted.
- Molly trades her land near the village for acreage within the original land purchase on Ragged Mountain.
- Joseph Elwell marries James and Molly's granddaughter Polly Wilson.
- Molly dies in 1818.

1820–1860

- William Wilson sells all of the Ragged Mountain property to William Murray, who then returns it to Wilson.
- William Wilson sells all of the Ragged Mountain property to Hiram Goodwin, who allows the Lighthouse community to remain on the land.
- Solomon Webster marries James and Molly's great granddaughter Mary Wilson.
- The Elwell and the Webster families of James and Molly's descendants constitute the core of the village's population.
- The village is abandoned by about 1860.

Chapter 7

DIGGING IN THE DIRT:
A Brief Introduction to
Archaeological Methodology
and Analysis

The summer of 1986 was the eighth field season of the Farmington River Archaeological Project. I had initiated FRAP in 1979. My goal was to conduct a multi-year study of a small, inland, upland river valley in north-central and northwestern Connecticut.

In the early years of our study, we focused much of our time on conducting an archaeological *site survey*—the actual search for sites—along the Farmington River itself. We also devoted considerable energy to the *excavation* of a sample of the prehistoric sites we had discovered, digging out of the ground the material remains people had left behind. We were extremely successful in documenting occupation of the valley from 10,000 years ago up to the historic period of European settlement. Funded only by the Department of Anthropology at my institution (Central Connecticut State University), we had excavated five sites.

In 1986 we expanded our geographical focus to the highlands bordering the valley on the west, searching for evidence of occupation of the rough, hilly region in what is now Peoples State Forest. Heretofore we had emphasized investigation of the floodplain of the Farmington River, where local inhabitants had been finding artifacts for years. Funded by a grant from the Department of the Interior (a federal agency) as administered by the Connecticut Historical Commission (a state agency), we directed our attention to the western hills of the Farmington Valley. Specifically, we conducted an archaeological survey of Peoples State Forest, approximately 3,000 acres of wooded uplands in the northwestern Connecticut town of Barkhamsted (Figure 7.1).

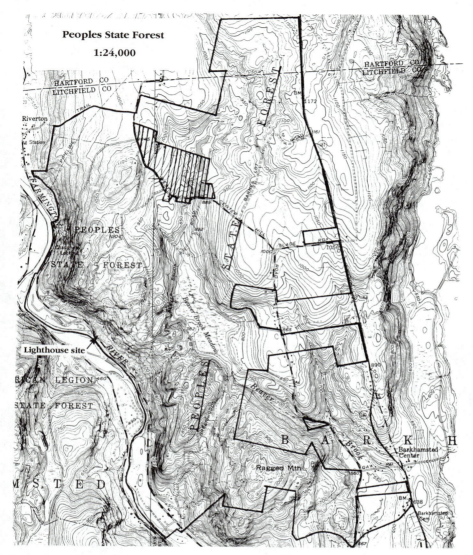

Figure 7.1   United States Geological Survey (U.S.G.S.) topographic map of Peoples State Forest. The location of the Lighthouse site is marked.

During the course of our investigation, we located 30 previously unknown prehistoric Indian sites dating from 4,000 to 600 years ago. We also identified the remains of six historic sites—mill and house foundations—in our survey of the thickly forested uplands.

The 1986 field project was geared toward the discovery of prehistoric sites. All our background research was aimed at putting together a strategy for finding such sites, focusing on the examination of localized features of the landscape that would have been attractive to prehistoric hunting and gathering people. We were aware of the existence of historical sites dating to the presence of European settlers in the northwestern hills of Connecticut in the eighteenth and nineteenth centuries, but these were not our primary concern. Certainly had we done more historical research we would not have been surprised with what we found while surveying the western part of the forest toward the end of the project. There we came across a site that both excited and perplexed us. On a flat, wooded terrace overlooking the floodplain of the Farmington River, we found peculiar-looking stone foundations. They clearly were not aboriginal, because the Indians in this region did not build in stone, but equally clearly they were not the remains of standard colonial structures; the foundations were small and irregular and the stonework was crude.

We were fascinated by this discovery and our imaginations ran wild as we crossed the road and sat down for lunch. Had we discovered a nineteenth-century camp of freed slaves? Had we stumbled on the village site of an ancient band of turnpike robbers? We were enthusiastic about our obviously significant discovery until one of my crew crossed back over the road, walked over to a boulder by the roadside, and called out to me, "Hey, Kenny, is this important?" I walked over to see what was so interesting about the rock and then saw the plaque set into it. It bore the following inscription:

THIS PORTION OF THE PEOPLE'S FOREST
WAS GIVEN BY THE CONNECTICUT
DAUGHTERS OF THE AMERICAN REVOLUTION
1929
NEAR THIS SPOT WAS THE
SITE OF AN INDIAN VILLAGE.

We figured out quickly that the remarkable archaeological discovery we thought we had made involved a site that the Daughters of the American Revolution and, as it turned out, most people in northwestern Connecticut were already aware of! We soon learned that the location of the crude foundations was locally known as the "Lighthouse."

The kind of archaeological field work we were conducting in 1986 when we happened on the Lighthouse is how most of the sites in FRAP have been located. Once sites are found in such site surveys and the decision is made to investigate further, as was the case with the Lighthouse, we have conducted the much more intensive work of an archaeological excavation. Chapters 8 and 9 will present the results of the excavation of the Lighthouse site. Before detailing the results of our field investigation of the Lighthouse site, it makes sense to provide a brief introduction to the methodology of such an investigation. This chapter will focus on the methods of archaeological analysis.

FIELD METHODS

Chapter 5 presented a concise discussion of the methodology of documentary research, preparing the reader for the discussion in Chapter 6 of the contribution made by such research to our investigation of the Lighthouse site and people. Paralleling that presentation, this chapter will entail a necessarily brief but concise introduction to archaeological research, laying a foundation for the presentation of the results of our archaeological investigation of the Lighthouse site. It is through the dynamic interplay of documentary and archaeological research that the lives of the Lighthouse people can be illuminated, and it is only by understanding both of these approaches that the results of our research can be fully comprehended.

As a cautionary note, it must clearly be stated that what follows is an intentionally and self-consciously incomplete outline of the methodology of archaeology. There simply is not enough space here to provide more than a brief introduction to the field. A number of fine introductory texts cover a broad range of topics in detail: Fagan 1991; Sharer and Ashmore 1992; Thomas 1991. My purpose here is to provide the reader with only a general discussion of archaeological methods so that the results of our investigation as presented in Chapters 8 and 9 can be better understood.

THE QUESTIONS OF ARCHAEOLOGY

In another book (Feder and Park 1993), I found it useful to present archaeology as an attempt to answer the kinds of questions a reporter might wish to resolve in a newspaper story: where, what, when, how, who, and why? The archaeologist wishes to be able to answer specifically the following questions:

1. *Where* did people live in the past?
2. *What* evidence of their presence did they leave behind?
3. *When* did past people live in a particular area or perform a particular task?
4. *How* did past people survive and how did they adapt to the world around them?
5. *Who* were a particular past people biologically?
6. *Why* did they live the way of life they did?

Using this list of questions as an outline, we can summarize the procedures archaeologists employ to understand a past people.

Where?

This fundamental step in archaeological field work is self-evident. We need to know where a group of people lived in the past, where they buried their dead, extracted resources from the environment, fought battles, worshipped their gods, and so on. These places where there is physical evidence of a past human presence are called *archaeological sites*. In attempting to answer the question "Where?" archaeologists devise methods to find archaeological sites.

To find sites, archaeologists consider the use of space by a prehistoric or historic group of people. Archaeologists use the term *settlement pattern* to describe that use of space. The settlement pattern refers to the strategy of land use of a past people: how they distributed themselves across a region, how they used different habitats, and even how they used space within their habitations.

As archaeologists search for sites in a site survey, they are, in fact, investigating the regional settlement pattern of a people—how they distributed themselves in a given region. If we can figure out a group's rationale, the rules they employed in deciding where to build villages, where to establish camps, where to bury their dead, and where to hunt, we can then apply those same rules to search for physical evidence of their presence in the different environmental zones of their territory.

In undertaking this task, archaeologists can employ any one of a number of techniques to find a sample of sites from which a settlement pattern can be generalized. In essence we are searching for the physical evidence of the past presence of people. Archaeologist Frank McManamon (1984) calls such evidence the "constituents" of archaeological sites. The constituents of sites are categories of archaeological remains. *Artifacts, ecofacts,* and *features* are all constituents of archaeological sites.

Artifacts are those items that a human being made and used. Spearpoints, pottery sherds, smoking pipe fragments, arrowheads, buttons, nails, and coins are all examples of artifacts (Figure 7.2). Artifacts are also often distinguished as being portable objects. Ecofacts are elements from the environment that display evidence of human activity (but not of human manufacture). The bone of an animal killed by a human hunter, the charred wood in a fireplace, and the nutshells discarded in a trash dump are all ecofacts. Artifacts and ecofacts are archaeological data that began their existence as tools, weapons, items of adornment, or the organic remnants of subsistence (bones, nuts, seeds). These cultural items became archaeological items through a number of processes including *loss,* in-ground storage or *caching, discard* (either *primary discard* right where the item was used or *secondary discard* in a dump, trash pit, or midden), or through simple abandonment. Once deposited in the ground or on the surface through these processes, natural processes are set in motion that can serve to bury and, at least partially, preserve the archaeological remains. The deposition of *alluvial* silt by flooding rivers, the downslope movement of *colluvium,* the deposition of soil by lakes, volcanic eruptions, and even the deposition of leaf and needle litter which then decays into humus and contributes to the soil matrix, all serve to cover material on the surface. These processes, to one degree or another, preserve archaeological artifacts and ecofacts.

Features are the archaeological reflection of discrete human activities (Figure 7.3). Usually consisting of a spatially defined cluster of artifacts, eco-

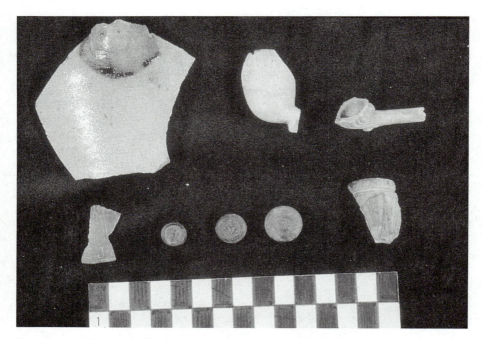

Figure 7.2   A sample of artifacts recovered in our archaeological investigation of the Lighthouse site.

facts, or both, a feature is a place where people performed a task like making a tool, cooking food, or burying the dead. In a sense, features are the equivalent of complex, non-portable artifacts. A stone toolmaking feature may consist of a spatial cluster of waste flakes, some partially finished tools, and a discarded hammerstone. A cooking feature may contain burned wood from the fire, fragments of burned animal bone, nut fragments, seed hulls, and *sherds* from broken cooking pots, along with discarded cooking utensils. A burial feature may consist of the physical remains of the individual, personal items included in the grave, and a stone to mark the location of the interment. A trash feature like a pit or a midden may consist of a dense cluster of all manner of items discarded when broken or used up. In attempting to answer the question "Where?" an archaeological survey is designed to identify the presence of these constituents of archaeological sites. The next question to be asked is, "How do we go about finding these constituents of sites?"

Background research.   Before venturing into the field, we study a number of potentially useful sources of background information. The history of an area may provide information about the presence of historical sites. History can also provide data about prehistoric sites previously uncovered intentionally by archaeologists and unintentionally by others.

Local informants are another valuable source of information. Collecting Indian or colonial artifacts is a hobby for many people, and such individuals

Figure 7.3   An example of an archaeological feature: here, a 4,000-year-old stone platform used for cooking deer meat.

are often, although unfortunately not always, willing to share their knowledge with a researcher. Some collectors walk farmers' fields searching for arrowheads, others root around in old trash dumps looking for antique bottles. Indian artifacts in a field or historical artifacts in a dump are indications of the previous presence of people and, therefore, of archaeological sites; some collectors are happy to share such information. It is unhappily the case that the more acquisitive of these collectors destroy valuable archaeological information, especially when they dig into sites.

There also is a category of informant I have called the "accidental archaeologist." These people are not intentionally searching for archaeological remains but come across the constituents of sites in their other pursuits. Farmers plowing their fields, geological survey teams digging test borings, highway construction workers excavating for roadways, and others commonly happen upon sites in the course of their work. People who, during their work day, move substantial amounts of earth, are a good potential source of information in archaeological survey.

Environmental factors also need to be taken into account for background research. When searching for sites, one needs to consider the constellation of environmental variables that would likely have attracted human settlement or exploitation. Factors such as availability of fresh water, presence of game animals, good soil for farming, and other natural resources, as well as areas easily protected from enemies or close to natural routes of transportation, all were considered by past and modern people when deciding where to settle; these factors must be considered by archaeologists when deciding where to search for settlements.

Field survey.   In field survey we apply the data gathered in background research to the actual search for sites. Field survey may include a *pedestrian survey*, which involves a walkover of an area involving a surficial inspection for aboveground remains or anomalous, visible ground disturbances. Pedestrian surveys are of particular use in prehistoric or historical research projects where past people built durable structures and where natural processes have not covered up site remains. They are also useful for getting a preliminary feel for a site, particularly in terms of site size and density of structural remains. Such a survey was conducted within the Lighthouse village and is discussed in Chapter 8.

Field survey may also include a subsurface investigation of a region. Here we look for buried evidence of the human presence. Technological advances have been made in noninvasive procedures or *remote sensing,* but archaeologists most often must rely on the decidedly "low-tech" process of digging holes called *test pits* to determine the presence of subsurface remains. Test pits are usually shovel-dug, small borings, typically 50 centimeters (about 20 inches) on a side. Maximum test pit depth depends on local conditions. For example, practical considerations ordinarily make digging below the water table impossible. It would similarly be impossible—and pointless—to dig into bedrock formed millions of years ago, long before people were present. In the case of New World prehistoric archaeology, it is likely that human beings arrived no earlier than the end of the Pleistocene (Ice Age). It would be unnecessary to dig deeply into materials left by the glaciers of this period before human occupation.

Test pit soil typically is passed through hardware cloth or screening with $1/4$ or $1/8$ inch mesh. The hope is that the soil will pass through the mesh while artifacts and ecofacts—at least those larger than the mesh of the screening—will not. Test pits are placed at regular intervals according to a particular sampling strategy. The optimum placement of test pits would be one in which all subsurface sites in a region would be found with the fewest possible number of test pits. Unfortunately there is no such perfect strategy that can be employed under all circumstances. It can be shown mathematically that the best general strategy is to place test pits at intervals that approximate the mean diameter of the sites in a region. Even employing this approach, test pit surveys are extremely time-consuming and imperfect. In our 1986 survey of Peoples State Forest, we excavated in excess of 1,000 test pits while discovering 30 buried, prehistoric sites. We do not expect that we found each and every site in our study, but we did not feel this was a reasonable goal. Our hope as well as our belief is that we located a *representative sample* of the sites present in the forest; in other words, a sample that consists of the same proportions of sites by age and type that exists in the entire *population* of sites actually there. A representative sample rather than an entire population of sites is often the most reasonable goal of a survey. Usually only when a survey is conducted in an area that is to be destroyed through construction or flooding is an attempt made to discover all sites in a region. Such surveys are the most intensive sort and can be quite time-consuming and expensive.

In the case of the Lighthouse, we did not need to conduct a test pit survey to determine *where* the site was—although as indicated at the outset of this chapter, we accidentally found the site while conducting just such a survey. We did, however, conduct a test pit survey *within* the site to determine where site constituents were clustered inside the village. This process will be detailed in Chapter 8.

Using these general procedures and many other specific ones, including chemical analysis of the soil and aerial photography, archaeologists can locate a representative sample of sites in a region.

What?

What people left behind are the constituents of archaeological sites discussed above: artifacts, ecofacts, and features. Human beings manipulate their world; they make and use tools, collect and prepare food, build structures, bury the dead, throw away trash, and so on. All of these tasks involve material items. These items become part of the archaeological record primarily through processes of loss and discard. Archaeologists rely absolutely on this fact; wherever people live, they leave a mess. In answering the question "What?" the job of the archaeologist is to recover the items left behind by a past people. The process of recovery is called *excavation*.

Excavation involves not only the recovery of individual items but the preservation of the *spatial contexts* of the remains. Knowing where things were found as well as what items were found together—their *associations*—as deposited by the people who lived at the site enables us to better understand their activities.

Consider the following example of a simple stone spear point. If the point had been found in an archaeological collection, bereft of site context, we might be able to examine the point itself to determine the source of the raw material, how it was made, and perhaps how it was utilized. But we wish to know more: What was the context of the tool in its culture? What was it used with? What other items were found nearby?

Imagine one possible context of the same spear point lodged in the bone of a food animal. Now imagine it in a grave as an offering to a dead hunter. Visualize it found in the skull of a human being. In each case the artifact is precisely the same in its material, form, and proportions, but its spatial context and associations are different. Without careful excavation and record keeping, such information would be irretrievable. All we would have is the artifact itself and a host of unanswerable questions about what the artifact meant.

Or how about this example: Imagine the archaeology of your room. Suppose the archaeologist was confronted with just a box containing the items recovered from that room. Now imagine being able to examine the room itself, with all the objects in place, exactly where you left them. Obviously you can learn far more about the behavior in a given place if you can examine the place itself rather than just the items found there.

Remember, we hope through excavation to be able to reconstruct the lives of the people who lived at the site (see the section "How?"). But ironically, in digging a site we destroy it. Therefore excavation is an exacting task. We wish to preserve the information in the artifacts, ecofacts, and features as we remove them from their spatial contexts. We accomplish this through meticulous record keeping.

Ordinarily sites are gridded into excavation units. This is the equivalent of superimposing a large-scale sheet of graph paper over a site. Each excavation unit is a square on the graph paper and is commonly one or two meters on a side. Each of those units is excavated by peeling back the soil in layers using a standard masons' trowel. Artifacts and ecofacts encountered during the excavation of a level are left in place—*in situ*—and their exact horizontal and vertical location—their *provenience*—is measured before they are removed to the laboratory for more detailed analysis. In this way, although we destroy the site in excavating it, we are able to reconstruct the site's appearance—the context, associations, and form of each artifact, ecofact, and feature—through our record keeping.

In many cases, archaeologists can detect naturally distinguishable soil layers from just a fraction of a centimeter to many centimeters in thickness, and may elect to peel back these natural strata one at a time. In many other cases, there are no discernible natural layers, or existing strata are quite thick and probably represent soil deposition over an extended time period. In these cases, archaeologists commonly excavate in layers of fixed thickness. All Lighthouse material was located in a single, fairly homogeneous natural stratum, probably deposited during the entire timespan of village occupation. Rather than peel back this entire layer at once, we decided to excavate it in three-centimeter-thick slices. Whether natural or fixed, the archaeological materials recovered from an individual level from an individual excavation unit constitute one analytical unit and ordinarily are stored together.

The point of excavation is not merely to recover archaeological items. Our goal is to reveal the material left by the people whose lives produced the site just as it was left by those people. In this way we can produce an accurate picture of what they left behind.

When?

We also wish to know when a site was occupied, when it was abandoned, and when important changes occurred in an ancient village. In essence, in answering the question "When?" archaeologists hope to be able to construct an accurate chronology of the lives of past people.

The numerous methods for dating the constituents of archaeological sites fall into two categories: *absolute dating* and *relative dating* techniques. An absolute technique provides an actual year date, or range of years, for an object or site. A relative technique provides only a sequence from older to younger, but no year or age. In prehistoric sites, dates can be directly determined for only a very few specific, individual objects. We may be able to determine that the charcoal found at a site from a particular fire is 1,000 years old. We then apply this directly derived date to all of the other materials found at the site as a whole or to a particular level or stratum of the site. (See the discussion of stratigraphy that follows.)

Some absolute techniques are based on the decay of radioactive isotopes—unstable varieties—of various elements. Carbon dating is probably the most common of these. A radioactive isotope of the element carbon (^{14}C) has a known rate of decay. By determining how much ^{14}C would have been present when the ancient item was alive (wood from a tree, seeds from a plant, and bone from an animal all contain carbon), by measuring the amount of ^{14}C left in the item, and by knowing the decay rate of ^{14}C (its *half-life* calculated at 5,730 years) we can determine its age.

There are several other of these *radiometric* techniques widely used in archaeology. Half-lives for all of the archaeologically important radioactive isotopes are measured in thousands of years or more. Because the Lighthouse site is no more than about 250 years old, such techniques are not applicable. Not enough time has elapsed for much radioactive decay to have transpired.

There are other absolute dating techniques valuable in archaeology. *Dendrochronology,* or tree ring dating, is extremely accurate, because it is based on the yearly addition of a growth ring in trees. Where entire logs or large sections of trees have been preserved, and where the tree ring sequence for the archaeological specimens can be overlapped with a *master sequence* covering many years in a region, archaeological sites—or, at least, the cutting down of a particular log by the people who lived at the site—can be dated to within a single year. This technique is most accurate under certain environmental regimes—primarily dry conditions—that do not apply to New England. This technique, therefore, has not been of use to us in dating the Lighthouse.

On the other hand, there are some specific procedures that fall into the category of *cultural dating* techniques that have been of great use to us in dating the Lighthouse occupation. In the case of some artifacts, it could be no clearer; they have actual year dates written on them. Coins are a good example, and we will discuss the presence of coins at the Lighthouse in Chapter 9.

Although such items are often rare, certain other artifacts, while not having actual dates on them, have chronological information essentially encoded in them. Certain specific kinds of *ceramics* with particular designs were made during narrowly circumscribed periods. Often there are clear historical records enabling us to assign these types and designs to a limited time span. Finding these items at a site like the Lighthouse allows us to state, at least, that people were at the site using the identified ceramic type after we know it was manufactured.

It is also the case in historical archaeology that we can often specifically identify the manufacturer of an item. Some styles or designs were unique to a particular manufacturer. In many cases, historical records enable us to determine when manufacturers were in business and even when they made specific kinds of items with specific styles. Finding such items at a site enables us to associate the date of the item with its use there some time after its manufacturing date.

As is the case today, manufacturers often placed their logo or company name on items they produced. Look at the bottom of the ceramic dishes made today and you will find the *maker's mark* (see Figures 9.1 and 9.11). Where historical records are good, we can determine when a particular manufacturer was in business, when that manufacturer made particular kinds of items, or when they used a specific logo or mark. Finding such materials at a site enables the researcher to assign a particular date to a site or to a part of a site. We can state with certainty that a particular item could have been present at a site no earlier than when it was being produced; it could have turned up any time after it was manufactured.

A number of valuable sources exist for dating logos and maker's marks in pottery. One of the standard references is G. Godden's (1964) *Encyclopaedia of British Pottery and Porcelain Marks*. For recent (nineteenth century to the present) ceramics of American manufacture, Louis Lehner's (1988) *Lehner's Encyclopedia of U.S. Marks on Pottery, Porcelain, and Clay* is useful. For American, British, and European marks dating to before 1850, Ralph and Terry Kovel's (1953) *Dictionary of Marks: Pottery and Porcelain* is an important reference, as is their *Kovel's New Dictionary of Marks* (1986) for the period after 1850.

Relative dating techniques do not provide a year date or age but do provide a sequence from older to younger. The most common relative procedure employed in archaeology is based on analysis of soil levels or *strata* (singular, *stratum*). Analysis of these strata is called *stratigraphy*. Remember that as we excavate a site we peel back the layers of soil that cover our archaeological material. We journey back in time, with each deeper slice of soil representing an earlier time period. Ordinarily we cannot assign a particular age to a layer simply because of its position or precise depth in the overall stratigraphy of a site, but we can determine the relative sequence of events at a site. Stratigraphic analysis enables us, at the Lighthouse and elsewhere, to develop an internal relative chronology for the occupation of the site, showing changes through time in the kinds of objects people used. The stratigraphic sequence of changes in behavior at the Lighthouse will be documented in Chapter 9.

Another relative dating technique relies on the tendency of artifact styles to slowly replace one another through time. The process of using the statistics of such changes to produce a relative chronological sequence is called *seriation*. In essence seriation is based on the following common pattern. A particular style or way of doing something is introduced in a culture. At first it is accepted by few individuals and its occurrence is rare. Slowly it gains in popularity, replacing some older style, until it becomes the dominant practice. While this is happening, another, newer method is introduced, slowly gaining in popularity, until it becomes dominant, and so on, and so on.

An excellent example of this process at work comes from historical New England and relates to tombstone design (Dethlefsen and Deetz 1966). Seventeenth-century settlers of New England adorned the tops of their gravestones with carved skulls (Figure 7.4). The skull or "death's head" motif reflects the pessimistic Puritan perspective, dominant at the time, that regardless of the good a person accomplished during his or her life, most were foreordained to burn in hell for eternity while a very small, select minority were bound to spend the hereafter in heaven. Puritans generally did not believe they could earn heaven through their works.

Toward the end of the seventeenth and beginning of the eighteenth century, people's perceptions about life and death began to change, as did the style of artifacts that reflected those changing perceptions. At this time gravestones began to display a happy, smiling cherub or angel face with feathered wings (see Figure 7.4) instead of a skull, reflecting a growing optimism about life and death, and, especially, ultimate heavenly reward earned by leading a good life, a concept rejected by the Puritans. The cherub face did not instantly become popular. It took time for people to accept it as Puritanism waned in popularity. Eventually, however, the cherub face with feathered wings soaring to heaven became the most popular tombstone design. The death's head became decreasingly popular until it disappeared completely.

In the second half of the nineteenth century, a new design emerged. The image of an urn with a weeping willow tree bending over it began its rise in popularity (see Figure 7.4). It eventually became the dominant mode, reflecting an interest in the architectural and artistic styles of classical Greece. The urn and willow design replaced the cherub as surely as the cherub had replaced the death's head before it.

When we graph this pattern of the introduction of new styles, their rise to a popularity peak, and their replacement by newer styles, we see a structure in its general form that reflects the histories of many kinds of artifacts (Figure 7.5, page 125). Along with depicting the rise and fall in popularity of certain artifact styles, we can use the general template of replacement to arrange a series of sites into a relative chronological sequence. Where there are a series of sites and where each site represents what amounts to a slice in time, we can determine the percentages of each style at each site. We then can arrange the pattern of percentages at each site into the most reasonable sequence: For each style, the change in time should proceed from low popularity upon its introduction, increasing popularity until it reaches its peak, and then decreasing popularity as another, newer style replaces it.

These techniques as well as many others help the archaeologist answer the question "When?" Not all techniques are applicable in all cases; some are specific to prehistoric archaeology, some are specific to historical sites archaeology. Some procedures can be used only for very recent sites, some for very old sites. Taken together, however, they provide archaeologists with a set of valuable tools for determining when a site was occupied.

Figure 7.4   Connecticut tombstones from the eighteenth and nineteenth centuries exhibit the symbols typical of their time periods: the death's head (top), cherub (middle), and urn and willow (bottom).

How?

In answering the question "How?" the archaeologist attempts to describe, as fully as he or she can, the way of life of a past people. How did the people at a given site survive? How did they provide the materials necessary for their subsistence? How did they manufacture or otherwise obtain the tools they needed? How did they find mates and raise their children? How did they relate

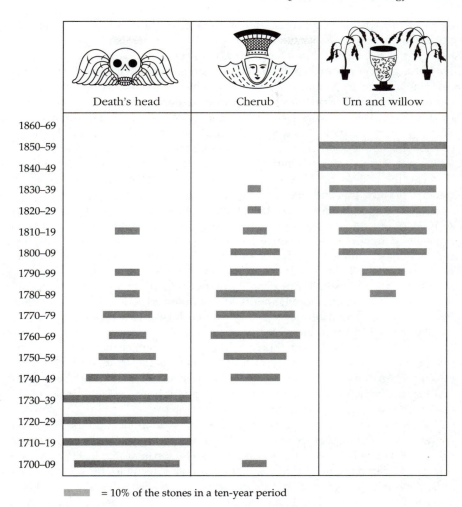

= 10% of the stones in a ten-year period

Figure 7.5 Seriation graph showing the change in tombstone style in southern New England from the late seventeenth through the late nineteenth centuries.

to human groups in the surrounding territory? How did they worship? How did they interrelate? Anthropologists who study living groups of people by living among them ask essentially the same questions and are said to be conducting an *ethnography*. In a sense, when archaeologists answer questions about how people lived, they are conducting an ethnography of a people who are no longer alive.

Obviously this presents quite a challenge. Archaeologists cannot interview past people or observe their behavior directly. We can attempt, however, to reconstruct their way of life indirectly by examining those things we can scrutinize directly: the constituents of archaeological sites produced by the behavior we wish to reconstruct and, in the case of historical archaeology, the documentary record associated with the people who lived at the site.

For example, certain artifacts directly reflect on the *technology* and *economy* of a group of people. Where people manufacture their own tools, we can examine artifacts to illuminate the ways in which items like stone spear points, pottery, iron swords, or bricks were made. If they obtained tools through a broader economic network by way of trade or commerce, implications can be drawn concerning their contacts with groups beyond their own and the nature of their economic system. As will be seen, analysis of the technology of the artifacts recovered at the Lighthouse has enabled us to assess the relationship between the people who lived there and the wider world around them, and to understand how this changed through time.

Diet is another element of people's lives that can be investigated directly. Animal bones, seeds, fruit pits or stones, nut and nut-shell fragments, or seashells commonly are preserved in food preparation features (fireplaces), storage features, middens (piles of kitchen refuse), and refuse pits; they can be recovered in the field or through separation techniques in the lab. Knowing the kinds of foods people relied on—whether hunting or gathering wild plant foods was paramount, and whether wild or domestic foods (or some combination of the two) constituted the subsistence base—can provide enormous insights into the way of life of a human group. We were extremely interested in how the people of the Lighthouse village lived, whether they lived primarily on the wild produce of their forest home or kept domestic animals and planted crops. Analysis of the bones and plant remains recovered at the site has enabled us to answer fundamental questions about how the Lighthouse inhabitants survived in their isolated hamlet. (See Chapter 9.)

It is said that humankind does not live by bread alone, and this is certainly the case. Anthropologists realize that culture represents the human *adaptation*, our strategy for survival. It should be readily apparent that technology, economy, and diet represent behaviors that contribute directly to the survival of the individual and the group, but it might not be so obvious that social, political, and ideological beliefs and behaviors are also crucial to human survival. Also, while it may be clear that technology, economy, and diet are behaviors that involve material objects that become part of the archaeological record in the form of artifacts and ecofacts, it may not be apparent that material remains— the archaeological constituents of artifacts, ecofacts, and features—would be found to be related to the more abstract categories of human behavior.

Social, political, and ideological systems are as much part of the cultural adaptation as are technology, economy, and diet. We humans are social creatures and our social networks define who we can rely on for help—and who can rely on us—in the struggle for survival. This was the case at the Lighthouse village where survival depended on the small group of individuals drawn to the outcast community. We humans also are political creatures because we live in groups, and the behavior of individuals living in groups needs to be coordinated and regulated for the survival of the group. It is readily apparent that this would have been the case at the Lighthouse. Also we are, in a sense, moral creatures. We have the intelligence to recognize the impacts of our actions on ourselves and on those among whom we live. Ideologies involving the definition of right and wrong and of responsibility are part of the human adaptation and, therefore, part of the constellation of behaviors that aid in our survival. It should be clear that this must have been the case in a small, isolated community like the Lighthouse.

In the case of historical archaeology, the documentary record will often provide direct insights into nonmaterial aspects of culture. In the example mentioned previously, we understand the symbolism behind the images on old gravestones because seventeenth-, eighteenth-, and nineteenth-century people wrote about their views of death. In ways both direct and indirect, they tell us what their symbols meant. In attempting to reconstruct life at the Lighthouse, although the inhabitants have left us no written information about their own lives (as shown in Chapters 4 and 6), some of their contemporaries did. The material record of the archaeological site and the written record of the documents each help us interpret the other and better describe life in the village.

There are two significant ways in which abstract aspects of human behavior become translated into the concrete archaeological record. In some instances, human beings manufacture, use, and discard objects whose primary purpose is expressly social, political, or ideological. A wedding ring, king's crown, or crucifix are obvious examples. Recognizing the social, political, or ideological functions of such objects allows for insights into those behaviors by the archaeological group being studied.

It is also the case that while the vast majority of items produced in a culture are not made explicitly for a social, political, or ideological purpose, all things are made within the context of a given society's social, political, and ideological beliefs and practices. For example, how you make a spear or pottery—and what the resulting artifacts will look like—depends very much on who has taught you, which is a social decision. The sources of raw materials or manufactured objects may depend on social and political forces that forge alliances and trading networks. Diet can be shaped by ideological considerations, as it may be for vegetarians.

Human behavior, in any one of the cultural systems we have defined here, does not develop in isolation from all other behaviors of the group. In this sense all activities are interrelated, and ideas that are part of those activities may leave material traces on the objects made and used in a given society. It is the challenge of archaeology to attempt to decode such nonmaterial information encoded in the material record.

Like prehistorians, historical archaeologists, with few exceptions, cannot directly question the inhabitants of sites on the meaning of their artifacts or the content of their lives. Historical archaeologists, however, do have significant sources of information unavailable to the prehistorian. The documentary record discussed in Chapter 6 is one of those data sources. Also, historical archaeologists sometimes can interview descendants of people who lived at a site to recover oral traditions passed down in families about the lives of the inhabitants. Ferguson (1992) uses early twentieth-century photographs and interviews with descendants of slaves recorded during the depression to better understand the culture of transplanted Africans in the American South. In an attempt to figure out the use of particular ceramic types, Russell Skowronek (1991) even used historical paintings where pottery is incidentally depicted. Ultimately, all archaeologists use whatever data they can to better understand the lives of past people and to answer the question "How?"

Who?

In asking the question "Who?" archaeologists wish to know about the specific individuals who lived at a site: their gender, age at death, nutritional status, health, and ethnic background. Prehistoric archaeologists can sometimes approach these questions with the data of *human osteology.* Where human skeletons have been preserved and excavated, biological anthropologists can analyze the human remains to provide the answers to some of these questions.

For example, we know that humans exhibit sexual dimorphism, that is, males and females exhibit differences even in nonsexual characteristics. Some of these differences can be seen in the human skeleton: The male tends to be larger than the female, with larger and rougher areas for muscle attachment; also, the skull of the male is larger than that of the female and tends to have bony ridges above the eyes. The *mastoid process,* a bony projection for muscle attachment just behind the ear, is large and broad in males, small and pointed in females. In perhaps the most obvious skeletal difference, the female pelvis is designed for childbirth and is almost always distinguishable from that of a male by its wider opening in what is called the *sciatic notch.* The notch angle determines the width of the birth canal and is generally larger in females than in males of the same group.

We also know that humans in general, and their skeletons in particular, go through a number of developmental stages. These stages, including tooth eruption and replacement as well as long bone fusion (when you are born, each of the so-called long bones in your arms, legs, hands, and feet are in three sections—a shaft and two end caps—that fuse to form a single bone), occur at fairly well-fixed points during our lives. These developmental time posts can be used to determine the age of death for individuals in their youth. For adults, skeletal changes still occur, but the time posts, including *cranial suture closure* and alteration in the *pubic symphysis,* are less certain. Cranial sutures—the wiggly lines that demarcate the junctures of the individual plates or bones of the skull—fuse slowly and with a degree of regularity until they disappear completely in aged individuals. In the case of the pubic symphysis (where the left and right pubic bones at the bottom of the pelvis meet), the wear and tear of a lifetime can be measured and an approximate age at death derived.

Biological anthropologists also look for telltale skeletal evidence of nutritional deficits, disease, injuries, and normal wear and tear. (See the discussion in Chapter 2.) Cracks in the surface of the ends of long bones and in tooth enamel indicate dietary deficiencies. Arthritis, tuberculosis, syphilis, and certain cancers leave telltale marks on bones. Minor variations in the skeleton in different parts of the world allow the geographic, ethnic, and racial source of individuals to be assessed on the basis of their skeletal remains.

We have not and will not excavate the cemetery at the Lighthouse (see the discussion in Chapter 8), but you may have noticed that some of the categories of information that fall into the category of the question "Who?" are the same kinds of *demographic* information included in census and vital records like those discussed in Chapters 5 and 6. We already have much of the information we wanted about many of the people of the Lighthouse: their gender, age at death, cause of death, number of children they had, ethnic identity, and so on.

Why?

The final question we will discuss is "Why?" Archaeologists seek to understand the fundamental reasons why people lived the way of life they did, why their culture changed in the ways it did, and perhaps why they did or did not survive. Archaeologists the world over wish to comprehend some of the large issues that might help us better understand humanity. Archaeologists are anthropologists, and anthropologists are social scientists. Remember at the very beginning of this book, I pointed out that the archaeologist's goal is *not* to fill museums with fabulous treasure but to contribute to an understanding of the human species.

Our particular and unique contribution toward understanding ourselves rests in examining the lives of past people. We accomplish this by recovering and examining the objects and records produced by these people that fortuitously have been preserved.

We think examining past people makes a significant contribution to the database of anthropology in particular and social science in general. After all, we human beings have been around in one form or another for more than two million and perhaps as many as four million years. To understand modern humanity, to fathom the mysteries about ourselves that perplex us so, to diagnose the ills that befall us, and to respond to the challenges that confront us, we need to illuminate the roots of our species. The modern world with its problems of environmental degradation, warfare, urban decay, drug abuse, poverty, infant mortality, and so on is the product of many millennia of cultural history. If we wish to understand the current state of human affairs and try to change it for the better, we must be able to grasp how this all came about. And the roots of these problems lie not in the recent past but in the antiquity of our species.

It is not likely in our study of a little hamlet in the hills of northwestern Connecticut that we will be able to answer the broad questions that social scientists might wish to answer about what makes humanity tick: Why do we kill each other in wars? Why are our modern cities in such bad shape? Why do we destroy the environment? Why are so many poor and hungry? Nevertheless, by understanding why the Lighthouse village was a successful community for more than a hundred years—a successful community of Indians, whites, and blacks in an isolated forest in the eighteenth and nineteenth centuries—perhaps we can begin in a small way to more fully understand the capabilities of our species. In answering our small questions "Why?" about the people at the Lighthouse, our hope is to better understand the big question "Why?": Why are we humans the way we are?

Chapter 8

DIGGING IN THE DIRT:
Archaeology at the Lighthouse Site

You will recall from Chapter 4 that Sol and Mary Webster were interviewed in 1900 by a reporter from the *Connecticut Courant*. They both claimed to be descendants of the Chaughams, but neither could document their relationship to the village's founding couple. As a result of the Websters' confusion about their own genealogy, and because they appeared to be the final living inhabitants of the community, the *Courant* reporter came away quite pessimistic about the possibility of the true story of the Lighthouse ever being known. He states:

> Inquiries into its history, when they were made by curious eyes, came too late; the true story of one of the last Indian resorts in the State will, perhaps, never be *unearthed* [emphasis mine].

"UNEARTHING" THE STORY OF THE LIGHTHOUSE

"Never be unearthed," indeed, a perfect challenge for an archaeologist. In the field seasons of 1986, 1990, and 1991, unearthing the story of the Lighthouse is literally what we did. Chapters 8 and 9 will detail the processes employed in and the results derived through the literal and figurative unearthing of "the true story of one of the last Indian resorts in the State."

BRINGING THE DEAD TO LIFE

I do not believe in ghosts. It might seem contradictory, therefore, when I tell you that in certain contexts I have encountered the spirits of human beings long since passed away. Not in the corner of my eye but rather in a corner of my mind. I have glimpsed them and yearned to view them more clearly.

I felt their tug at the edge of my consciousness when as a child I visited the monumental site of Stonehenge in England. Years later I recognized their presence while on a visit to the site of the Battle of the Little Big Horn in Montana (see Chapter 2). I have espied their spectral presence at each of the many prehistoric archaeological sites I have worked on. And I have heard the dim echoes of their voices, seen the pale wisps of their phantasms, and felt the soft trace of their spirits every day I have worked at the Lighthouse site.

I mean none of this literally. Would that we truly could transcend the barrier that separates the dead from the living. The finality of death prohibits absolutely a virtual or literal contact between the curious living and the silent dead. But, although the dead may leave no personal phantom behind, they sometimes leave a fossil essence of themselves in the kinds of documentary data discussed in this book and, especially, in the physical, archaeological detritus of our lives. We archaeologists know full well—and believe me, we despair of it—that we cannot truly contact the builders of Stonehenge, the soldiers who were at the Little Big Horn, or the prehistoric inhabitants of New England. And I know full well that Molly Barber and James Chaugham, Mercy and Isaac Jacklin, Polly and William Wilson, and all of the rest of the residents of the Lighthouse are forever silenced. And yet as I walk about the ruin of their village, I feel their presence; it permeates the site on the terrace at the foot of Ragged Mountain. In the foundations of their homes, in the stone mortar in which they ground their corn meal, in the cemetery where they laid their dead to rest, and even in the bits and pieces of material objects that were part of their existence, the Lighthouse people yet live and can still teach us of the content of their lives. It is the goal of every archaeologist to resurrect, if only in a metaphorical sense, the essence of those long dead. That was my goal at the Lighthouse.

MAPPING THE SITE

One of the most important tasks we accomplished in 1986 was to produce a detailed and accurate topographic map of the Lighthouse village. A team of five people began by demarcating the area to be mapped on the basis of the location of aboveground remains of the sort discussed in the next section of this chapter. The crew conducted an informal pedestrian survey, locating the kinds of visible, surficial remains that alerted us to the presence of the site in the first place. (See the introduction to Chapter 7.)

Once the crew identified the general area of the site, they established a site *datum*. The datum in this case was an arbitrary point from which all other points at the site would be measured—the 0,0 point on an imaginary, large-scaled X,Y grid superimposed on the site. That same datum has been used throughout our excavation of the site as the reference point for all excavation units as well as for the provenience measurements of all site features. A stake was driven into the ground at that point to serve as a permanent marker for any subsequent examination of the site.

The mapping crew utilized a *plane table, alidade*, and *stadia rod* to produce the site map. A plane table is simply a wooden table mounted on a tripod that can be leveled with a carpenter's bubble and then horizontally aligned by using a compass. The plane table was set up initially directly over the site datum point. The alidade is a telescopic sighting device with cross hairs mounted in its lens. The sighting device itself is mounted on a flat base that serves as a measuring scale and straight edge. The alidade rests on a sheet of graph paper that has been affixed to the plane table surface. The stadia rod is an expandable metric scale, divided into meter and centimeter units. When mapping, the rod holder places the base of the stadia rod at a determined point at a known distance from the alidade. Sighting through the alidade, once the rod is visible and then centered in the cross hairs, the crew member takes an elevation reading. This reading represents the precise distance from the plane of the alidade cross hairs to the surface of the ground on which the rod is resting. Because we can easily measure the height above datum of the alidade sighting line, a simple calculation allows us to measure the depth or height of the spot on which the rod is resting relative to the datum point.

In mapping the site, the crew set up an imaginary grid, positioned north-south and east-west, with intersections of north-south and east-west lines at every ten meters. Topographic measurements were taken at each of these intersections, designating datum as elevation zero. After all measurements were taken, topographic lines called *isopleths* were drawn, connecting all measurement points of equal value with a line and by interpolation between measured points. The resulting map shows the topography of the Lighthouse village and served as the base map onto which all site features and the location of all our archaeological work were mapped (Figure 8.1). For a useful and brief introduction to field mapping, see Robert Spier's (1970) book, *Surveying and Mapping: A Manual of Simplified Techniques*. Another thorough treatment of surveying and mapping is J. C. Pugh's (1975) *Surveying for Field Scientists*.

THE PEDESTRIAN SURVEY

As discussed in Chapter 7, one important technique in archaeological site survey is the *pedestrian survey*, or *surface survey*. A pedestrian survey can locate and identify the materials where past people built structures using durable

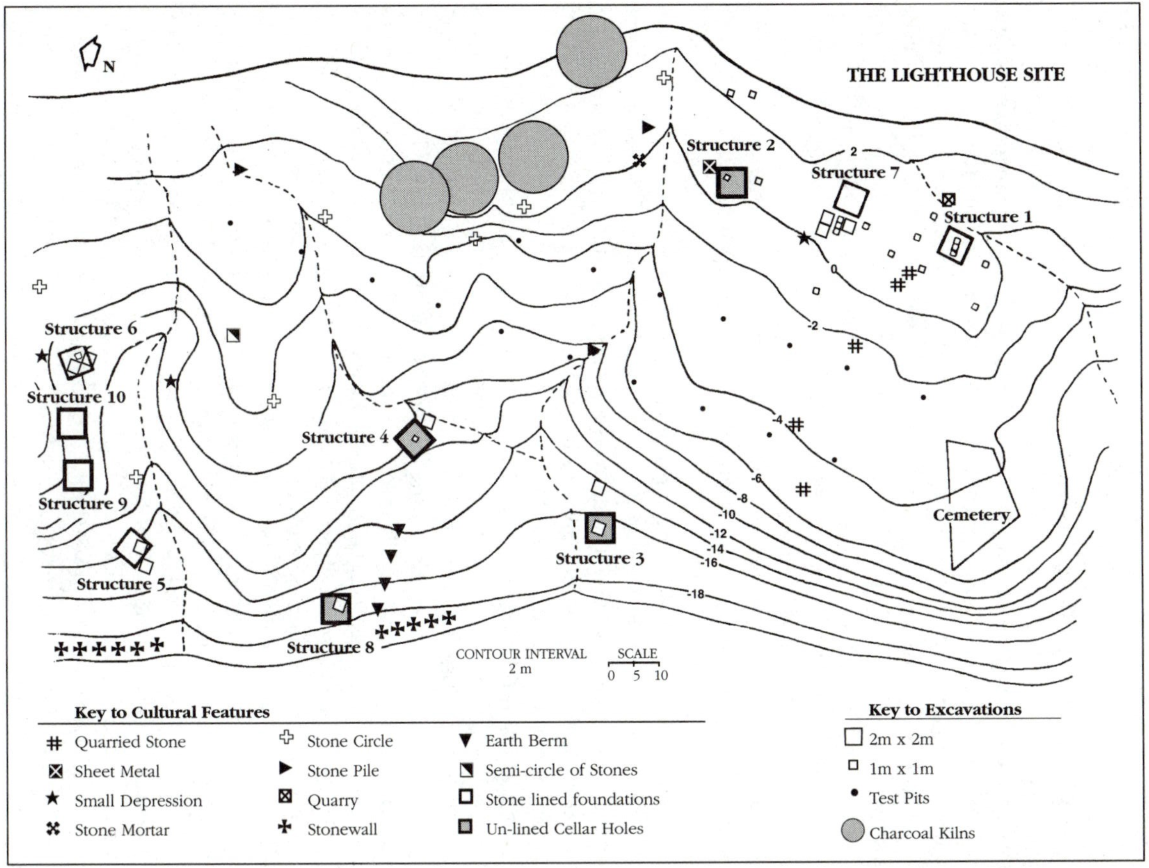

Figure 8.1 Map of the Lighthouse site. (Map drawn by R. Klonis Dardzienski.)

materials, where they permanently altered the landscape, where natural conditions have served to preserve their material remnants on the surface, or where natural processes have exposed their buried remains. Once a site is found, the distribution of aboveground remains within the site can be assessed using the same procedure.

A pedestrian (or foot) survey involves walking over the surface of a region and visually inspecting that surface for the constituents of archaeological sites. In 1986 and 1990 we did not conduct a formal, inclusive pedestrian survey of the entire site, although because we often walked over the site area, we did note a number of surficial features. These included four stone foundations, one square earth berm enclosure, two rectangular depressions, one large stone mortar, a small rock quarry, and four charcoal mounds (see Figure 8.1).

Wishing to be more thorough in our surface investigation, we initiated a formal pedestrian survey at the Lighthouse in 1991. We began by dividing the flat terrace on Ragged Mountain, where we knew the site to be due to surface indications, into a series of 30-meter by 30-meter (900 square-meter) units, or boxes. We staked out 17 complete and 5 partial units across the flat terrace. A crew of 6 people, regularly spaced at 5-meter intervals, then walked over each of these units. The total area covered in this survey was approximately 17,425 square meters (a little less than 188,000 square feet or a little more than 4.3 acres).

Each person in the 6-person crew was responsible for scanning the surface 2.5 meters to their right (east) and 2.5 meters to their left (west) as they walked north 30 meters in each of the surveyed boxes. All surficial indications of occupation of the area were flagged with surveyors tape and recorded and labeled in field notebooks.

This was a time-consuming and difficult task. The vegetational history of Ragged Mountain is similar to that of much of the uplands of Connecticut. Prehistorically such areas were largely wooded. Although there likely were small villages, hamlets, or wigwam clusters scattered throughout the region (Handsman 1990), even after horticulture became an important element in the subsistence of local natives, mountainous areas were not cleared for planting because cultivation of the stony soil was far too difficult. It has been estimated that up to 90 percent of Connecticut was covered with forest when Europeans first entered the area in the early seventeenth century. Most of the 10 percent of the land that was cleared was in broad river valleys.

During occupation of the Lighthouse village, it is likely that the slope of the mountain was largely cleared not for farming, but for firewood and construction material. After the Lighthouse village was abandoned, the land was allowed to return to forest. The same happened throughout much of Connecticut as firewood was replaced by fossil fuels and as efficient transportation systems made agricultural produce from other, more fertile parts of the country less expensive than homegrown products. Today it is estimated that more than 60 percent of Connecticut is forested.

Table 8.1   Surface Features—Pedestrian Survey

Surface Features	Number
Stone foundations	4
Four-sided depressions/cellar holes	6
Quarried stone	5
Rock circles	8
Rock semicircle	1
Stone piles	3
Stone walls	2
Earth berm	1
Metal accumulation	1
Small, amorphous depressions	3
Charcoal mounds	4
Stone quarry	1
Stone mortar	1
Total	40

All this means is that pedestrian surveys in Connecticut are often difficult. Thick vegetation renders even walking in a straight line impossible for any distance. Leaf litter and thick ground cover often obscure surface material, and the roots of fallen trees tend to disturb surface material. The slope of Ragged Mountain is covered with hemlock, pine trees, and thick, nearly impenetrable stands of mountain laurel, which produces Connecticut's quite lovely state flower as well as terrible conditions for surveyors.

The crew encountered 40 site features visible on the modern surface, all of which are listed in Table 8.1. Most of these features were produced by the inhabitants of the Lighthouse while carrying out the activities of their everyday lives. So, what was once a thriving village of dozens of individuals now appears to be little more than piles of stone, vague depressions in the ground and foundation ruins. Yet, as will be shown, to the archaeologist such things can speak to us when the residents of the village no longer can.

Categories of the Pedestrian Survey

We can categorize the features in the pedestrian survey and in previous informal site walkovers into a number of types and suggest the nature and function of each. The meaning of these features in relation to our interpretation of life at the Lighthouse will be addressed in Chapter 9.

Stone foundations.   The stone foundations are just that: the foundations of structures, almost certainly houses inhabited by members of the Lighthouse community. The four stone foundations are for the most part crudely constructed and irregular in size (Figure 8.2; and see Table 9.1). Both in terms of size and complexity, they contrast greatly with another foundation found elsewhere in Peoples State Forest built by a white farmer toward the end of the eighteenth century (Figure 8.3).

All of these features were noted before the formal surface survey of 1991. The foundation for what we will designate Structure 1, immediately west of the stone quarry, is the most elaborate of the structural remains, consisting of quarried stone surrounding a relatively deep depression. The foundation of Structure 7, on the same terrace as Structure 1 and just 32 meters north of it, is also stone lined, but only a few of the stones show quarry marks. The foundation of Structure 5 (see Figure 1.1) is to the north of the permanent stream that flows through the site, draining the uplands to the east. Structure 5 is a three-sided stone wall built into the side of a hill about 14 meters northeast of what is now East River Road, and was, after 1789, the Farmington River Turnpike. None of the stones in this foundation exhibit quarry marks.

The foundation of Structure 6 is just uphill from Structure 5, about 40 meters to the northeast. It is similar to Structure 5, with three walls of dry-laid, unquarried stone built into the side of the hill. The openings of the foundations of Structures 5 and 6 face roughly to the south.

Cellar holes. The sizeable (several square meters), rectangular depressions in the ground at the Lighthouse are also the bases of structures. These are cellar holes of houses that no longer exist. We have labeled these Structures 2, 3, 4, 8, 9, and 10, respectively (Figure 8.4). Although a stone foundation provides a far greater degree of permanence to a structure, it was common, especially for the poor, to build houses with no solid stone foundation. It is therefore not surprising that a good proportion (60 percent) of the structures identified at the Lighthouse site possessed simple, unadorned cellar holes.

The remnants of the houses at the Lighthouse as represented by the four stone foundations and six plain cellar holes can tell us quite a bit about the people who built and lived in them. We will discuss the significance of these structural remains in Chapter 9.

Quarried stone. Five individual pieces of quarried stone bearing actual quarry marks (Figure 8.5) were located in the pedestrian survey. As seen on the survey map (see Figure 8.1), all five quarried rock fragments were directly west of and downhill from Structure 1, which contained by far the greatest proportion of quarried stone in its foundation when compared to the other stone foundations at the site. Quarried stones found west of Structure 1 likely were transported down-slope by gravity.

Circular accumulations of stone. One semicircular and eight circular accumulations of stone were identified in the surface walkover. These accumulations were all small, less than 75 centimeters across, and appear to have been outdoor fireplaces.

Figure 8.2   Typical of the stone-lined Lighthouse foundations, Structures 1 (top) and 7 (bottom) are small and irregular in their proportions.

Figure 8.3 Late eighteenth-century foundation in Peoples State Forest. This foundation is far more typical of the period than any of those at the Lighthouse site.

Figure 8.4 The cellar hole of Structure 2 shows the small size and subtle remains of Lighthouse structures that lacked stone foundations.

Figure 8.5   Stone from the foundation of Structure 1. Note the quarry marks.

Rock pile.   The three rock piles identified at the site are small (less than 50 centimeters across) and amorphous. Their function, if any, is unknown. Rock piles often result from the attempt (and "attempt" is the operative word here) to plant vegetable gardens in the stony soil of northwestern Connecticut. In trying to create a patch of even vaguely productive, clean soil, the rocks were removed and piled up to the side of the garden. We do know that Molly, at least, kept a garden at the site. In a land transaction between Nathaniel Weed, an outsider who owned land in the village (see Chapter 6), and Joshua Youngs on March 19, 1806, measurement of his property is noted in reference to "Molly Chaugham's garden."

Stone walls.   Small parts of two stone walls were found in the surface survey of the site. Both are immediately next to East River Road. Although stone walls as property boundary markers are ubiquitous throughout New England, there are no other stone walls in the Lighthouse village. The significance of this lack of stone boundary markers will be assessed in Chapter 9.

Raised berm.   The raised earth berm is part of the trail system in the forest. It may be a product of trail establishment during the depression in the 1930s.

Metal trash accumulation.   The accumulation of metal trash on the surface is a small, modern trash dump consisting of a pile of rusted sheet metal.

Small depressions.   We know of at least one instance where amateur diggers have searched for artifacts at the site. The three small, round depressions seem to be the remnants of pits excavated by artifact collectors.

Figure 8.6   The stone quarry directly east of Structure 1. This quarry was used by residents of the Lighthouse to supply stones used in the foundations of some of their structures.

Charcoal mounds.   Four circular, low mounds of charcoal surrounded by a shallow ditch were first identified in the 1986 investigation of the site. Such features have been found elsewhere in Peoples State Forest and are fairly common in upland areas of New England. Rolando (1989) noted 45 such mounds in a survey in Vermont. These are the remains of outdoor charcoal kilns where charcoal was produced primarily for use in the local iron, copper, and brass industries. The significance of these features will be detailed in Chapter 9, although charcoal production on Ragged Mountain likely postdates the Lighthouse settlement.

Stone quarry.   Immediately next to the east wall of the stone foundation of Structure 1 is a small stone quarry (Figure 8.6). Almost certainly the quarried rock that makes up this foundation and the other quarried rock found at the site in other foundations and in the cemetery come from this spot. Several large slabs of bedrock in the quarry—a granitic schist—bear clear quarry marks. These marks are cross-sectional remnants of holes drilled into rock. See Chapter 9 for a detailed description of the stone quarrying process.

In one case the quarrying process did not work precisely as planned. The bedrock source of the rock—the "parent" piece—is in place and quarry marks can be seen. Just to the side, right where it split off, is the "daughter" piece. Apparently, it was too big or too irregular as broken. In any event it was not used and remains where it was split off from the bedrock.

Figure 8.7   The stone mortar found in our surface walkover and likely the same feature noted by Lewis Mills in his poem, *The Legend of the Barkhamsted Lighthouse.*

Stone mortar.   In his poem about the Lighthouse legend, Mills mentions that Molly pounded the corn they grew at the site in an "ancient mortar" (Mills 1952:70). We likely have found that mortar. To the north of Structure 2 is a large boulder that shows clear evidence of wear on its top surface (Figure 8.7).

Corn or other grain may have been ground on the flat, worn surface of the boulder using a round or cylindrical stone to produce a coarse meal, or flour. The process is time-consuming. The end product is nothing like the fine cornmeal you can buy in a supermarket, or even much like the coarse, stone ground meal you can purchase at a health food store. Although not just a little ground-up rock ends up in your meal, where there is no grist mill available to grind grain between millstones, there is little choice but to use a stone mortar. This mortar must have been used by inhabitants of the site, at least early in its history before Europeans moved into the area with their water-powered mills.

PEDESTRIAN SURVEY INDICATIONS

As a result of the generally thick vegetation that covers the New England landscape, pedestrian surveys do not often contribute greatly to archaeology. In this case, however, the pedestrian survey provided us with a useful perspective of the general appearance of the Lighthouse village, and the context needed to determine the best strategy for site excavation (discussed later in this chapter).

Of primary importance, we know there were at least 10 structures at the site and we know where they were. Compare this to the assertions of Mills and his sources that there were 30 or 32 cabins in the village. There may have been, but most left no physical evidence visible on the surface. Further, we know that there were two basic forms to the foundations of these structures: stone lined and simple unlined cellar holes. We also know that a number of fireplaces unassociated with particular houses were scattered throughout the village.

Beyond the surficial features mentioned, there was a cluster of stones in an area about 40 meters southwest of Structure 1. Because these constituted a particular aspect of behavior at the site, they were analyzed separately and will be treated separately in the next section of this chapter.

THE LIGHTHOUSE CEMETERY

The Lighthouse cemetery is discussed in the Mills poem and in a number of his sources. Mills states that the cemetery was "southward" from the village and that it contained about 50 unmarked stones, including the grave markers of James, Molly, and their young daughter Sally. Mills likely takes his estimate of the total number of stones in the cemetery from William Wallace Lee who published that estimate in his 1868 article in the *Winsted Herald*. Lee had visited the cemetery and counted the stones. He located the cemetery "about thirty rods south of the Chaugham house site" (Lee 1881:42). A rod is about five meters or 16.5 feet, so the distance of the cemetery to the Chaugham homestead was about 150 meters or about 500 feet. Lee may have been measuring from our Structure 5, which is easily recognized on the ground and is, indeed, about 150 meters—Lee's "thirty rods"—north of the cemetery.

Other estimates of the size of the cemetery have been published. Solomon Webster told the *Connecticut Courant* in 1900 that there were 200 people buried in the cemetery. There even is a rumor that there is no real graveyard at the site, but that depression-era Civilian Conservation Corps workers encamped just across the Farmington River in what is now American Legion State Forest created a false graveyard to make work for themselves. These workers were responsible for trailblazing and maintenance in both American Legion State Forest and Peoples State Forest. With this sort of confusion about the Lighthouse cemetery, we made it an important goal of our project to determine how many probable gravestones were at the site.

A crew of five people established a datum point within the cemetery. This datum was an arbitrarily selected point in the cemetery, measured relative to the site datum (see the discussion earlier in this chapter). All measurements within the cemetery were made directly from the cemetery datum point.

The crew erected our alidade and plane table directly over the cemetery datum. Using the alidade and plane table along with a 30-meter tape, every possible grave marker—that is, all upright stones or possible knockdowns—

were mapped, photographed, drawn, and examined. In this way, 93 possible grave markers were located. The resulting map appears as Figure 8.8.

Not all of the recorded stones are grave markers, and not all graves were marked with stones. The ground across the entire Lighthouse village site is littered with stones of various sizes and shapes. The steep cliff immediately to the east of the site has several areas of bedrock exposure, and this bedrock erodes and works its way down-slope. Even acknowledging this, of the 93 stones recorded, about 76 can be identified as likely markers. These were flat, roughly rectangular stones, clearly chosen for their shape, and set into the ground (Figure 8.9). A few exhibited quarry marks, but none bore any writing or marking of any kind, just as Lee maintained in 1868.

That there are perhaps 76 grave markers in the cemetery does not necessarily mean there are that many bodies buried there. In a few of these cases, we may have been overgenerous in designating stones as grave markers rather than fortuitously shaped and located natural rocks. It is also possible that in some cases there were headstones and footstones placed over individual graves. Although there could be additional unmarked graves, the flat area of

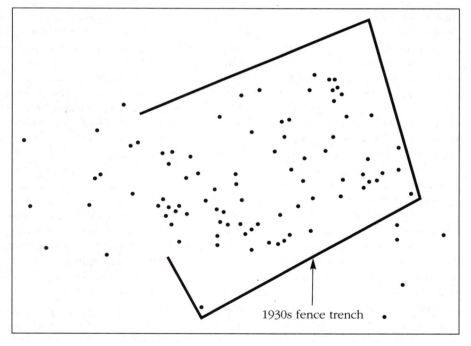

1930s fence trench

Figure 8.8   Map of the Lighthouse cemetery. The locations of more than 90 stones are indicated. Many of these were actual headstones, some likely were footstones, and some may simply be talus from the adjacent slope. There likely were a minimum of 50 graves in the Lighthouse cemetery (R. Klonis Dardzienski).

the cemetery is nearly filled to capacity; therefore we probably did not miss many gravesites. Based on the cemetery survey, an estimate of about 50 burials, the same as that counted by William Wallace Lee a little more than 120 years ago, is probably not far from the truth.

Lewis Mills includes two photographs of the graveyard in his book. The photographs clearly show a number of upright fieldstones surrounded by a wooden stockade fence (Figure 8.10). The sign fastened to the fence reads:

THESE ARE THE GRAVES
OF THE INDIANS
WHO LIVED HERE FOR OVER A CENTURY,
BEGINNING ABOUT 1740.
DO NOT DISTURB THESE GRAVES
NO IMPLEMENTS ARE BURIED HERE.

This fence was erected by the Civilian Conservation Corps, which certainly was not the creator of a cemetery that William Wallace Lee already had described as early as 1868. None of the fence remains today, but our cemetery crew did find a shallow trench around almost the entire graveyard. In the trench were the rotted remains of fence posts. The location of the trench has been included in the cemetery map.

Figure 8.9   A sample of some of the obvious headstones (all unmarked) in the Lighthouse cemetery.

Figure 8.10   A photograph taken in the 1930s of the Lighthouse cemetery. A sign that was hung from the fence read: These are the graves of the Indians who lived here for over a century, beginning about 1740. Do not disturb these graves. No implements are buried here.

SUBSURFACE SURVEY

In 1986, soon after we happened onto the Lighthouse, we conducted a test pit survey of the terrace on which the site is located. As discussed in Chapter 7, such a survey entails the excavation of small test holes, in this instance 50-centimeter squares down to bedrock, water, or glacial deposit. We had been conducting such a survey to search for evidence of the prehistoric occupation of Peoples State Forest when we accidentally came upon the surficial remains of the Lighthouse village. Once we had determined the historical significance of the site, we conducted a test pit transect survey of the area to determine whether further excavation would be worthwhile.

We initially excavated 17 test pits within the village itself. These pits were excavated at approximately 15-meter intervals in two north-south transects. (Their locations in relation to site features are indicated in Figure 8.1.) We also excavated 30 test pits on the island in the Farmington River, next to the site.

We knew there were aboveground remains at the site; the features discussed earlier in this chapter, and located before the pedestrian survey of 1991, were first recognized by us in 1986. We also knew a small amount about the

CEMETERY EXCAVATION?

An obvious question might be asked at this point: Why not simply dig up the burials to find out how many were buried there and perform the kind of osteological analysis mentioned in Chapters 2 and 7? In response to such a question I might ask, How would you feel if these were your relatives we were excavating?

As an archaeologist, as a scientist, and as a researcher who is ready to travel any avenue to learn more about the people of the Lighthouse, I would very much like to examine the skeletal remains of those people. On the other hand, I can certainly understand the perspective of those who might feel that such an excavation would be a violation of the peace of the dead. I cannot imagine that many of the descendants of James and Molly, the descendants of people who knew them as friends, or even the people who know them now only from the legends and stories that have been handed down, would be eager to see their skeletal remains disinterred.

In recent years several Native American groups have protested vehemently about the perceived desecration of their ancestors' burials by scientists who are, almost exclusively, of European descent. Archaeologists have found themselves placed in a position where they have to defend their life work—work they view as being of great value, particularly to the native peoples who are so upset by it. Ultimately the argument goes far beyond questions of respect for the dead and involves political issues outside the scope of this book. We are learning much about the inhabitants of the Lighthouse by examining their archaeological remains. We will leave their biological remains alone. James and Molly and their descendants are safe in their graveyard. We shall leave them in peace.

history of the site—basically what was contained in the Lewis Mills poem. It seemed certain there would be a subsurface, archaeological component of the village, but we needed to be sure before committing time, effort, and personnel to an intensive excavation.

From the test pit results it was clear there was an extensive, material subsurface component to the site. Of the 17 initial pits excavated, artifacts and, in some cases, ecofacts were found in 10 of the pits. Material included ceramic sherds, iron nails, brick fragments, a *gunflint* (used as part of the spark-producing mechanism in a gun or rifle), and charcoal. The people who lived at the Lighthouse, like people everywhere, lost and disposed of many things through the cultural processes described in Chapter 7, and that material became incorporated into the ground they walked on. The most productive test pits in terms of numbers of artifacts recovered were those in the vicinity of Structures 1 and 2. This pattern of artifact clustering near structural remains was repeated in additional site testing and served to direct our more intensive efforts at subsurface excavation.

Although there were no foundations or other structural remains located on the island, we tested there. We know the island was considered part of James Chaugham's estate. It is specifically mentioned in Nathaniel Weed's sale of land to Joshua Youngs—"lying on the east branch of the west river lying on the island that was formerly owned by James Chaugum's heirs. . . ." We laid-in a test pit transect across the north-south length of the island, placing pits at intervals of 10 meters. Of the 30 pits excavated, only 5 produced artifacts; their total number was just 9, including a few ceramic sherds, nails, and pieces of more or less modern shingle. The material record indicates that the island was not intensively occupied by the Chaughams or their descendants. We have not investigated the island further due to the sparseness of material recovered in testing.

The significance of the items recovered in the test pits excavated in the heart of the village will be discussed in greater detail in Chapter 9, where we will focus on the material culture of the Lighthouse people. Even from a cursory inspection of the material recovered in the 1986 testing of the site, the number and variety of artifacts convinced us that the site had great potential from an archaeological standpoint and that there was information yet to be learned about the Lighthouse and its people, much of which only the material record could tell us. This encouraged us to excavate a few one-meter by one-meter units at the site in 1986 and to return in 1990 and 1991 to conduct a full-scale archaeological excavation using the procedures discussed in Chapter 7. Our exact approach at the Lighthouse is detailed in the next section.

ARCHAEOLOGICAL EXCAVATION OF THE LIGHTHOUSE SITE

We conducted preliminary excavations of the site in 1986 and extensive archaeological excavation in the summers of 1990 and 1991. In 1986 we excavated 6, one-meter by one-meter squares at the site. In 1990 we excavated 15, one square-meter units, and in 1991 we excavated 12, two-meter by two-meter (four square-meter) units. Above and beyond the initial 17 test pits in the heart of the village and the 30 test pits excavated on the island, we excavated a total of 75 square meters of the site (about 740 square feet). Because we have defined the site through our pedestrian survey as encompassing an area of 17,425 square meters, our total excavation of the site comes to about a .4 percent subsurface sample. This is quite misleading, however, as it is clear from the test pit survey that artifacts were not spread out evenly across this area but were clustered in and around the structural remains of the dwellings of village inhabitants. This was crucial in planning a strategy for site excavation and provided significant information about cultural practices in the village. (See Chapter 9.)

As a direct consequence of our test pit survey, we placed our excavation units close to the structural remains. In most instances we excavated at least

Figure 8.11   Photograph showing the process of excavation at the Lighthouse site.

one unit inside the structure and one next to it. Figure 8.1 shows the excavation units in reference to site features. Each unit is designated by its location in relation to datum. By convention, each unit is defined as the position of its southwest corner. For example, unit N73W81 has its southwest corner 73 meters north and 81 meters west of datum (N0E0).

Excavation units were excavated in three-centimeter levels in the manner discussed in Chapter 7 (Figure 8.11). Where possible, artifacts and ecofacts were left in place as members of the field crew excavated the soil in these levels using masons' trowels. All soil matrix was passed through ⅛-inch mesh hardware cloth screening. Many of the artifacts, particularly smoking pipe stem fragments, were difficult to distinguish from nonartifactual material present in the soil. Screening the soil dramatically increased the likelihood of recovering some of these less readily recognizable remains.

Other procedures utilized are standard for archaeological sites in general and historical sites in particular. Each two-meter square was excavated in quadrants. In other words, each of the four one-meter by one-meter quarters of a two-by-two-meter unit were taken down by three-centimeter levels. Each artifact and ecofact category recovered from each three-centimeter level from each quadrant of the excavation unit was bagged separately, and those bags were then placed in a level bag, and all of the level bags for an individual unit were bagged together in a unit bag. For example, all ceramics recovered from the northwest quadrant of unit N27W13 for level 8 were bagged together; all pipe fragments from the same quadrant, level, and unit were placed in a separate bag. In this way all materials could be assigned to a particular quadrant, a particular three-centimeter level, and a particular excavation unit of the site.

When we excavate an archaeological site, we destroy it, and the excavation of the Lighthouse was no different. By keeping obsessively accurate track of where all the materials we recover originated, we can put the pieces of the site back together in our notes and in our minds. The archaeological constituents of the Lighthouse site have been reposing in the earth for at least 130 years and as many as 250 years. It would be a terrible irony if, in our desire to extract these items from the soil to recover the information they can provide us, we were to destroy that information. The approach of archaeology is to minimize destruction and to preserve as much of the information as possible. We hope and feel that we have accomplished this in our excavation of the Lighthouse.

CONCLUSION

You now should have a good idea of how we went about the task of investigating the archaeological site of the Lighthouse village. It remains for us to enumerate and discuss in greater detail the meaning of the material culture that was reflected in the archaeological assemblage. In this chapter we have told you how we coaxed the data out of the ground. Still to be approached are questions about the things we found and what they tell us about the people who lived on the side of Ragged Mountain.

Chapter 9

MATERIAL CULTURE AT
THE LIGHTHOUSE

We try to make it a regular habit to spend at least one day every other week in the lab during a field project. As obsessive as we are about keeping accurate records of everything we do in the field, it must be admitted that as the time between the excavation of a particular area and the recording of the recovered materials increases, it becomes progressively more difficult to remember all the potentially important details with precision.

One day one of my field crew, Jeff Dahlstrom, was working on the material from his excavation unit N128W87, washing artifacts, assigning each an accession or inventory number, and recording in the artifact catalogue information on the location and depth of each artifact found in his unit. N128W87, immediately south and east of Structure 6 (see Figure 8.1), had been extremely rewarding, producing lots of pipe fragments, nails, and ceramic *sherds*.

Jeff was admiring one sherd in particular. It was nothing more than a standard piece of whiteware, typical for the early and middle years of the nineteenth century. On one face it bore a *transfer print* design, an innovation of the eighteenth century, where an often finely wrought pattern or picture is printed onto the body of the ceramic and then covered with a clear glaze.

On the reverse side was a part of a maker's mark, the name and logo of the company that produced the artifact (Figure 9.1, top right). Because it was only partially intact, we could not determine the actual name of the manufacturer. All we could make out was ". . . ANOVA." Beneath that were the letters "L-O-N-G-P." We had no idea what either meant.

At the same time another of my students, Cathy Labadia, was working on the rather meager material from unit N102W118, immediately south and west of Structure 5, down-slope from Jeff's unit and about 40 meters away. Earlier that day she had found a small sherd with a part of a maker's mark with the potter's name "T. MAYER" clearly visible. She had catalogued the piece and put it away, hoping that perhaps the microscope might help tell her more about the mark. Remember from the discussion in Chapter 8, maker's marks are valuable because we can use them to trace the source of the ceramics at a historical site, and the marks are helpful in dating the site itself.

I told Cathy that Jeff had found another fragment with a maker's mark— and I teased her that Jeff's mark, although incomplete, was "much better" than the one from her square that she had shown me previously.

When she glanced across the lab and spotted the sherd from Jeff's unit, she immediately recognized the pattern and color of the transfer print design on the front of the sherd as being similar to those on the sherd she had processed earlier in the day. She asked me to bring over the piece so she could compare it to the fragment from her unit. As soon as I handed it to her, she told me she was certain that her fragment, from a square some 125 feet away, was from the same dish and that, in fact, it would fit together with the piece from Jeff's unit. I thought she was joking. In her field notebook she wrote:

> While I furiously rummaged through all our bags I glanced up to see
> Kenny laughing and I realized that he thought I was joking or having
> "delusions of grandeur." Even as I turned the bag over and that piece of
> ceramic fell into my hand, Kenny looked on in disbelief. I don't think I
> could ever describe how the expression on his face changed as he took
> the piece from my hand and put the two together. That was one of those
> moments that would seem trivial to anyone that is not an archaeologist,
> but for those of us that were there, it was beyond magical, beyond words."

Cathy's piece can be seen in Figure 9.1, top left.

The two pieces fit together precisely, providing us with a nearly complete and fully readable maker's mark: "CANOVA, T. MAYER • LONGPORT" (Figure 9.1, bottom). It turns out that Thomas Mayer was a well-known potter in Staffordshire, England in the first half of the nineteenth century. "Canova" is the name of one of the ceramic patterns he used—in this case a black transfer-print design with classical scenes of European temples or churches. Mayer owned several potteries and took in a number of different partners through the years, but we can narrow down the age of the sherd with the maker's mark shown here. We know that Thomas Mayer owned a pottery in Longport, Staffordshire between 1826 and 1838. That is likely when the plate, whose fragments we found at the Lighthouse, was made.

Some of this ware ended up in the outcast outpost of the descendants of James and Molly Chaugham. We have the sharp eyes of one of my crew to

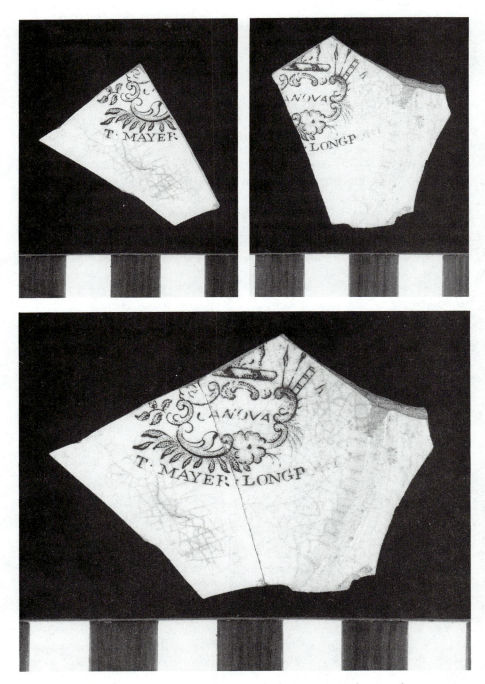

Figure 9.1   Two fragments of a transfer-printed whiteware (top) that together provide a nearly complete maker's mark (bottom).

thank for putting this together. It may seem a minor point, but in a very specific way it allows us to more clearly perceive life at the Lighthouse. We now know where some of their dishes came from. We can imagine the dish falling to the ground and breaking just outside one of their homes. Some of the pieces may have worked their way down the slope to the stream just to the south. That stream feeds the Farmington River and these pieces of plate are gone forever. At least one of the fragments, however, was washed down the path, ending up in the cellar hole of a different house. And now, many years later, archaeologists have recovered two pieces of the dish, can join the pieces, and read the maker's mark.

Even when the material record can provide nothing more than this—a glimpse at a seemingly inconsequential event in the lives of a long dead people—it can make a significant contribution to our work. Where it can do more—and it almost always does—is to allow us a far more intimate perspective of the lives of people like the inhabitants of the Lighthouse.

To hold an object buried for more than 150 years that belonged to, was touched by, and was part of the daily lives of the people we have come to know at the Lighthouse is a remarkable part of the process of trying to illuminate their story. There is an undeniable visceral, emotional element to this part of the work.

Beyond simply making a direct connection with these people long dead, the artifacts, ecofacts, and features also tell us things about their lives that we might not otherwise have known. Archaeologists often joke that "garbage is knowledge," and this is a fundamental tenet of our discipline. People, especially those without a historical voice of their own, have left us their personal histories in the everyday, mundane, material items of their lives. In this chapter we will attempt to convey the story the artifacts, ecofacts, and features tell of the lives of the people of the Lighthouse.

MATERIAL CULTURE: ARCHAEOLOGICAL FEATURES AT THE LIGHTHOUSE

Archaeological features were defined in Chapter 7 as the archaeological reflection of discrete human activities, consisting of spatially defined clusters of artifacts, ecofacts, or both. A feature is a place where people performed a task like making a tool, cooking food, or burying the dead. In a sense, features are the equivalent of complex, nonportable artifacts. Most of the items found in the pedestrian survey can be categorized as features. Some of these provide us with a unique perspective of life in the Lighthouse village. Among the most informative features were the remains of structures (foundations and cellar holes), the meager remains of stone walls, the quarry (and the resulting quarry stones), charcoal kilns, exterior fireplaces, and the cemetery. We can discuss these features and examine their implications individually.

Foundations

In his insightful book, *Pattern in the Material Folk Culture of the Eastern United States*, historian Henry Glassie (1968) surveys material culture, the items made and used by people who lived in the eastern part of the United States in the seventeenth, eighteenth, and nineteenth centuries. Although he is not an archaeologist, in examining material culture Glassie provides a detailed description of exactly the kinds of things that archaeologists regularly find. His focus is on the homemade and the common, the things people made themselves and used in their daily lives.

Glassie investigates many categories of historic items in his book: tools, furniture, toys, baskets, gravestones, fences, and so on. He also devotes a good deal of space to architecture, the homes and outbuildings people built for themselves in various regions of the United States.

In a later work focusing on architecture in Virginia, Glassie (1975) found that in the English tradition of "vernacular" architecture (in the sense of common or ordinary kinds of construction), house building was based on a 16-foot square. This unit was used extensively in the Virginia colony. The 16-foot standard measurement may have been based on the rod, a now obsolete unit of length that equals about 16.5 feet.

Archaeologist James Deetz (1977) found that this same 16-foot unit was used in New England as well. Houses were built on 16-foot square foundations and were added to in 16-foot modules. As Deetz maintains, "The sixteen foot unit pervades Anglo-American folk housing. Rooms tend to be sixteen foot square, chimney sections of houses eight feet (half the unit) wide" (1977:109). Measurement of a stone foundation in another part of Peoples State Forest and partially contemporary with the Lighthouse shows that it conforms to the 16-foot standard (see Figure 8.3).

Eighteenth- and nineteenth-century structures of non-European Americans appear to be different. Deetz (1977) found a pattern of smaller than standard foundations at the community called New Guinea or Parting Ways in Plymouth, Massachusetts. The Parting Ways community consisted of four families of freed African-American slaves. Joan Geismar (1982) in New Jersey (at the Skunk Hollow site mentioned in Chapter 2) and S. L. Jones (1985) in Maryland also see smaller than standard colonial foundations in other free black communities.

The structures at the Lighthouse (see Figures 1.1, 8.2, and 8.4), or at least their stone or earth foundations, as well as their cellar holes, do *not* conform to the English 16-foot standard. Like Parting Ways, the Lighthouse structures are uniformly smaller than 16-foot squares. In fact the Lighthouse foundations and cellar holes are so varied they seem not to conform to any standard at all.

Although precise measurement is impossible, particularly for the six foundations at the site that are little more than eroded depressions, Table 9.1 shows that the houses at the site are a hodgepodge of sizes and shapes. The stone-lined foundation walls of Structures 1, 5, 6, and 7 range in length from 6 feet to

Table 9.1   Lighthouse Structure Size

Structure type	Structure number	Dimensions of each wall			
Stone foundations	1	12'	14'6"	9'10"	14'6"
	5	13'9"	9'10"	13'9"	9'10"
	6	10'6"	15'1"	9'2"	13'5"
	7	6'	6'5"	6'6"	7'2"
Cellar holes	2	9'10"	8'10"	8'6"	7'2"
	3	10'2"	7'2"	9'2"	9'2"
	4	—	—	—	—
	8	7'2"	7'6"	8'9"	8'6"
	9	7'10"	5'3"	6'6"	4'11"
	10	6'6"	8'2"	8'6"	8'10"

more than 15 feet. The walls of the cellar holes of Structures 2, 3, 8, 9, and 10 range from less than 5 feet to nearly 10 feet in length. The cellar hole marking Structure 4 was too vague to obtain an accurate measurement of size.

Foundations or cellar holes need not be perfectly rectangular, but ordinarily even in crude colonial architecture, opposite walls were of nearly equal length and adjacent walls met at nearly right angles. This was not the case at the Lighthouse. Not only was there no standard size to the Lighthouse structures (see Table 9.1), there were few right angles and rules of symmetry were not adhered to. Only Structure 5 has a rectangular foundation. The rest are only vaguely rectangular.

All this should not be surprising. The inhabitants of the Lighthouse were certainly not eighteenth- and nineteenth-century, middle-class European-Americans. English individuals married into the family, but the ethnic blend of Native American and African American contributed to a mixture of material cultures as well as building practices. Add to this the fact that the settlers were poor and, at least initially, had little access to outside technology, and it is to be expected that their house remains look unlike those of contemporary, mainstream, English settlers.

In many ways the foundations at the Lighthouse are reminiscent of seventeenth-, eighteenth-, and nineteenth-century examples found in the southeastern part of Connecticut on the Pequot Indian reservation. In both cases, foundations are smaller than the European 16-foot standard, are crudely constructed, and often are excavated into the sides of hills. In fact when archaeologist Kevin McBride (1990a;1990b), who has focused much of his research energies since 1983 on Pequot culture history, visited the Lighthouse site in 1990, he was immediately struck by the similarities between the architectural styles of reservation structures and at least some of those at the Lighthouse.

As McBride describes them, Pequot houses in the mid-eighteenth century:

were built into south-facing hillsides with a fieldstone retaining wall constructed against the hillside. A low stone wall two to three feet wide was then built in a U or D shape from the back of the retaining wall. It is not known whether a sapling frame and mats were used in these structures, or if they supported some kind of more formal frame structure with shingles (McBride 1990a:113).

Note that McBride's description of mid–eighteenth-century Pequot dwelling foundations matches quite closely the appearance of structures at the Lighthouse, especially Structures 5 and 6 as described in Chapter 8. Houses on the reservation and at the Lighthouse thus appear to have been an amalgam of English and Native American architectural forms. Remember from Chapter 4 that J. E. Mason calls the Lighthouse structures that he saw "wigwams," and the reporter for the *Mountain County Herald* described the dwellings at the Lighthouse as being "built after a style of architecture about half-way between a wood-pile and a log fence." McBride is far more charitable—and likely more accurate—when he describes the eighteenth-century houses on the Pequot reservation as being "intermediate between wigwams and Euro-American frame houses" (1990:113). This description is apt for Lighthouse village houses as well. A similar process of "creolization" or mixture of house construction styles is noted by historical archaeologist Leland Ferguson (1992) on plantations in South Carolina where there, too, the cultures of Africans, Native Americans, and Europeans intersected.

Stone Walls

The dearth of stone walls (many New Englanders call them "stone fences," and they are nearly everywhere) at the site as noted in Chapter 8 is perhaps a more significant fact than the presence of a wall or walls separating the property from the roadway. Stone walls were built in New England partially to demarcate property boundaries. In most regions—Ragged Mountain being one of these areas—there is an ample supply of stone. Piling up stones serves the multiple purposes of clearing a field for plowing and planting, restricting animals to certain sections of a property, and indicating a property boundary. Elsewhere in Peoples State Forest, stone walls do appear, associated with family-owned farmsteads and mills. The area around the colonial structure seen in Figure 8.3, for example, is crisscrossed by stone walls.

The lack of stone walls at the Lighthouse village, therefore, is significant. There were no owners (or, at least, no occupant owners) before the Chaughams. Sometime after 1740, when the legend says James and Molly arrived, by 1779–1782 when land records indicate that James Chaugham and his son Samuel bought much of the side of Ragged Mountain, and before 1836 when much of the property was sold off, Chaugham family members owned nearly all the property where the village was located. Individual family lines possessed title to tracts within the village, and family members bought and sold these tracts among themselves as shown in Chapter 6, but it seems they felt no need to demarcate the boundaries of their various landholdings with stone walls. This may signify a generally communal attitude toward ownership of village land, at least in terms of Chaugham descendants and in-laws.

It is an English practice to clearly mark land ownership on the ground; it is essentially alien to Native-American cultures. Deetz (1977) at Parting Ways in Massachusetts and Jones (1985) at freed slave communities in Maryland found that land ownership, or at least use, also was communally based. In both studies, habitation structures were clustered within a larger tract of communally held land, instead of being laid out in the English pattern of individual family houses separately located within distinct, individually-owned and demarcated plots. The structures identified at the Lighthouse were confined to an area of a bit more than four acres; the lands owned by James Chaugham and his children consisted of about 100 acres. This is reminiscent of the pattern seen at these free black communities. The lack of stone walls marking individual tracts at the Lighthouse seems a further indicator that although land may have legally and formally been distributed to individual heirs of James Chaugham, the land was not divided up for individual use. The lands were likely used communally by members of the Chaugham family.

Stone Quarry

As noted in Chapter 8, immediately to the east of Structure 1, at the base of the slope leading to the top of Ragged Mountain, are the remains of a small stone quarry (see Figure 8.6). Large rocks bearing evidence of quarrying—the remnants of the drilled holes or quarry marks used to break the rock apart (see Figure 8.5)—can be found at the base of the slope. The large in-place boulders are talus—stone that has shifted downslope as a result of gravity, accumulating at the base of the incline. The rock left in place essentially represents the "parent rock" or source of "offspring" that have been quarried out, shaped, and then used in construction or gravestone production. In one case, the quarrying was unsuccessful; apparently the offspring broke off in too large or irregular a chunk and was left where it fell, next to the parent boulder.

The appearance of the quarry itself, as well as the form of the quarried rocks, indicates that the process used by the quarriers at the Lighthouse was typical for eighteenth- and nineteenth-century New England (Cramb 1992; Kennedy 1988). Quarrying with hand tools required two people and four tools: a sledgehammer, a drill, a plug, and "feathers." (Feathers are pairs of half-cylindrical pieces of metal that together have a diameter about the size of or somewhat smaller than the drill holes.) To break off a piece of rock for a foundation stone, a series of holes was drilled in a straight line along the parent rock using a hardened steel bar with a star point. The bar was held in place by one worker while the other struck it with the sledgehammer. The bar was turned about one quarter of its circumference with each hammer blow. After many blows and turns, a narrow hole was produced.

After a number of holes were finished in a line along the length of the rock, each hole was filled with feathers and a plug. A feather pair was placed inside each hole with the junction between them placed on the line along which the rock was to be broken. Plugs, which were simply metal wedges, were placed inside the feathers. Pounding on the plugs with a sledgehammer caused the two feathers to push apart against the sides of the drill hole. With enough pounding on the plugs, the rock would split along the line of drill holes, producing two fairly straight rock faces, one on the parent piece and one on the offspring piece. It was (and still is for those who quarry and cut rock in this traditional way for historical restoration) tedious, time-consuming, and back-breaking work. Nevertheless, it is an effective way to cut even very hard rock without the benefit of power equipment. The Lighthouse people produced squared-off stones for their foundations in this manner. That they quarried their own rock for use in their foundations indicates their self-sufficiency in this aspect of house construction.

Charcoal Kilns

As mentioned in Chapter 8, four charcoal kilns were discovered in the pedestrian survey. Although called kilns, no structures are used in such on-site production of charcoal. For a detailed discussion about the process of on-site charcoal manufacturing during the eighteenth and nineteenth centuries, refer to a booklet produced for the Hopewell Village National Historic site in Hopewell, Pennsylvania, by Jackson Kemper (n.d.).

Until interstate transportation systems like the railroad made coal available, charcoal was an important source of fuel in Connecticut for the copper and brass industries as well as for small-scale iron producers and blacksmiths.

The on-site charcoal mounds cannot be dated (they are too recent to date using the radiocarbon method discussed in Chapter 7). Local naturalist Walter Landgraf has counted more than 60 such kilns while conducting hikes through Peoples State Forest (O'Brien 1992). No documentary evidence exists to suggest that the Chaughams were producing charcoal or that they leased their land for this purpose. It is possible that charcoal production postdated occupation of the Lighthouse village.

Exterior Fireplaces

We found one semicircular and eight circular accumulations of stone in the pedestrian survey. Each of these contained some evidence of burning in the form of charcoal. In most of the cases it was clear that much of the charcoal we saw was fairly recent. Open air fires are generally forbidden in Peoples State Forest (no camping is permitted), but some still get built. It is difficult to determine whether each of these stone accumulations represents outdoor fires of Lighthouse residents or merely the recent fires of forest visitors. It is conceivable that some might date to the Depression when Civilian Conservation Corps workers trailblazed, built the fence around the cemetery, and generally cleaned up the site. Subsurface testing revealed no artifacts in these features that would help us date them.

The Cemetery

Burial grounds of European settlers of the New World are abundant in southern New England. They vary from enormous cemeteries of hundreds and even thousands of people to small church graveyards with the remains of a few dozen parishioners to small family plots of just a handful of graves.

Individual stones within these burial grounds are extremely variable, ranging from simple, upright markers with little more than a name and a date to huge, elaborately carved family memorials with detailed designs and expansive epitaphs. Certainly the size, expense, and elaborateness of a tombstone was contingent on the social and economic position of the deceased or the family of the deceased.

Some designs were more or less standardized on grave markers of the seventeenth, eighteenth, and nineteenth centuries. As discussed in Chapter 7, death's heads, cherubs, and urns and willows were common motifs that appeared regularly on gravestones. In Connecticut raw materials varied but consisted primarily of red sandstone (technically, arkose), black or gray slate, granite, and marble. (For detailed discussions of seventeenth-, eighteenth-, and nineteenth-century tombstone designs, see the many fine articles published in two volumes edited by Peter Benes [1977, 1978].)

The kinds of gravestones erected by individual families in individual communities depended on religious affiliation, ethnicity, location, time period, and, as noted, the wealth and social standing of the individual and his or her family.

Early in the colonial period, gravestones were carved as a sideline by individuals involved in other full-time pursuits. Farmers, bricklayers, roofers, and even surveyors engaged in part-time tombstone manufacturing (Duval and Rigby 1978). Later, full-time specialists began to dominate the market.

Aboriginal, native burial practices in southern New England varied depending on time period and location; and they were fundamentally different from European practices. Cremation was common a few thousand years ago. In late pre-contact times, flexed burials, where the body was bent with knees drawn up to the chest, were standard. The European practice of extended burials with the body laid out on the back, along with a stone marking the grave, was alien to native cultures. With the spread of Christianity through proselytizing by European missionaries in the seventeenth, eighteenth, and nineteenth centuries, many native people adopted these European burial practices. It is common in these centuries to find Indians interring their dead in cemeteries that follow the basic European pattern. Indian cemeteries like those at Fort Shantok in southeastern Connecticut (Salwen and Bridges 1976; Williams 1972) and the King site in Rhode Island (Robinson and Gustafson 1982; Robinson, Kelley, and Rubertone 1985) reflect these changes.

Literacy was not common among Indians, and poverty was rampant during these centuries. Few Indians could write well enough to produce inscriptions on stone. Most could not afford to purchase a slate gravestone imported from Massachusetts or a marble stone imported from Vermont. Equally few could afford to pay a part- or full-time specialist to carve their stone for them. In this sense, Indians were comparable to impoverished Europeans of the same time, who might erect simple wooden crosses or homemade grave markers. Thus it is fairly common to find Indian graveyards that mimic European cemeteries, with extended burials and stone grave markers; but these markers are simple fieldstones bearing no written inscription.

The Tunxis Indian cemetery in Fort Hill in Farmington, Connecticut is a good example of this. Several Tunxis graves dating to the early eighteenth century are marked by uninscribed, upright fieldstones. In this cemetery there also is one grave of a Tunxis woman, obviously of greater wealth than most, with a typical, professionally carved tombstone bearing an inscription and cherub design. Had the woman, Sarah Wimpey, not been buried in a historically-known Tunxis cemetery, and had she not shown up in town land records as a Tunxis Indian, her grave would be indistinguishable from those of her European-American contemporaries.

The Lighthouse cemetery can be seen in this context as typical of native and poor white burial places of the eighteenth and nineteenth centuries. Individuals were interred in European fashion, their bodies extended, their graves marked with stone memorials. The markers, as can be seen in Figure 8.9, are crudely hewn, flat, rectangular stones, roughly following a European pattern. Most of the stones are made of the same granite schist used in foundation construction at the site. This is the predominant rock type on Ragged Mountain. A few of the markers are made of red sandstone, another common rock type.

In contrast to European stones and typical of native grave markers, there is no writing on the Lighthouse gravestones. We know from the land records discussed in Chapter 6 that in every instance where the Lighthouse people were required to sign a deed, they did so with an "X." This is a good indication of the lack of even *signature literacy* among Lighthouse inhabitants; in the centuries preceding our own, many people who could not read or write nevertheless possessed the skill of writing their own name to enable the execution of such legal documents as deeds, wills, and contracts (Gilmore 1982). The people of the Lighthouse do not exhibit even this ability, and this explains, along with their apparent poverty, why their gravestones bear no written inscriptions.

William Wallace Lee noted the lack of any gravestone inscriptions when he visited the Lighthouse cemetery in 1868. He counted some 50 stones. As noted in Chapter 8, we identified close to 100 stones that are potential grave markers. Not all of these mark individual graves, some may simply be fortuitously shaped stones and others may be footstones. Fifty graves is likely an accurate, conservative estimate for the number of graves in the Lighthouse cemetery; there may be as many as 75.

MATERIAL CULTURE: ARTIFACTS

When archaeologist Vern Baker (1978) analyzed the ceramic assemblage from the Black Lucy's Garden site (Bullen and Bullen 1945; and see Chapter 2 of this book), he was struck by how similar that element of the material culture of freed slave Lucy Foster seemed to the ceramics of local white inhabitants:

> Upon initial examination, the ceramics as well as other cultural materials retrieved from Black Lucy's Garden appear identical to those from Anglo-American sites. (Baker 1978:110)

After more detailed scrutiny of the patterns reflected in the ceramic assemblage, Baker concluded:

> . . . compared to recent findings from other Afro-American sites, these materials are seen to fit patterns not previously observed on sites of Anglo-Americans (1978:110).

At first glance too, the material culture of the Lighthouse seems indistinguishable from that of poor people of European ancestry in eighteenth- and nineteenth-century southern New England. We will see here that just as was the case for poor, nineteenth-century African Americans, the material culture of the Lighthouse, like the foundations of their houses and the stones they used to mark their graves, reflects their different cultural character.

Lighthouse Artifact Assemblage

We can begin with a listing of the general categories, frequencies, and percentages of artifacts found at the Lighthouse site (Table 9.2). Historical archaeologist Ivor Noël Hume's *A Guide to Artifacts of Colonial America* (1969), although focusing on an earlier period, was useful in categorizing the kinds of artifacts we unearthed. This general list, including ceramics, smoking pipes, coins, bricks, glass, firearms, buttons, nails, cutlery, miscellaneous metal

Table 9.2   Lighthouse Artifact Assemblage

Artifact	Number	Percent of total
Ceramics	4,733	38.47
Pipes	398	3.23
Coins	5	0.04
Bricks	191	1.55
Window glass	737	5.99
Bottle glass	876	7.12
Lamp glass	745	6.05
Glass beads	4	0.03
Unidentifiable/burned glass	461	3.75
Gun related	45	0.37
Stone tools	71	0.58
Buttons	178	1.45
Metal fragments	1,396	11.35
Nails	2,439	19.82
Cutlery	22	0.18
Slate pencils	3	0.02
Total	12,304	100.00

objects, slate pencils, and stone tools, would, with the exception of stone tools, be similar for most other eighteenth- and nineteenth-century communities in southern New England. The counts and percentages in Table 9.2 provide a preliminary and admittedly subjective feel for the kind of material culture found at the site—the material items that were part of the daily lives of the Lighthouse inhabitants.

There are more than 12,000 artifacts in the Lighthouse artifact assemblage. As can be seen in Table 9.2, the most abundant artifacts are ceramic sherds (4,733 individual fragments), which make up more than 38 percent of the assemblage. The next largest class is nails, with 2,439 whole nails and fragments, about 20 percent of the assemblage, followed by 1,396 miscellaneous metal fragments, about 11 percent of the total artifact count. Bottle glass fragments account for about 7 percent, and window glass and lamp glass (fragments from oil lamps) each account for about 6 percent of the total. The rest of the categories combined make up the remaining 11 percent of the total artifact assemblage.

We can clearly see that the assemblage is overwhelmingly European in its content. Only a little more than .5 percent consists of stone tools almost certainly made by Lighthouse inhabitants. The other 99.5 percent is made up of items from the outside. In other words, nearly everything we found at the Lighthouse was European or American manufactured goods purchased or traded for by Lighthouse residents. This by itself is an interesting insight about life in the village. Although the inhabitants of the Lighthouse were a marginal group in both the literal and figurative sense because they were at the geographic and social margins of eighteenth- and nineteenth-century Connecticut, the vast majority of their material culture was obtained from the larger society. In terms of categories of items and their percentages, material culture at the Lighthouse was not unlike that in European-American society.

A more detailed analysis of the specific kinds of artifacts we recovered is needed to describe the kind of life led by inhabitants of the Lighthouse village. First we need to describe each of the artifact categories we have used here and note the specific characteristics of the Lighthouse assemblage. Then the artifact assemblage can provide us with insights about activities in the daily lives of the inhabitants, the social and economic status of the Lighthouse people in comparison to that of the surrounding English communities, and a chronology of the occupation of the individual structures at the site.

Artifact Categories

We will proceed by following the list of artifact categories from Table 9.2.

Ceramics.   Ceramics includes a wide variety of fired clay objects serving a broad range of functions. The world's oldest fired clay objects are figurines that date to more than 20,000 years ago in Europe; the earliest use of the technology to produce pottery is dated to about 12,000 years ago in Japan. Native Americans independently invented pottery probably close to 7,000 years ago in South America. Prehistoric New Englanders were manufacturing pottery by about 3,000 years ago. Pottery provides a more or less waterproof, fireproof, chemically inert, and relatively durable, inexpensive container for storing, cooking, and serving food. It is no wonder that wherever people were exposed to ceramic technology, pottery quickly became an indispensable part of their material culture.

At the time of the founding of the Lighthouse settlement, Indians in New England were making their own pottery, but no aboriginally made ceramics have been found at the Lighthouse. This is not surprising; archaeologist Kevin McBride (1993), who has worked on numerous Native-American sites that date to after the period of European settlement of southern New England, has never found any aboriginally made ceramics dating to after the seventeenth century. The pottery recovered in our excavations was commercially produced and kiln-made. Some was made in America, some in England—for example, the Canova ware discussed at the beginning of this chapter.

Differences in paste composition, color, hardness, manufacturing technique, and firing temperature are used to divide commercially produced ceramics like those found at the Lighthouse into the classes *earthenware, stoneware,* and *porcelain* (Spargo 1974; Turnbaugh 1983, 1985; Brown 1982; Frye et al. 1991).

Common clays fired in kilns with temperatures of about 1100°C (2000°F) produce ceramics called earthenwares. Earthenware color commonly ranges from red to yellow-tan or buff. The earthenware class of ceramics is divided into various types on the basis of paste refinement and glazing. Unglazed and lead-glazed earthenwares are called *redware*. Tin-glazed earthenwares include delft, faïence, and majolica. Other earthenwares use a refined clay paste; these include *creamware, pearlware,* and *whiteware.*

Redware was a common, generally coarse, inexpensive ceramic type. Lead-glazed redware was initially produced in Europe in the sixteenth and seventeenth centuries. Redware manufacture began in America in about 1625 (Turnbaugh 1985). Its popularity declined with the introduction of finer wares in the eighteenth century.

Creamware was introduced in England around 1740. This refined earthenware had a yellowish or buff paste, was often covered with painted or printed designs, and was ordinarily coated with a clear glaze with a yellowish cast. It remained popular until it was replaced in about 1830 by a whiter ceramic type discussed below.

Pearlware was introduced in 1779 (Noël Hume 1978). Its look was an explicit attempt to emulate Chinese porcelain. The addition of cobalt blue to the paste and glaze gave pearlware its white or pale blue tint, as opposed to the yellower look of creamware. Pearlware also lent itself to various design techniques. Its popularity waned after 1820, and it too was replaced by about 1830.

After 1820 an even whiter ceramic type was introduced by potters in Staffordshire, England. The use of white kaolin clay reduced the blue appearance of the ceramics and made it a truer white; this type was appropriately called whiteware. Whiteware largely replaced creamware and pearlware in the nineteenth century. As we will see, the great majority of the ceramic objects recovered at the Lighthouse is whiteware.

Stoneware is a separate class of ceramic objects, fired at somewhat higher temperatures (1200–1400°C or 2200–2500°F). It is a generally denser, heavier class of ceramic than earthenware, ranging in color from gray to brown to buff. A salt-glaze commonly was applied. After 1810 some potters coated stoneware vessel interiors with a brown slip, called "Albany slip." Many of the stoneware objects recovered from the Lighthouse are of this style. Stoneware was manufactured in North America by the middle of the eighteenth century and largely replaced lead-glazed redwares after 1780. The durability of stoneware rendered it useful for storage. Note that most of the stoneware objects recovered at the Lighthouse were jugs.

Porcelain is made from a translucent paste fired at a temperature of 1400°C (2500°F). Porcelain is an advanced ceramic and generally was more expensive than either the earthenwares or stoneware. We found no true porcelain in our excavations at the Lighthouse.

Our analysis of the ceramics recovered at the Lighthouse began with the statistic called *minimum vessel count.* The reason for this is simple. One object may break into dozens or even hundreds of small fragments while another may be intact or may have broken into a small number of large pieces. Using simple sherd counts in analysis can be misleading by overestimating the impor-

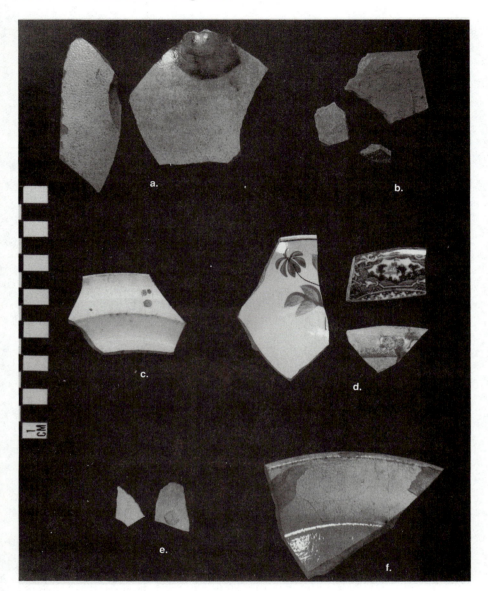

Figure 9.2   Sample of ceramics from the Lighthouse site: (a) stoneware;
(b) redware; (c) creamware; (d) whiteware: hand-painted polychrome (left)
and transfer print (right); (e) pearlware; (f) yellowware.

tance of some categories of ceramics that happened to have broken into more
fragments. To avoid this problem, the entire ceramic assemblage has been
examined to produce a minimum vessel count for the various categories of

objects. Historical archaeologist Robert F. Gradie divided the assemblage into ceramic classes, types, patterns, colors, functional categories, and location of discovery. Next he analytically combined sherds that, on the basis of these considerations, could have come from the same object. In this way he provided a count of the minimum number of objects that we recovered of each of the functional and ware types seen at the site. To be sure, this almost certainly underestimates the counts; in some cases sherds that were combined in the analysis may have come from different objects that were the same (or nearly so) in terms of shape, color, and so on. But it is better to be conservative and use the minimum count in the analysis, for in this way we avoid exaggerating the number and significance of any or all ceramic categories found at the site.

The ware types recovered at the Lighthouse include those discussed earlier: redware, creamware, pearlware, whiteware, and stoneware (Figure 9.2). Sherds of two other types, *ironstone* and *yellowware*, also were recovered. Using the numbers produced in our minimum vessel count, it can be seen that the ceramics used by the inhabitants are varied (Table 9.3).

Again using the minimum vessel count, we can determine the number of vessels or objects of each ceramic functional type recovered at the Lighthouse: plates, saucers, cups, bowls, pans, jars, jugs, bottles, pitchers, teapots, and mugs. There was even a single fragment of a chamber pot (one of the objects in the type "other" in Structure 3 in Table 9.4). The breakdown of the minimum number of each of these types of objects recovered in excavations at each of the Lighthouse structures is presented in Table 9.4.

Smoking pipes.   Another common artifact recovered at the Lighthouse was fragments of kaolin (a fine, white clay) smoking pipes (Figure 9.3). These common, long-stemmed white pipes are familiar to any visitor to a colonial restoration. They were originally manufactured in England at the end of the sixteenth century when smoking tobacco brought to Europe from the Americas became popular (Oswald 1951). These pipes were cheap, expendable items; Ivor Noël Hume (1969:296) estimates that pipes were sold by manufacturers for as little as two shillings for a gross in the first decade of the eighteenth century. The average pipe, Noël Hume suggests, was manufactured, sold, smoked, broken, and discarded all within a matter of a year or two.

The pipes were inexpensive, and even poor people could afford them. It nevertheless surprised me that people so far out at the geographical and economic margins of eighteenth- and nineteenth-century society had access to the pipes or even the small disposable income necessary to obtain them. They are abundant at the site, dating to a period late in the occupational history of the Lighthouse. Among the 398 smoking pipe fragments recovered were pipe bowls and parts of their long, tapering stems. Some of the bowls bore various designs, and three of the stems revealed the name of the same manufacturer: Peter Dorni. The presence of such a large number of pipe fragments indicates that smoking tobacco was common at the site. It also indicates that, at least after a time, the inhabitants of the Lighthouse had access to manufactured items like pipes that they could purchase or trade for.

Table 9.3 Number and Percentage of Minimum Number of Vessels of Each Ware Type for Each Structure at the Lighthouse

Structures Ware types	1		2		3		4		5		6		7		8		Whole site	
	No.*	%	No.	%	No.	%	No.	%	No.	%	No.	%	No.	%	No.	%	No.	%
Redware	2	3.5	0	0.0	3	3.8	5	13.5	1	3.8	1	1.2	3	3.8	3	5.0	18	4.2
Creamware	3	5.3	0	0.0	6	7.6	1	2.7	0	0.0	1	1.2	9	11.3	12	20.0	32	7.4
Pearlware	1	1.8	3	37.5	2	2.5	4	10.8	0	0.0	2	2.4	11	13.8	18	30.0	41	9.5
Whiteware	31	54.4	5	62.5	53	67.1	23	62.2	14	53.8	68	81.9	42	52.5	21	35.0	257	59.8
Stoneware	15	26.3	0	0.0	8	10.1	3	8.1	8	30.8	8	9.6	9	11.3	6	10.0	57	13.3
Ironstone	2	3.5	0	0.0	5	6.3	0	0.0	2	7.7	1	1.2	3	3.8	0	0.0	13	3.0
Yellowware	2	3.5	0	0.0	1	1.3	1	2.7	1	3.8	2	2.4	1	1.3	0	0.0	8	1.9
Unidentified	1	1.8	0	0.0	0	0.0	0	0.0	0	0.0	0	0.0	2	2.5	0	0.0	3	0.7
Other	0	0.0	0	0.0	1	1.3	0	0.0	0	0.0	0	0.0	0	0.0	0	0.0	1	0.2
Total	57		8		79		37		26		83		80		60		430	

*Number of vessels

Table 9.4 Number and Percentage of Minimum Number of Vessels of Each Functional Type for Each Structure at the Lighthouse

Structures / Functional types	1		2		3		4		5		6		7		8		Whole site	
	No.*	%	No.	%	No.	%	No.	%	No.	%	No.	%	No.	%	No.	%	No.	%
Plate	11	19.3	5	62.5	25	31.6	12	32.4	8	30.8	29	34.9	21	26.3	9	15.0	120	27.9
Saucer	6	10.5	0	0.0	14	17.7	3	8.1	4	15.4	18	21.7	18	22.5	11	18.3	74	17.2
Cup	2	3.5	2	25.0	10	12.7	5	13.5	2	7.7	9	10.8	10	12.5	11	18.3	51	11.9
Bowl	15	26.3	1	12.5	12	15.2	7	18.9	1	3.8	10	12.0	12	15.0	15	25.0	73	17.0
Pan	2	3.5	0	0.0	2	2.5	3	8.1	1	3.8	2	2.4	1	1.3	0	0.0	11	2.6
Jar	0	0.0	0	0.0	0	0.0	0	0.0	1	3.8	0	0.0	1	1.3	0	0.0	2	0.5
Jug	12	21.1	0	0.0	0	0.0	3	8.1	4	15.4	5	6.0	6	7.5	5	8.3	35	8.1
Bottle	2	3.5	0	0.0	3	3.8	0	0.0	1	3.8	1	1.2	1	1.3	0	0.0	8	1.9
Pitcher	2	3.5	0	0.0	3	3.8	0	0.0	0	0.0	1	1.2	0	0.0	2	3.3	8	1.9
Mug	1	1.8	0	0.0	0	0.0	1	2.7	0	0.0	0	0.0	0	0.0	0	0.0	2	0.5
Teapot	0	0.0	0	0.0	2	2.5	1	2.7	0	0.0	3	3.6	1	1.3	1	1.7	8	1.9
Other	0	0.0	0	0.0	2	2.5	0	0.0	1	3.8	3	3.6	4	5.0	3	5.0	13	3.0
Unidentified	4	7.0	0	0.0	6	7.6	2	5.4	3	11.5	2	2.4	5	6.3	3	5.0	25	5.8
Total	57		8		79		37		26		83		80		60		430	

*Number of vessels

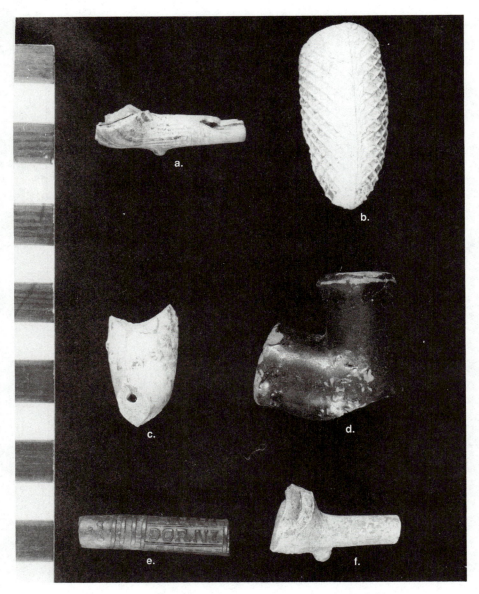

Figure 9.3   Sample of smoking pipe fragments recovered at the Lighthouse site: (a) and (f) kaolin bowl base and stem; (b) and (c) pipe bowls; (d) redware pipe; (e) kaolin pipestem with the mark of Peter Dorni.

Coins.   The first federal coinage in the United States was minted between 1785 and 1787, with individual states (Connecticut was one of them) minting their own low denomination coins in the same period (Noël Hume 1969:169). Coins are extremely useful for dating purposes, obviously, since most bear

Figure 9.4   All five coins recovered at the Lighthouse: four Indian head cents and one larger British half-penny token.

their dates of minting or possess designs that can be ascribed to often narrow time ranges.

Five intact coins were recovered in our excavation of the site (Figure 9.4). All five were found in the same excavation unit within Structure 3 and can be dated to the nineteenth century. (See the section on dating later in this chapter.) The presence of nineteenth-century coins at the Lighthouse is a clear indication that its residents were participants in the broader economic system of the surrounding European-American communities.

Bricks.   Few bricks or brick fragments were found at the site. The sample of 191 pieces of brick constitutes just a bit more than 1.5 percent of the entire artifact assemblage. Although bricks from abandoned structures are commonly appropriated for reuse, the small and fragmentary sample at the Lighthouse is a good indication that brick was not a major construction material in the village. Even for chimneys, the residents relied on local fieldstone for their primary raw material; for example, the surface next to the southeast corner of Structure 2 is littered with the fieldstones that made up the chimney. Not a single brick was found here. This situation can be compared to that of the late eighteenth-century structure in Peoples State Forest northeast of the Lighthouse village (see Figure 8.3). The area around that foundation is littered with bricks from the structure's chimney.

None of the recovered brick fragments bore any marks that might be used to trace their source or determine their precise age. Most bricks found on eighteenth- and nineteenth-century sites in America were made in the United States, so it is a good bet that the few bricks used at the Lighthouse were American-made. Although size, color, and coarseness of the clay used to produce bricks do correlate with time, usually an accurate date cannot be derived from such a small, broken-up sample.

Glass.   Totaling 2,823 very fragmentary artifacts, the glass assemblage can be broken down into five categories: window, bottle, lamp, bead, and burned beyond recognition.

A little less than one third of the glass assemblage consists of broken fragments of window glass. The presence of window glass and, hence, windows at the site provides some insight into the kinds of structures built and the degree of contact with the outside world; certainly window glass was purchased and not manufactured by site inhabitants.

Window glass manufacturing developed at the beginning of the seventeenth century with the production of small, geometric shapes of flat glass held together with strips of lead. Blown "crown glass" evolved in the late seventeenth century and then the mass production of "broad glass" developed through the "sheet process" in 1832. As Noël Hume (1969:233) says, glass found at archaeological sites usually can be dated no more precisely than in this general chronology.

At the Lighthouse the entire lack of lead strips that held the small glass shapes together in early seventeenth-century windows is due to the site being occupied later than this period. Also none of the glass examined is crown glass, which was blown and spun in a circle and then cut to shape for a window frame. Crown glass typically exhibits evidence of its manufacturing process, with air bubbles arrayed in concentric circles as a result of being spun. All window glass recovered at the site appears to have been manufactured by the sheet method, which produced flatter glass with a more regular thickness than the crown method. This fact indicates that the windows at the site all dated to after 1832, when the sheet process was invented. Some of the structures may date to before 1832, although most, likely, did not have glass windows before this date.

The next category of glass is bottle glass. The history of bottles and bottle making is complex and beyond the scope of this book. Once again, Ivor Noël Hume's *A Guide to Artifacts of Colonial America* provides a succinct summary of the interpretation of glass bottles as archaeological artifacts found at seventeenth-, eighteenth-, and nineteenth-century sites in America. The *Parks Canada Glass Glossary* (Jones and Sullivan 1985) was particularly useful in the identification of the very fragmentary bottle glass assemblage at the site. Encyclopedic works by McKearin and McKearin (1941) and McKearin and Wilson (1978) are extremely useful in the identification of historical glass objects.

Noël Hume points out that glass bottles went through a series of regular changes in their development. Changes in the manufacturing process between 1650 and 1820 enable bottles to be dated to within two or three decades of their actual date of manufacture (Noël Hume 1969:60; McKearin and Wilson 1978).

No complete bottles were found at the Lighthouse, and even the small percentage of the entire artifact assemblage represented by bottle glass—just under 6 percent—is misleadingly high. Nearly all bottle glass fragments were extremely small, and together represent a very small number of whole bottles present at the site. This conforms well with the data from the free black community of Skunk Hollow mentioned earlier. There, too, bottle fragments were infrequently found. As Geismar indicates:

> Ceramics in the form of creamware were available to the general public beginning in the 1760s whereas bottles were not common until improvements occurred in transportation in the 1830s and in general technology in the 1850s (1982:151).

Bottled items became fairly common only by the end of the occupation of the Lighthouse village.

Most of the bottle glass assemblage consisted of small pieces of clear, light green, and dark green glass. We recovered the base of one octagonal bottle, a fragment of a molded circular bottle, a few pieces of patent medicine bottles, and several fragments of a single pictorial flask. These few bottles that could be identified all date to the nineteenth century.

A sizeable portion of the glass assemblage consisted of fragments of lamp glass, the very thin glass that shrouds the flame of an oil lamp. The largest fraction (almost 86 percent of all the lamp glass recovered) came from excavation units in and around Structure 3. The large number of fragments likely resulted from the breakage of only a few or even a single lamp. Oil lamps were common sources of illumination in the nineteenth century.

Also in the glass assemblage were four glass beads. Three of these were a faceted type called Russian beads manufactured in the nineteenth century (Kidd 1970; Fogelman 1991). Each of these was a different color: blue, red, and clear. The fourth bead was a variety called "donut," after its shape. This bead was amber in color and also dates to after 1800. The beads were each found in a different structure at the site. The small size of the bead sample makes it difficult to draw very many conclusions about bead use at the site. At best, we can say that beads were present, but apparently not used to any great extent by the inhabitants of the Lighthouse.

A final glass category includes those fragments too badly burned to otherwise identify. About 16 percent of the entire glass assemblage fell in this category. The presence of burned glass in a house foundation is often evidence of a fire in the house, and such evidence was not evenly distributed across the site. More than two thirds of the burned glass at the site was recovered from the excavation of Structure 5. There is other clear evidence of a fire here; a substantial deposit of burned wood was found in this structure. Structures 6 and 7 also produced substantial quantities of burned glass; together they produced nearly the rest of the remaining one third of the burned glass artifacts. From the evidence of burned glass as well as burned wood, it seems clear that Structure 5 and perhaps Structures 6 and 7 were substantially destroyed by fire, perhaps after the site was abandoned.

Gun related.   During the course of excavation, we recovered 5 *gunflints*, 17 balls of lead shot, 5 percussion caps, several pieces of lead from shot, and one gunpart called a *frizzen* (Figure 9.5). Gunflints are small, worked pieces of flint used in flintlock firearms. Flintlock firearms were perfected in the first half of the seventeenth century and did not change much through succeeding centuries. Basically, flintlocks replaced matchlock guns, where a burning fuse was used to ignite the gunpowder that powered the shot or bullet. In a flintlock a piece of flint held tight in a little vise on the gun is cocked in a spring-powered device. Pulling the trigger releases the lock on the spring and the flint smashes down onto a steel platform on the frizzen, producing a spark that ignites the gunpowder on the pan below the frizzen, which then explodes, propelling the shot or bullet through the barrel of the gun or rifle.

We have been able to identify the gunflints through reference to Ivor Noël Hume's (1969) guide and archaeologist John Witthoft's (1966) detailed analysis of these artifacts. Two of the gunflints are English and three are French. Both of the English flints as well as two of the French flints are of a size and shape that conform to nineteenth-century pistols. The other French flint is larger and probably was part of a long gun or rifle. The frizzen is also almost certainly dateable to the mid-nineteenth century.

Stone tools.   The term "lithic" refers to any item made of stone. Not counting foundation stones or gravemarkers as individual lithic artifacts, and including European gunflints in the separate category "gun related," we recovered 71 stone tools manufactured from local raw materials at the site (Figure 9.6). Most

Figure 9.5   Gunflints and frizzen recovered during excavation of the Lighthouse: (a) and (c) are English gunflints; (b), (d), and (f) are French gunflints; (e) is a frizzen.

common were quartz and granite schist cutting and scraping tools. The natives of New England did not possess metallurgy; they produced most of their cutting, scraping, and piercing tools from stone.

It appears that people at the Lighthouse relied to some degree on stone tools. The tools are both varied and simple; we found nothing like the often finely-flaked, symmetrical stone tools that characterize the prehistoric record of

Figure 9.6   Sample of the stone tools found at the Lighthouse. These tools must have played an important role in survival during the early years of occupation, before European-American technology became available to village residents.

southern New England. The tools we found seem to represent a pragmatic and practical response to the lack of metal tools, at least during an early stage in the site's occupation. Stone was available and metal was not. The only technological pattern is reflected in the small number of granite schist cutting tools. These are blade-like and appear to have been sharpened on a single face (that is, unifacially) of both lateral edges. This does not correspond with any known, local native stone tool-making tradition. In the presence of stone tools, however, we have an aspect of the Lighthouse assemblage that distinguishes it absolutely from the material culture of eighteenth- and nineteenth-century European Americans.

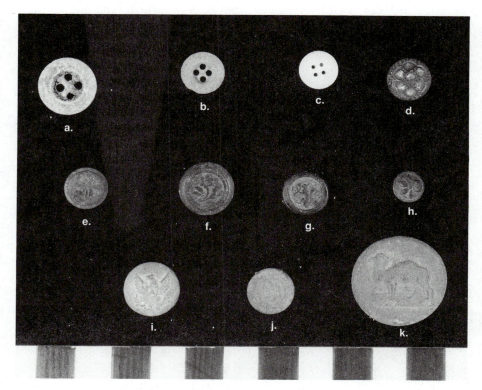

Figure 9.7   Sample of the buttons found at the Lighthouse. The compara-
tively large button assemblage may be an indication that residents were
supplementing their income by selling other people's discarded items of
clothing to paper manufacturers. Buttons (a) and (b) are soft metal, (c) is
white glass, and (d) through (k) are brass.

Buttons.   Noël Hume (1969:91) provides a short synopsis of eighteenth- and
nineteenth-century button making based on the research of historical archaeologist Stanley South (1964). South defined 32 common button types for those
centuries from the archaeological assemblages recovered at the sites of
Brunswick Town and Fort Fisher in North Carolina.

Figure 9.7 presents a sample of the buttons found at the Lighthouse site.
Table 9.5 summarizes the entire Lighthouse button assemblage using South's
typology. As can be seen in Table 9.5, most of the buttons recovered at the
Lighthouse were manufactured in the nineteenth century. Only four buttons
can be ascribed to the eighteenth century, and even these might actually date
to the early years of the nineteenth century. Sixty-five of the buttons, a little
more than one third of the assemblage, are brass (South's types 9, 16, 18, 26,
27, 28, and 32); some have various designs stamped onto their faces. About an
equal number (57) are plain glass (primarily white; South does not type these),

Table 9.5   Button Assemblage at the Lighthouse

Button types*	Year ranges	Structures								Total
		1	2	3	4	5	6	7	8	
9	1726–1776	—	—	—	—	—	—	3	—	3
13	1726–1776	—	—	—	—	—	—	1	—	1
16	1726–1865	—	—	—	—	—	—	1	—	1
18	1800–1865	—	—	3	1	—	—	7	3	14
19	1800–1865	1	—	—	1	—	—	3	—	5
21	1800–1865	—	—	1	—	—	—	14	—	15
22	1800–1865	—	—	—	—	—	—	1	—	1
25	1837–1865	2	—	8	2	—	—	4	1	17
26	1837–1865	1	—	2	—	—	—	3	2	8
27	1837–1865	1	—	1	—	—	—	2	1	5
28	1837–1865	1	—	—	—	—	1	10	—	12
30	1837–1865	—	—	—	—	—	—	1	—	1
32	1837–1865	—	—	1	—	—	—	4	—	5
Glass		6	—	34	3	—	11	3	—	57
Unidentified		1	—	6	—	—	—	11	1	19
Other fasteners		3	—	1	—	—	—	11	—	15
Total		16	—	57	7	—	12	79	8	179

*Button type numbers and dates taken from South (1964).

with assorted bone (type 19), shell (type 22), soft white metal (type 30), faceted glass (type 13), iron-backed (type 25), and iron-faced (type 21) buttons making up the remainder of the assemblage.

Metal fragments.   The 1,396 fragments of miscellaneous metal recovered in the excavation are an extremely varied lot. These pieces include small, very rusted, unidentifiable fragments of iron, pieces of oil lamps, a small sherd of pewter, horseshoe and bridle buckle fragments, and even a piece of a woodstove.

Nails.   Metal nails represent the second most abundant artifact type at the Lighthouse site: 2,439 complete nails and fragments, or nearly 20 percent of the entire assemblage.

Until about 1790 nails were all handwrought, usually made by a black-smith. After 1790 nails could be mass-produced by a machine that cut them from sheet iron—hence the name "cut nails"—but these were inferior to hand-wrought nails until technological improvements came about after 1830 (Frurip et al. 1983). Handwrought nails can usually be distinguished from machine-made nails by reference to the direction of their metal fibers: the grain of the metal of handwrought nails runs parallel to the length of the nails, whereas the fibers in cut nails run perpendicular to the length (Nelson 1968). Round, steel

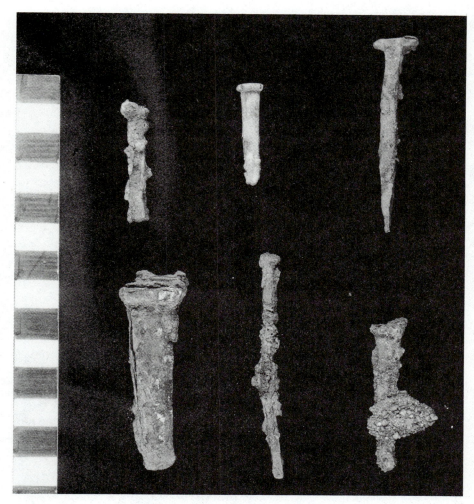

Figure 9.8   Sample of cut nails that predominated in the Lighthouse nail assemblage.

wire nails like the kind we are accustomed to seeing were not manufactured until the 1850s. To complicate matters, handwrought nails continued to be made well into the nineteenth century, and antique-style cut iron nails are still made for use in historic restoration or merely for the antique look they provide. The Tremont Nail Company of Wareham, Massachusetts makes such nail replicas; they even produce a chart that contains a sample of each historic replica nail type they produce. This chart is useful in identifying the kinds of nails found at archaeological sites like the Lighthouse.

Nearly all the nails we recovered at the site were cut nails, although a very few appear to have been handwrought (Figure 9.8). This is a good indication that much of the nail use at the site occurred in the very late eighteenth century and during the first half of the nineteenth century. This corresponds with the period of site occupation when contact with the outside world was accelerating because of construction and use of the Farmington River Turnpike. We are fairly certain that the site was occupied before 1790, but the lack of a more substantial portion of handwrought nails indicates that these metal fasteners were not being used in early house construction at the site.

Cutlery.   We recovered 21 complete and fragmentary cutlery items in our excavation of the site. The assemblage included the fragmentary remains of six spoons, five knives, and two forks (Figure 9.9). The other fragments could not be assigned a specific function. In some cases the material was too rusted to identify and in other cases all we recovered were the bone handles of utensils. These included bone-handled forks, spoons, and knives, as well as iron utensils. Two of the items were broken, but otherwise well-preserved, brass utensils. One of these was a fork, the other was the handle of either a fork or a spoon. The items found were all inexpensive; there was no genuine silverware found at the site.

Slate pencils.   We recovered three fragments of slate pencils in our excavation of the site. These pencils were made from a relatively soft slate and were used to mark on harder school slates before inexpensive paper and modern

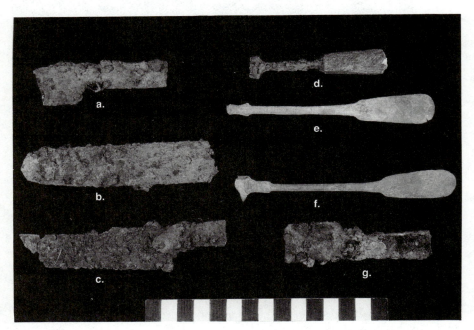

Figure 9.9   Sample of cutlery, including forks, spoons, and knives found in excavating the Lighthouse site: (a), (b), (c), and (g) are knife fragments; (d) is a bone-handled utensil; (e) and (f) are brass handles—(f) is a brass handle to a fork.

graphite pencils became widely used. As seen from the few surviving school registers from Barkhamsted discussed in Chapter 6, a number of Chaugham descendants were attending local public schools in 1858 and 1865. It is not surprising, therefore, to find school-related objects in the village, likely dating to the end of its occupation. Two of the pencils were recovered in the vicinity of Structure 7. The other was found in Structure 3.

Activity Analysis

By analyzing the functions of the various artifacts recovered in the excavation of the Lighthouse site, we can determine the daily activities of the Lighthouse village people. We find that the activities include food serving, preparation, and storage; stone quarrying and house construction; transportation; smoking; the wearing of clothing; hunting; and a number of other miscellaneous categories.

Food. The preparation, serving, and storage of food is clearly reflected in the ceramic assemblage. Included among the ceramic fragments are pieces of plates and bowls. These make up between one third and one half of the ceramic assemblage in each structure (see Table 9.4). Ceramic jars, jugs, and bottles likely used in the storage of food and beverages represent another 10 percent of the ceramic assemblage. Fragments of cups, mugs, and teapots constitute 14 percent of the ceramic artifact total. We have also recovered fragments of metal cooking pots. Cutlery including knives, forks, and spoons were found as well. It is not surprising that a large number of artifacts at a village site occupied for more than a hundred years relate to food.

Stone quarrying and house construction. Also in the artifact assemblage were a few items related to stone quarrying. There is a small quarry at the site, and some of the foundations, fireplaces, and grave markers contain quarried rock. In the cellar hole of Structure 1, we recovered two iron plugs that fit precisely into the quarry marks on the rocks that make up the foundation of that structure (see Figure 8.5). Although we have not recovered fragments of sledgehammers, drills, or feathers, the quarry marks on the stones and the presence of plugs indicate that stone was quarried in a traditional way in the village.

Transportation. A small proportion of the miscellaneous metal assemblage included fragments of horseshoes and bridle buckles. No documents show ownership of horses by any of the village inhabitants, but it would not be surprising that a community of people, at least some of whom engaged in farming, used horses in their agricultural activities.

Smoking. As indicated previously, nearly 400 fragments of smoking pipes were found at the site. This is a clear indication that smoking was a pastime of at least some of the village's inhabitants.

Wearing of clothing.   The existence of buttons in the assemblage is an obvious indicator of the wearing of clothes at the site. In this sense, certainly, the recovery of buttons is to be expected at a site occupied in eighteenth- and nineteenth-century New England. On the other hand, it cannot be said that the clothing worn at the Lighthouse was altogether typical of European Americans of this period. Remember the description of the clothing of Lighthouse villagers provided by J. E. Mason in 1855 mentioned in Chapter 4: "Their dress was of a singular fabric. It consisted of a coat, hat, waistcoat, all made from the same kind of cloth."

The recovery of buttons at the Lighthouse site may be an indication of something beyond merely the possession of clothing. Historical archaeologist Robert Gradie (1992) suggests that the large number of buttons may indicate that the Lighthouse inhabitants supplemented their income by "ragpicking." Poor people in the nineteenth century collected discarded clothing, removed and disposed of the buttons or other fasteners, and then sold the rags to paper manufacturers who used the cloth in paper making. No historical documentation exists for such a practice among the Lighthouse inhabitants, but the large number of buttons at least suggests this possibility.

Hunting.   Hunting or shooting of firearms is in evidence in the material culture of the site. The presence of a frizzen, gunflints, lead shot, and bullet caps directly attests to the use of firearms. Based on our analysis of the faunal assemblage, we know that the Lighthouse residents hunted animals. (See the section "Ecofacts: The Faunal Assemblage," later in this chapter.)

Social and Economic Indicators

James Deetz (1977) showed at the Parting Ways community of freed slaves that even though aspects of material culture such as house construction bore a superficial resemblance to standard European practice, there were fundamental differences. Vern Baker (1978) at Black Lucy's Garden and John Otto (1977; 1984) at Cannon's Point Plantation in Georgia have similarly shown that the material culture of ceramics at these communities might look the same as that of local whites at first glance, but there are significant differences that betray the nature of nineteenth-century socioeconomic systems in North America.

Essentially these researchers found that when compared to the crockery of wealthier whites, the ceramics of poorer blacks—slave and free—contained a far greater proportion of serving bowls or hollowware and a lower proportion of flatware or dishes. At Black Lucy's Garden, 51 percent of the tableware recovered in excavation was flatware, while 41 percent was serving bowls (Baker 1978:111). At Cannon's Point Plantation slave quarters, 49 percent of the excavated tableware was flatware and 44 percent was hollowware (Otto 1977:99). When Otto excavated the plantation owner's house, he found that 84 percent of the tableware consisted of flat dishes, but only 7 percent represented serving bowls (Otto 1977:99).

Serving bowls were used when serving soups, pottages, and stews; flatware was used when serving cuts of meat, such as roasts. Today, as well as in the nineteenth century, stews, pottages, and soups are less expensive dishes to prepare than steaks or roasts. Stews and pottages commonly are served in an attempt to stretch the food budget. Both Baker and Otto conclude that the predominance of serving bowls in the slave and free-black sites they excavated is an indication of poverty. This can be contrasted with the situation at Skunk Hollow. Geismar (1982) notes that when this same sort of analysis is applied to the ceramic assemblage at this New Jersey site, the results are more similar to those obtained from the assemblages recovered at excavations of plantation whites.

A somewhat different explanation for this pattern is suggested by Ferguson (1992). He hypothesizes that although black slaves used European glazed ceramics, they incorporated these alien objects into their lives within their own African cultural context. General African and Native American practice was to treat food in a communal way, with individuals in a family sharing meals from larger serving bowls of earthenware. Ferguson suggests that the abundance of European-American glazed ceramic serving bowls shows a persistence, in South Carolina plantations, of an African or Native American cultural practice of a more communal approach to meals. Deetz (1977) points out that a similar pattern of a higher proportion of serving bowls and, therefore, more communal approach to meals is present in European-American sites that date to the seventeenth century.

Proportions of flat to hollow serving vessels at the Lighthouse.   Determining the ratios of flat to hollow serving vessels at each of the Lighthouse structures was quite simple. Essentially following John Otto's methodology, I counted the total number of serving vessels—the kinds of items food would be served on or in (plates and bowls)—recovered in each structure, and determined the percentage of flat objects (plates) to hollow objects (bowls).

The proportions of flatware to hollowware in the ceramic assemblages of each of the structures at the Lighthouse as well as for the entire site conform to the pattern seen for poor African Americans in the nineteenth century. Overall at the site, serving bowls constitute a little less than 38 percent of the total serving ware; two structures exhibited hollowware percentages of more than 40 percent (Table 9.6). Only Structure 5 contradicts this pattern with about 11 percent hollow serving objects.

The ceramic assemblage in its flat-to-hollow ratio matches the pattern seen at Cannon's Point, Black Lucy's Garden, and other African-American sites. Their poverty and, perhaps, a cultural preference for a more communal approach to meals likely explains the abundance of hollow serving vessels at the Lighthouse. The archaeological record indicates this interesting fact not mentioned in the historical documents: The people of the Lighthouse seem to have practiced a generally non-European pattern of food serving and eating—or, at least, a non–eighteenth- or nineteenth-century European pattern.

Table 9.6   Percentage Comparisons of Flatware to
Hollowware for Each Lighthouse Structure

Structures	Percent flatware	Percent hollowware
1	42.31	57.69
2	62.50	37.50
3	67.57	32.43
4	63.16	36.84
5	88.89	11.11
6	74.36	25.64
7	63.64	36.36
8	37.50	62.50
Whole site	62.18	37.82

Ceramic values in the Lighthouse assemblage.   Another interesting consideration concerns the value, quality, or worth of the ceramics found in various Lighthouse structures. As mentioned previously, no porcelain was found in the excavations. Porcelain is a more expensive product than earthenwares and stonewares; it is not surprising that Lighthouse residents seem not to have owned any.

Not all earthenwares were of equal value or cost. Historical archaeologist George Miller (1980:3–4) has listed the general value of nineteenth-century ceramics from lowest to highest: undecorated, shell-edge and sponge wares, painted, and then transfer printed. Going beyond just this relative value listing, Miller (1980; 1991) went right to the sources, examining eighteenth- and nineteenth-century price lists, bills, and account books and found the actual costs of such items as plain creamware bowls, transfer-printed whiteware plates, and hand-painted whiteware cups. From these prices, he derived ceramic *index values* for various ceramic form and design types for different years. He expressed these values as multiples of the value of creamware objects for those years. For each ceramic form, for each year where prices are available, creamware objects are set at a value of 1.0; the values of all other ware and design types are expressed as multiples of that. For example, for 1833 the index value of a creamware plate is set at 1.0, a shell-edge whiteware plate (9 to 10 inches in diameter) is determined by Miller to have an index value of 1.33, and a transfer-printed plate of the same size has an index value of 2.67. Obviously, the higher the index value, the more expensive the object.

A mean index value can then be determined for each vessel form (plates, cups, bowls) at a site or for each structure within a site. These mean values, reflecting the mean value or cost of the ceramics found, can be compared to those derived for other structures within a site, or to other sites.

Using Miller's (1991:12–22) data, we can determine the mean index values for the plates, cups, and bowls from each of the Lighthouse structures

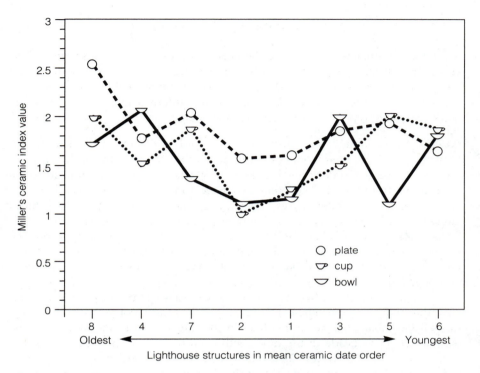

Figure 9.10   Change in ceramic index values through time.

(Figure 9.10). Arranging the structures by their mean ceramic date (see pages 188–191) along the horizontal axis of the graph as done in Figure 9.10 then provides us with a perspective on the value of ceramics used at the site through time and a view of changes in the wealth or poverty of the residents.

There are definite trends discernible in Figure 9.10. Interestingly, the index values for plates, cups, and bowls show relatively high levels in the oldest structure (Structure 8, with a mean ceramic date of 1814). From there, a definite downward trend in the value of ceramics occurs until about 1827 (Structure 2, as determined by mean ceramic date), with a gradual upward trend and then a stable level thereafter. All three kinds of objects—plates, bowls, and cups—seem to follow this basic pattern, though imperfectly.

The mean ceramic dates should not be taken too literally—they are merely statistically derived figures and some are quite close together in time. Also each date was derived from a different structure and each structure housed a different family, so differences in ceramic index values may just as likely be functions of differences in the wealth of different families in the village. Nevertheless, it can be determined that there were variations in the wealth of different families living in structures occupied at somewhat different times. Stretching the data about as far as possible, we can suggest that there was a general downward trend in ceramic values for a time and then a gradual increase, attaining eventual stability until the village was abandoned.

Chronology of Occupation

A number of artifacts help us date the occupation of the Lighthouse and either verify or call into question the dates provided by the legend (Chapter 3), by historical references (Chapter 4), and by documentary evidence (Chapter 6). We will assess the chronological information inferred from coins, maker's marks, smoking pipes, and the ceramic assemblage.

Coins.   As mentioned previously, we recovered five coins at the site, all in Structure 1. All five were copper coins. Four of the five were Indian head cents and two of these had decipherable dates: 1859 (the first year Indian head cents were minted) and 1861. The other two were too damaged after years in the wet, acidic soil of southern New England to determine their dates. The fifth, larger coin is a King George III halfpenny token with an impression of the British monarch on one face and Britannia (a seated woman holding a trident) on the other. The coin is badly damaged and the date has been destroyed, but enough of the design is visible to place its mint date between 1806 and 1807 (Tallman 1993).

Clearly four of the five coins date to the last years of village occupation, after the middle of the nineteenth century. The King George token indicates that village inhabitants were involved in the larger cash economy at least as early as the first decade of the nineteenth century. Because we know that the Chaughams were involved in land purchases as early as 1770, it is not surprising to find material evidence to show that this was the case nearly 40 years later.

Smoking pipes.   As Oswald (1951) points out, kaolin smoking pipes reflect the period of their manufacture and probable use in a number of ways. Some pipes had their actual year of manufacture stamped into the soft clay; like ceramics, some exhibit maker's marks that can sometimes be traced through historical records. Pipes with no maker's mark can be dated through analysis of the design type that may appear on the bowl. (See Noël Hume's chart [1969:303].) Pipes went through a number of changes in shape and size that also can be used to date pipes found in archaeological contexts. Using these general dating methods, it can be determined that the smoking apparatuses recovered at the Lighthouse site date to no earlier than the late eighteenth century. Most of the recovered pipe fragments that can be dated by reference to bowl shape and design almost certainly were manufactured in the early through middle years of the nineteenth century. Pipes with the "Peter Dorni" impression —we found four at the site—were manufactured in the middle years of the nineteenth century.

Another way of dating pipes is based on design, as the stem became longer and the draw hole in the pipestem became smaller over time. As Ivor Noël Hume (1969) points out, the holes were made by pushing a wire through the stems while they were still in the mold. As the stem became longer for cooler smoke, it became increasingly difficult to push a thick wire through without damaging the stem. Thus, thinner wires were used and holes became regularly smaller through the first half of the eighteenth century. J. C. Harrington (1954) developed a method for dating pipestems to five successive periods on the basis of the diameters of their holes; and archaeologist Lewis Binford (1962) refined the technique by producing a mathematical equation for the same analysis, useful in producing a mean-year estimate for a group of pipes ($Y = 1931.85 - 38.26X$, where X is the mean hole diameter for a group of pipes and Y is the estimated date for the group).

The Harrington and Binford methods work only for pipe assemblages dating from about 1680 to 1760 (Noël Hume 1969:300). After this, pipe manufacture became far more idiosyncratic, and pipe hole diameters vary too much from manufacturer to manufacturer. Because only a short segment of occupation of the Lighthouse village overlaps this period, the method is not applicable here.

Datable ceramic styles and patterns.   Particular ceramic designs, design methods, or even the colors used can provide chronological information when dating a site or structures within a site. At the Lighthouse some of the ceramic objects recovered from Structure 6 were part of a tea set with a green transfer print design traceable to W. T. Copeland during the period 1832–1847. In another instance a grouping of objects found in Structure 4 can be traced to the famous Spode family pottery (Copeland and Spode were partners) on the basis of its light blue transfer print design, manufactured sometime during the period 1834–1847. (Both of these transfer print designs were identified using Lynne Sussman's 1979 guide to Spode/Copeland patterns.)

In a more general approach, more than one fifth of the 430 ceramic objects identified at the Lighthouse exhibit the design method of transfer printing, described earlier. Objects with transfer print designs can be divided by the color of the print: Dark blue, light blue, black, green, red, brown, and purple are the colors represented in the Lighthouse assemblage.

The color, design and technology used in a transfer print have clear chronological implications. Archaeologist George Miller (1991) has summarized the timing of transfer printing. The technique was patented in England in 1751, first used in 1756, used on English porcelain in 1760, used on refined earthenware by 1780, and, finally, used as an underglaze (a dark blue color) in 1783. A technological advance was made in 1807 that allowed the use of dots in the image (stippling) for shading, giving a greater feeling of depth in the transfer print image.

Early transfer print wares exhibited dark blue images; many of these are found on pearlware objects. According to Miller (1991:9), in America dark blue prints were extremely popular between 1818 and 1829. The 1830s saw the increasing popularity of light blue, brown, green, red, black, pink, and purple transfer prints.

If we look at the distribution of transfer print color in the Lighthouse assemblage, we can see that dark blue, light blue, and black prints on whiteware dominate, and stippling is fairly common in the assemblage. The presence of these colors and of stippling reflects the occupation of the site during the late eighteenth century and throughout the first half of the nineteenth century.

Maker's marks.   We found only seven identifiable printed maker's marks (including the single mark on the two conjoinable pieces discussed at the beginning of this chapter) in our assemblage of more than 4,700 ceramic fragments (Figure 9.11; Table 9.7). Along with the mark of Thomas Mayer on the conjoined piece of Canova ware, we identified three other Canova ware marks: another mark from T. Mayer—a precise match to the first one we found—and two more Canova marks from two other potteries. One of the Canova marks, "Canova Stoneware," was a trademark name for a variety of pottery made by the American Pottery Company of Jersey City, New Jersey (Ripley 1942; Ramsay 1976; Lehner 1988:228).

We also recovered a partial Canova mark (specifically, "anovan") of a potter named Clews. Because there were several potters in the Clews family, we cannot tell definitively whose mark it was. However, based on the style of the ceramic, it almost certainly was manufactured by the English potters James and Ralph Clews, who were in business between 1818 and 1834.

Another mark found was that of John Ridgway, a British potter; this particular mark dates to after 1841. We also recovered two partial marks that we as yet have not been able to identify. On one we could make out only the name of the ceramic pattern, "Venture." On the other were the blue letters CA, which may indicate a Canova pattern. We cannot ascribe these marks to a particular potter or specific year or range of years.

We also found two impressed marks on Lighthouse ceramics (see Table 9.7). As the term implies, the mark is impressed in the soft clay of a ceramic object before firing, rather than being printed on the vessel. One of the marks, an impressed anchor, is probably the logo of potter Thomas Fell in Newcastle upon Tyne, Northumberland, England. Fell used an impressed anchor between the years 1817 and 1830. It was found on a piece of whiteware recovered from Structure 4.

The other impressed mark is difficult to read because insufficient pressure was applied when the metal die bearing the mark was pushed into the base of the pre-fired plate. A guess is that the mark is from the pottery of George S. Harker, East Liverpool, Ohio. The sherd with the mark is a piece of ironstone found in Structure 6. Harker did manufacture this hard, dense ware after 1853. It may be his mark, but we simply cannot be certain.

Not unexpectedly, all the marks date to the nineteenth century, covering the years from about 1818 to 1850. Certainly, some—but not many—of the ceramics found at the site predate this, but the evidence of the maker's marks conforms nicely to the dates from the coins and is likely another indication that the inhabitants of the site became fully incorporated into a European-American economic sphere beginning only in the early years of the nineteenth century.

Mean ceramic date.   In historical archaeology, artifact analysis ordinarily affords researchers more precise chronologies than those available to the prehistorian. Prehistoric artifact styles usually exhibit some degree of persistence

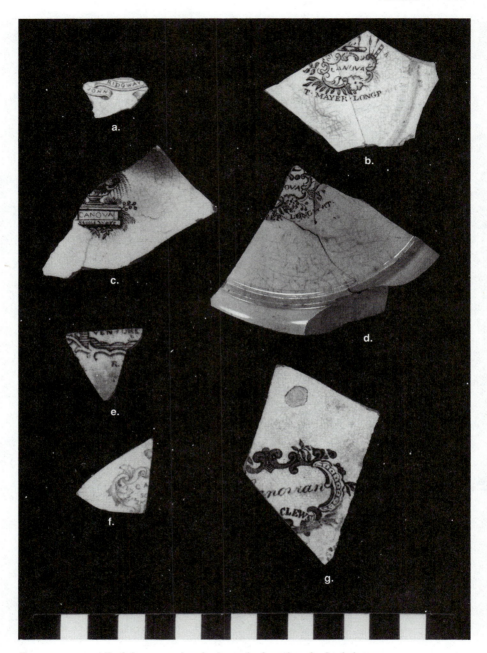

Figure 9.11   All of the printed maker's marks found at the Lighthouse:
(a) John Ridgway; (b) and (d) Thomas Mayer; (c) American Pottery;
(e) Venture pattern; (f) may be Canova; (g) Ralph Clews.

Table 9.7 Maker's Marks

Maker's marks	Location	Years in operation	Mark years	Pattern	Structure
Printed					
T. Mayer	Staffordshire, England	1826–1838	?	Canova	5, 6
T. Mayer	Staffordshire, England	1826–1838	?	Canova	3
American Pottery Company	Jersey City, N.J.	1825–1829 and 1833–1892	1840–1850	Canova	3
James and Ralph Clews	Staffordshire, England	1818–1834	?	Canova	6
John Ridgway	Staffordshire, England	1830–present	post-1841	?	1
R. ?	?	?	?	Venture	6
?	?	?	?	Ca. . .(Canova?)	6
Impressed					
Thomas Fell	Newcastle, England	1817–1890	1817–1830	?	4
George S. Harker	East Liverpool, Ohio	1854–1890	?	?	6

so that artifacts made hundreds, thousands, tens of thousands, and even hundreds of thousands of years apart are sometimes indistinguishable on the basis of technology, raw material, or style. Historical artifacts like eighteenth- and nineteenth-century ceramics changed relatively rapidly. Individual types or styles tend to have been restricted, at least in terms of their manufacture, to often quite narrow temporal ranges.

Archaeologist Stanley South (1977) used this fact to devise a technique for determining the *mean ceramic date* for historic sites (1977:207–221). South assigned year ranges for 78 ceramic types (the dates were provided by historical archaeologist Ivor Noël Hume and his wife Audrey Noël Hume). Each year-range for each type has a median date at the midpoint of the range. In this application of the technique, the minimum number of each object of each type is counted. Using the count of objects instead of sherds eliminates the possibility that a small number of objects that happened to break into lots of pieces will distort the resulting mean date. The number of each type found is multiplied by that type's median date and these products (each of the counts for individual types multiplied by the median date for that type) are added together and then divided by the total number of objects of that type in the assemblage. This procedure can be expressed mathematically:

$$Y = \frac{\sum\limits_{i=1}^{n} X_i f_i}{\sum\limits_{i=1}^{n} f_i}$$

(South 1977:217)

X_i is the median ceramic date for each type; f_i is the number of sherds or objects recovered for each type; and the result (Y) is the mean ceramic date of the site being analyzed.

The same kind of analysis can be performed to produce what are called *terminus post quem* and *terminus ante quem* dates for the site. Terminus post quem refers to the recognition that a site cannot date to before the age of the oldest artifacts found there; in other words, the site must date to sometime after the age of the oldest artifacts. A terminus ante quem date uses the youngest artifact found at a site as an estimate for the end date of occupation; the site must have been abandoned sometime earlier than the date of the youngest or most recent artifact found there.

Based on the same mathematical procedure outlined for mean ceramic date, we have derived mean terminus post quem and terminus ante quem dates for each of the structures at the site (Salwen and Bridges 1976). For terminus post quem dates, we inserted into South's formula the beginning dates

Table 9.8   Mean Ceramic, Terminus Post Quem and Terminus
Ante Quem Dates for Each Structure at the Lighthouse

Structure	Terminus post quem	Mean ceramic date	Terminus ante quem
1	1806	1831	1855
2	1806	1827	1849
3	1801	1832	1855
4	1789	1818	1847
5	1812	1836	1860
6	1822	1841	1860
7	1801	1825	1849
8	1786	1814	1841

Ceramic beginning and end dates used in the calculations that produced these dates
were taken from: Baker (1978); Brown (1982); Frye et al. (1991); Gradie (1992); Miller
(1980, 1991); South (1977); Turnbaugh (1985).

for each of the ceramic types found at the site. For terminus ante quem dates
we used the final years of availability for each of those types.[1]

Mean ceramic terminus post quem and terminus ante quem dates are
presented in Table 9.8. These dates conform to the other archaeological data
for the Lighthouse occupation. Interpreted most broadly, at least two of the
structures, Structures 4 and 8, may date to soon after 1786 and 1789 respectively. This is just after the Chaughams obtained legal title to the land on Ragged
Mountain. Terminus post quem dates show structures added to the village during the first three decades of the nineteenth century, a period of village growth
according to the documentary record, in the following rough order: after
Structures 4 and 8 in the 1780s come Structures 7 and 3, Structures 1 and 2,
Structure 5, and then Structure 6.

The mean dates for these structures show the fundamentally nineteenth-
century character of the material culture exhibited at the site. Although we are
certain the village has its roots some 30 or 40 years earlier, the inhabitants
were not obtaining European ceramics much before the late 1780s.

Terminus ante quem dates, although artificially clustered around the
1860s as a result of our application of South's technique, do show an order of
house abandonment in the 1840s through 1860. Structure 8 seems to have
been abandoned first, followed by Structure 4, then Structures 2 and 7,
Structures 1 and 3, and Structures 5 and 6. Using terminus post quem and ter-

---

[1]Because we know from historical records that the Lighthouse was abandoned by about 1860, we
used that as the final date for those types that continued to be manufactured later than 1860. Obviously, Lighthouse residents did not obtain these types after the site was abandoned. This renders
interpretation of the terminus ante quem dates problematic, but they can be compared one to another to get a sense of the lateness of occupation of a structure relative to other structures at the site.

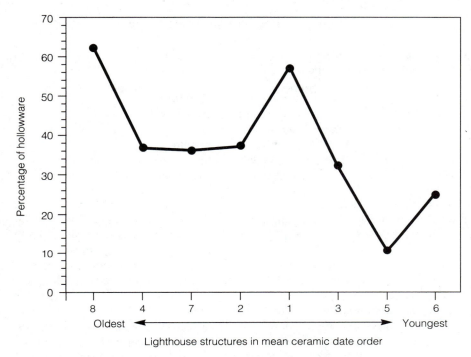

Figure 9.12   Percentage of hollowware at the Lighthouse through time. Structures are arranged along the horizontal axis from oldest to youngest, as determined by mean ceramic date.

minus ante quem dates, Lighthouse structures were inhabited for a minimum of 38 years (Structure 6) and a maximum of 58 years (Structure 4). We cannot take these figures literally, but they do provide a general sense for how long each structure was occupied.

Tableware change through time.   We can combine the data of the mean ceramic date with the ratio of hollowware to flatware to suggest the possibility that through time the Lighthouse inhabitants became a little better off economically and, perhaps, began to adopt a more European mode of meal taking. When we graph the hollowware percentage against structures arranged from oldest to youngest according to the mean ceramic date, we see a suggestive pattern (Figure 9.12). Although not absolutely clear-cut, there does seem to be a general trend at the site, through time, toward a decreased use of bowls. For the more statistically inclined among you, there is a fairly strong correlation (r^2 = .411) between mean ceramic date and hollowware percentage for each structure. Structure 1 and, to a lesser degree, Structure 6 contradict the general trend. What cannot be determined is whether they reflect poorer or more traditional families, short periods of rough economic times, or if the perceived pattern of a decrease in hollowware use is merely a statistical artifact.

Ecofacts: The Faunal Assemblage

In his poem, Mills states that the people of the Lighthouse subsisted in part on the natural resources of the forest:

> Oft they hunted through the forest
> For the rabbit and the squirrel.
> Oft they labored by the river
> Building swift canoes for sailing.
> Often in the shallow water,
> Spearing eels and trout and suckers (Mills 1952:55).

This is another element substantiated, at least in a general sense, by the archaeological record. An assemblage of more than 1,100 animal bone fragments was recovered in the 1991 excavation of the Lighthouse site. Nearly three quarters of these remains exhibited evidence of burning, almost certainly resulting from cooking. As a combined result of various food preparation processes, as well as post-depositional deterioration in the acidic, biologically active soil of southern New England, the great majority of the faunal remains are fragmentary and, therefore, the species are unidentifiable. In fact only about 3 percent (34 bones) of the entire assemblage could be assigned to a species. The majority of those (22 bones) are from white-tailed deer and a few are from small mammals, fish, and dogs. A handful of cow bones round out the faunal assemblage. Although the numbers are small, the notion that the inhabitants of the Lighthouse subsisted, at least in part, on local game is borne out by the archaeological record.

Artifact Spatial Distribution

As mentioned earlier, testing of the site in 1986 showed quite clearly that material remains of the Lighthouse occupation were clustered in the vicinity of the structures. Inhabitants of the Lighthouse were, perhaps, not quite as fastidious as we are concerning trash disposal and do not appear to have had a separate, designated village dump where all trash was disposed of. This kind of ad hoc, in-place primary refuse pattern was the dominant mode among English colonists in the seventeenth century, but not in the eighteenth and nineteenth centuries during occupation of the Lighthouse. Historic sites archaeologist James Deetz refers to this pattern as *broadcast refuse* or *sheet refuse* disposal. "Apparently," as Deetz points out, "all waste materials were simply thrown out, and often at what to us would be an alarmingly short distance from the door" (1977:125).

By Deetz's estimation, after 1750 this pattern changed among European Americans. It was no longer polite for an increasingly ordered American society simply to throw trash out of the nearest door or window. By the middle of the eighteenth century, English settlers in New England were disposing of their refuse in a more orderly way, digging square, often quite deep, trash pits, into which the trash was neatly deposited. These pits are secondary in nature as opposed to the primary nature of sheet refuse as defined in Chapter 7. As discussed in that chapter, Deetz (1977:126–127) sees some "deep" philosophical significance to the mid–eighteenth-century practice of disposing of one's trash in deep pits, but this need not concern us too much here. What is important to us is that the people of the Lighthouse were practicing in the eighteenth and nineteenth centuries what was, fundamentally, an anachronistic pattern of refuse disposal. Simply put, from the mid-eighteenth through the mid-nineteenth centuries, the inhabitants of the Lighthouse were dealing with their trash in a way that had been acceptable to English colonists living in towns only before the middle of the eighteenth century. Apparently for a group of outcasts in an uninhabited wilderness, the niceties of "modern" (eighteenth- and nineteenth-century) trash disposal were not seen as necessary or practical.

We now know something we did not know previously about the settlement, something no contemporary chronicler, no eighteenth-century town clerk, or nineteenth-century census taker recorded. The people of the Lighthouse did not conform to the accepted practice of trash concentration. Instead, not unexpectedly, they followed a pattern of sheet refuse disposal that was adhered to in rural settlements through the eighteenth and nineteenth centuries. It is a routine pattern in such areas even today.

Culture Change at the Lighthouse

As shown in the historical documentation, the people of the Lighthouse were not ordinary eighteenth- and nineteenth-century inhabitants of northwestern Connecticut. Their material culture provides further evidence of their unique character.

From the historical record discussed in Chapters 3, 4, and 6, occupation of the Lighthouse can be divided into three chronological phases in relation to contact with the outside world. The first period begins with the inception of the village circa 1740, the date mentioned in legendary accounts; admittedly, there is no hard evidence for this date. The first period lasts until 1789 when the Farmington River Turnpike next to the village was improved for stage travel (Wood 1919).

From 1740 to 1789 the village was largely isolated from the outside world. The relatively small number of inhabitants would, of necessity, have been essentially self-sufficient. Contact would have been restricted to Indians living in scattered settlements in the northwestern hills of Connecticut and the small number of white settlers in the area. Artifacts of European-American origin would be limited to those items James and Molly brought with them and whatever they could obtain through trade with intermediary Indians or from the few white settlers.

The second phase of occupation begins with the opening of the Farmington River Turnpike for regular stage travel in 1789 and lasts until about 1815. This period was marked by accelerating and intensifying contact with the outside world, because stagecoaches regularly drove by the village. The artifact assemblage reflects this, as European-American artifacts increasingly became available to the Lighthouse inhabitants.

The third phase of occupation begins roughly in 1815 and lasts until the village is abandoned sometime in the early 1860s. The 1815 date is an approximation; it represents the inception of rather rapid expansion in population and industry in the village of Riverton (first called Barkhamsted Forks, then Hitchcock's Mill, next Hitchcocksville, and finally Riverton, a village within the incorporated town of Barkhamsted). The first white settlement in Riverton occurred in 1782, but it remained sparsely inhabited until the 1820s. Then began a period of growth as Riverton became an industrial base in northwestern Connecticut with the opening of the Hitchcock Chair factory, the Stephens Ruler factory, and the Eagle Scythe Company. The population of Riverton grew from a few families in the early nineteenth century to 700 people by 1846 (Smiley 1934). The center of Riverton is less than two miles north of the Lighthouse, along the Farmington River Turnpike. After 1815 contact between inhabitants of the Lighthouse and European-American society was no longer an occasional event but an everyday occurrence. Inhabitants of the Lighthouse were no longer physically at the margins of society, and within a short period they were to become incorporated into the dominant culture.

A very small number of artifacts that may be datable to the eighteenth century have been recovered at the Lighthouse: Lead-glazed redware (in particular, the few sherds of so-called Jackfield ware, a redware with a deep black glaze and largely restricted to the eighteenth century), creamware, pearlware, and salt-glazed stoneware may date to the eighteenth century, but these, with the exception of Jackfield, also were manufactured in the nineteenth century. Perhaps the few handwrought nails and some of the kaolin pipes are eighteenth century, but here too there is too much overlap with the nineteenth century to be certain.

One might conclude from this that the legend simply is wrong about the dates and that the Lighthouse village was not occupied until very late in the eighteenth century. I think that the documentary evidence is clear that the site was occupied earlier, but there is just very little in the way of material evidence for this earlier time.

This is not surprising, however, considering how isolated the villagers were. James and Molly likely arrived with no more than they could carry. They were isolated from the colonial economy of the middle eighteenth century and their only contacts would have been with the very few whites living in isolated farmsteads in the northwestern hills and with hamlets of Native Americans. Also it is not until rather late in the eighteenth century that the village begins a period of growth, as James and Molly's children get married and begin having children of their own. The small population combined with their geographic isolation may have kept the earlier European-American assemblage sparse. It is always possible that an older part of the community lies elsewhere on the mountain and only further study will reveal its location. The presence of some eighteenth-century material is good, physical evidence that James and Molly, indeed, were there. The paucity of it merely indicates how hard it was for them to obtain any of the material culture of the larger society.

As indicated we found a number of stone tools made and used by the inhabitants. These tools are simple but may have made the difference between life and death in the earliest occupation of the village. The ability to use the natural environment in their immediate surroundings to produce tools was crucial to their survival, and the archaeological record shows that this was the case. In fact, Mills anticipates such a discovery regarding the Lighthouse people when he states in his poem: "Many hunting in the forest/Many making bows and arrows."

As a result of the inception of regular stagecoach traffic past the Lighthouse village and the later growth of surrounding towns like Riverton, European-American items became readily available to people living in the village. Such objects found at the Lighthouse dating to the nineteenth century are abundant. Most of the ceramics, brass buttons, kaolin pipe fragments, iron nails, bottle glass, horseshoes and bridle parts, gunflints, gun parts, cutlery, and coins found at the site were nineteenth-century objects.

The artifact assemblage seems to reflect the evolution of the site from a settlement on both the geographic and the social margins in the early eighteenth century to a settlement at least confluent with the mainstream in the middle of the nineteenth century. As surely as James and Molly adapted to their isolated forest home in the eighteenth century, the later Lighthouse residents adapted to the economic environment of the nineteenth century. These people, materially poor by any measure, were nevertheless able to obtain a broad spectrum and large number of material goods made available by the Industrial Revolution.

INSIGHTS FROM THE MATERIAL RECORD

The archaeology of the Lighthouse has provided us with unique insights. It has illuminated the lives of the residents of the community in ways that the documentary record could not. We have seen that the material culture of the Lighthouse people was essentially European American in its content but not in at least some contexts. The lack of stone walls dividing the property on Ragged Mountain into individual homesteads, the clustering of houses in the community, the high proportions of serving bowls in nearly all of the structures, and the size and configuration of the homes of residents and their reliance on hunting for a part of their subsistence are all indicators of the non-European aspect of the lives of Lighthouse residents.

Archaeologist Kevin McBride (1993) has noted a similar quality in the eighteenth- and nineteenth-century archaeological sites of the Pequot Indians of southeastern Connecticut. There, too, the material culture as reflected in the inventory of objects they used and in the catalogue of archaeological specimens that results is largely European. According to McBride, their own unique cultural contexts were maintained in the character of their social lives, rather than in their hardware. In their village sites, as in the village site of the descendants of James and Molly, this is reflected in how European material culture is used and how it is expressed.

The residents of the Lighthouse, although their roots were largely Native American (with some admixture of African and European) clearly adopted the material culture of European America. Nonetheless, reflected in their incorporation of this material culture into their lives are elements of deeper aspects of their own native or "creole" social system. In their manner of use of items provided by European technology, we can see that their native culture endured.

Polly Elwell was right when she told J. E. Mason in 1855 that those people buried at the Lighthouse cemetery and those who still inhabited the site were "Narragansett," at least as she understood the term. The people at the Lighthouse truly represented a remnant of native culture, with a blend of African and European, enduring in the northwestern hills of Connecticut well into the nineteenth century. The material record of archaeological artifacts and features at the Lighthouse site, in its subtle way, provides us with this crucial insight.

Chapter 10

EPILOGUE

I was sitting on the back of one of our vehicles when an old pickup truck, kicking up gray dust in its wake, pulled into the parking area along East River Road. At first I thought little of it; people often stopped to relax along the river, to fish, or just to talk.

Out of the truck stepped a rather imposing, older gentleman, tall and broad, wearing a dirty T-shirt and a baseball cap. With him was a sizeable but friendly black dog. The old man gruffly told "Rags" to sit in the truck, slammed the pickup door, and came directly up to me, looking me over bemusedly with his hands on his hips. After what seemed like an eternity, he thrust out his large, calloused hand and said in a very serious tone, "Shake my hand." Needless to say I did. Then he placed his hand on my shoulder and with a big smile said, "My name is Ray Ellis and you've just shaken hands with one of them," and he pointed up the hill to the Lighthouse village site. "I am a descendant of 'Jimmy' Chaugham."

I was at first taken aback, but then my curiosity grew. According to an article that appeared in the *Winsted Evening Citizen* on March 3, 1933, there were many descendants of the Chaughams still living in Barkhamsted and the surrounding towns as late as the fourth decade of the twentieth century. The Chaugham name had disappeared, but several families whose ancestors had married direct descendants of the Chaugham line a few generations after James and Molly died were still around. So it was quite possible that in 1991, nearly 60 years after the article was written—and more than 170 years after Molly Chaugham had died—there still were descendants living in the area.

Ray Ellis gave me the details of his genealogy as best he could. Of course he knew his parents' names, as well as the names of his aunts and uncles, grandparents, and even great grandparents. But he could not go further back than this. He did know one thing for certain; all of his life he had been told that he was a descendant of "Jimmy" Chaugham and Molly Barber. Remarkably, when he was a child, Mr. Ellis told me, his great grandmother had taught him a handful of words she said were Indian!

He wondered if I could help him fill in his family genealogy. I could. Ray Ellis, who visited us that day on the mountain, is the son of Lillian and Ernest Ellis. His mother's maiden name was Cochran. Her father, Edward, was the son of Andrew and Susan Cochran. Susan Cochran's maiden name was Webster; she was the daughter of Solomon Webster and Mary Wilson, the couple who lived at the Lighthouse in the 1850s and who were interviewed by the *Connecticut Courant* in 1900. Ray Ellis is the great-great-great-great-great grandson of James and Molly Chaugham! (You can find Ray Ellis on the genealogical diagram in Figure 6.7.) The Lighthouse "tribe" has not disappeared. Descendants of James and Molly, like Ray Ellis (Figure 10.1), continue to live throughout western Connecticut and continue to pass down the intriguing history of their ancestors.

THE LIGHTHOUSE LEGEND CONTINUES

The Legend of the Barkhamsted Lighthouse is an entrenched part of the oral history of northwestern Connecticut. One nineteenth-century newspaper maintained that a thousand versions had already been told, passed down through the generations in southern New England. Most local people have long known that the story presented in the legend of the Indian James Chaugham and his white wife Molly Barber was fundamentally true. The village was, after all, occupied until only about 130 years ago. Even today some of the older locals can remember their grandparents telling them anecdotes about the occupied village and the "Lighthouse Tribe."

As the decades have passed, however, published versions of the tale have added elements that bear little relationship to the original story. For example, in David E. Philips' book *Legendary Connecticut,* published in 1974, he retells the standard story of the elopement of James and Molly but then passes along the rumor that the Lighthouse tribe was wiped out by a group of robbers who moved into the village. From this base, the story goes, the robbers committed various heinous crimes against surrounding communities. The ghosts of the Chaughams, Philips relates, are rumored to have returned to the village where they scalped the robbers, killing them all to avenge their own deaths. Philips, of course, doesn't believe that version, but he does suggest that the descendants of James and Molly themselves were robbers and cutthroats who terrorized neighboring towns.

Figure 10.1   Raymond H. Ellis and his dog Rags at the Lighthouse cemetery. Ellis is a seventh-generation descendant of James Chaugham and Molly Barber.

In Glenn E. White's version, recounted in his book *Folk Tales of Connecticut,* published in 1977, the interracial aspect of the love story is only briefly mentioned, but the supposed mysterious disappearance of the Chaughams is emphasized. In his account, after the bodies of the robbers are found, 40 more bodies turn up! Incredibly these turn out to be the corpses of members of the Lighthouse tribe who had vanished and presumably been murdered years before. It is said that to this day, on moonless nights a ghostly signal fire can be seen burning on top of Ragged Mountain as a beacon left by the spirits of the people of the Lighthouse.

More recently the legend has taken an interesting turn. In an oral version that seems to have surfaced in the 1980s, it is said that Molly eventually was able to claim her fortune as the heir of a wealthy father, and that a chest filled with the gold that was Molly's inheritance is buried somewhere on the Ragged Mountain hillside. Although this new mythical element seems to predate our excavations at the site, I cannot help but wonder if our presence on Ragged Mountain has contributed to its acceptance. After all, who in their right mind would spend the greater part of two years meticulously sifting through the soil on the mountain looking only for old brass buttons, bits of pottery, and fragmentary pipe stems? There must be something really valuable up there—like a chest of gold, perhaps? We are still looking into this new twist on the legend of the Lighthouse. It would be ironic if in the process of trying to illuminate the legend, we contributed to it.

CONCLUSION

Barkhamsted, the Connecticut town in which the Lighthouse is located, was established in 1779. In 1879 the town threw itself a big party that culminated in a historical address given by local historian William Wallace Lee. Lewis Mills relied on Lee for many of the facts that he incorporated into his poetic account, and we have relied on Lee here to provide us with a historical rendering of the truth behind the legend.

In the address Lee presented at Barkhamsted's centennial, he was disdainful of those who expand upon the Lighthouse legend:

> Every few years some city chap, with a pen behind his ear, comes out among these plain country folk, puts on airs, shows off large, and in return gets badly sold . . . and forthwith is launched a new version of the Lighthouse story and doubtless this process will be repeated for years to come (Lee 1881:41).

Whenever I read that, I check to make sure there is no pen behind my ear. In one sense we are fulfilling Lee's prophecy in our research. Ultimately, however, I think Lee would applaud our following in J. E. Mason's footsteps by attempting to illuminate the lives of the people of the Lighthouse. It is important in the 1990s to be reminded that at one time Native Americans, African Americans, European Americans, and various mixtures of these three groups, having in common only that they had nowhere else to go, created a thriving community on the banks of the Farmington River in northwestern Connecticut. I hope and trust that in our integrated study of historical documents and the material record of the archaeological site that resulted from the settlement, we have not been "badly sold" and our rendition of the Lighthouse story is a veritable history of, as Mills calls it, the "Home of the fearless Molly Barber/And her spouse, the Honest Chaugham."

The story of the Lighthouse, ultimately, is one of survival and cultural persistence. There is great dignity, I think, inherent in the maintenance of cultural traditions, as well as pride in persistence in the face of enormous pressure to conform to a different cultural pattern. Archaeologist Leland Ferguson (1991), speaking of the persistence of African cultural behaviors and values among black slaves, categorizes this as "unconscious resistance" to slavery and oppression. Keeping to the old patterns is a way of maintaining "self" in a world where that is often difficult and sometimes dangerous. Viewing the culture of the Lighthouse people, as we have been able to reconstruct it here, in the same light is useful.

During the period of occupation of the community, the people at the Lighthouse were disparaged by reporters, defamed by historians, and viewed with pity by local European Americans. Lewis Mills did not romanticize the Lighthouse story until nearly a hundred years after the village was abandoned, and even with that, his enormous respect for James and Molly Chaugham and their descendants was and may yet be a minority view. Even today, many locals will refer to the Lighthouse residents as drunks, beggars, and no-accounts.

But we have seen the pride of self in the Lighthouse residents' vigorous and apparently unpublishable response to the *Mountain County Herald* reporter who was surprised at how happy they seemed to be with their way of life. I saw that same pride generations later in the face of Ray Ellis in our first conversation when he told me: "I am a descendant of Jimmy Chaugham."

The Lighthouse is one of the largely forgotten or too often ignored elements of American history. The village is just one of many examples of historical communities across the United States where those outside of the mainstream carved out a niche for themselves and lived out their lives. We saw this at Skunk Hollow and at Parting Ways. We saw it at Black Lucy's homestead and on the Pequot Indian reservation. We can also see it at the many nineteenth-century, post-Civil War communities of freed blacks scattered throughout the American South (Orser 1991) as well as in urban settings in the North (Bower 1991). And we can see it in communities like

Schaghticoke in western Connecticut, where Native Americans today, following traditional ways in a modern world, remind us by the persistence of their culture as well as in their own words: "We are still here!" (Richmond 1993).

Although the diversity of the lives of such people reflects directly on our celebration of the unique character of America, it has largely been forgotten in our mainstream narratives of American history. Much time is spent in colonial restorations and outdoor museums attempting to recapture the texture of the lives of European settlers to these shores, but rarely do we see restorations of slave communities, Indian villages, or multiracial settlements. And so, in a sense, we are all cheated in our celebration of the American experience. If my work here has caused you to reconsider the importance of the lives of Native Americans and African Americans, as well as poor European Americans, then my time has been well spent and this book has been a success.

James Chaugham and Molly Barber and their descendants were not important historical personnages, yet their lives were of enormous value and they can teach us much about the human spirit. Their modern descendants have ancestors to be proud of:

> On the side of Ragged Mountain
> In the town of fair Barkhamsted
> By the rolling Tunxis River
> Generations speeding onward
> In an ever widening circle
> Carry far the blood of Chaugham
> And his spouse brave Molly Barber . . .
> Through the ages still they journey
> Ever more and more descendants
> From that Ragged Mountain cabin
> Home of fearless Molly Barber
> And her spouse, the Honest Chaugham (Mills 1952:97).

Appendix 1

DATES USED IN MEAN CERAMIC DATE CALCULATION

Beginning, Ending, and Mean Dates for Ceramic Types and Designs Used in Mean Ceramic Date Calculation

	Beginning date	*Ending date**	*Mean date*
Shell edge	1830	1860	1845
Flow blue	1844	1860	1852
Sponge blue	1830	1871	1851
Elaborate edge	1820	1843	1832
Annular	1795	1820	1808
Hand-painted polychrome	1830	1860	1845
Salt glaze stoneware	1795	1860	1828
Brown stoneware	1820	1860	1840
T-print (dark blue)	1818	1830	1824
T-print (colors)	1830	1860	1845
Redware	1620	1840	1730
Yellowware	1830	1860	1845
Jackfield	1745	1790	1768
Creamware	1740	1830	1785
Pearlware	1779	1830	1805
Whiteware	1820	1860	1840
Pearlware annular	1795	1820	1808
Pearlware T-Print	1787	1830	1809
Pearlware shell edge	1800	1830	1815
Ironstone	1800	1860	1830

*Where end dates for a ceramic type occur after the abandonment of the Lighthouse, the date of abandonment (1860) was used as an end date.

Beginning and ending dates taken from: Baker (1978), Brown (1982), Frye et al. (1991), Gradie (1992), Miller (1980, 1991), South (1977), and Turnbaugh (1985).

Appendix 2

MILLER INDEX VALUE CALCULATIONS

Structure	Form	Decoration	Index value	Number	Product	Mean index value
1	Plate	Cream	1.00	1	1.00	
		Shell edge	1.33	2	2.66	
		T-print	2.67	2	5.34	
		Plain	1.20*	5	6.00	
		Flow blue	2.64	<u>1</u>	<u>2.64</u>	
				11	17.64	1.60
	Cup	Painted	1.43	1	1.43	
		Plain	1.00	<u>1</u>	<u>1.00</u>	
				2	2.43	1.22
	Bowl	Cream	1.00	1	1.00	
		Painted	1.60	1	1.60	
		Sponge	1.20*	1	1.20	
		Annular	1.20*	3	3.60	
		Plain	1.10*	<u>5</u>	<u>5.50</u>	
				11	12.90	1.17
2	Plate	Plain	1.20*	3	3.60	
		T-print	2.67	<u>1</u>	<u>2.67</u>	
				4	6.27	1.57
	Cup	Plain	1.00*	2	2.00	1.00
	Bowl	Plain	1.10*	1	1.10	1.10
3	Plate	Cream	1.00	2	2.00	
		Flow blue	2.64	1	2.64	
		Shell edge	1.33	5	6.65	
		Sponge	1.20	3	3.60	
		T-print	2.67	8	21.36	
		Plain	1.20*	<u>2</u>	<u>2.40</u>	
				21	38.65	1.84
	Cup	Cream	1.00	1	1.00	
		Painted	1.43	3	4.29	

(continued)

Structure	Form	Decoration	Index value	Number	Product	Mean index value
3		Sponge	1.50	1	1.50	
		T-print	2.83	2	5.66	
		Plain	1.00*	3	3.00	
				10	15.45	1.55
	Bowl	Cream	1.00	1	1.00	
		Painted	1.60	1	1.60	
		Flow blue	2.50*	1	2.50	
		T-print	2.80	4	11.20	
		Annular	1.20*	1	1.20	
		Plain	1.10*	2	2.20	
				10	19.70	1.97
4	Plate	Cream	1.00	1	1.00	
		Shell edge	1.43	2	2.86	
		T-print	2.86	3	8.58	
		Plain	1.20*	5	6.00	
				11	18.44	1.68
	Cup	Painted	1.25	2	2.50	
		Annular	1.20*	1	1.20	
		T-print	2.25	1	2.25	
				4	5.95	1.49
	Bowl	Annular	1.20*	1	1.44	
		T-print	2.80	3	7.84	
		Plain	1.10*	1	1.21	
				5	10.49	2.06
5	Plate	Shell edge	1.33	3	3.99	
		T-print	2.67	4	10.68	
		Plain	1.20	1	1.20	
				8	15.87	1.98
	Cup	Painted	1.43	1	1.43	
		T-print	2.57	1	2.57	
				2	4.00	2.00
	Bowl	Plain	1.10*	1	1.10	1.10
6	Plate	Cream	1.00	1	1.00	
		Shell edge	1.33	8	10.64	
		Sponge	1.20	3	3.60	

(continued)

Structure	Form	Decoration	Index value	Number	Product	Mean index value
6		T-print	2.67	7	18.69	
		Flow blue	2.64	1	2.64	
		Plain	1.20*	8	9.60	
				28	46.17	1.65
	Cup	Painted	1.50	5	7.50	
		Sponge	1.50	1	1.50	
		T-print	3.00	2	6.00	
		Annular	1.22	1	1.22	
				9	16.22	1.80
	Bowl	Painted	1.80*	1	1.80	
		Sponge	1.20*	2	2.40	
		Annular	1.20*	1	1.20	
		T-print	3.00	3	9.00	
		Plain	1.10*	3	3.30	
				10	17.70	1.77
7	Plate	Cream	1.00	2	2.00	
		Shell edge	1.33	8	10.64	
		Painted	2.00*	1	2.00	
		T-print	3.00	9	27.00	
		Plain	1.20*	1	1.20	
				21	42.84	2.04
	Cup	Cream	1.00	1	1.00	
		Painted	1.50	3	4.50	
		T-print	3.00	3	9.00	
		Plain	1.00	2	2.00	
				9	16.50	1.83
	Bowl	Cream	1.00	4	4.00	
		Painted	1.60	1	1.60	
		T-print	2.60	2	5.20	
		Annular	1.20*	1	1.20	
		Plain	1.10*	3	3.30	
				11	15.30	1.39
8	Plate	Cream	1.00	1	1.00	
		Shell edge	1.33	1	1.33	
		T-print	3.33	5	16.65	
		Plain	1.20	1	1.20	
				8	20.18	2.52

(continued)

Structure	Form	Decoration	Index value	Number	Product	Mean index value
8	Cup	Cream	1.00	1	1.00	
		Painted	1.50	5	7.50	
		T-print	3.00	4	12.00	
		Plain	1.00	<u>1</u>	<u>1.00</u>	
				11	21.50	1.95
	Bowl	Cream	1.00	7	7.00	
		Painted	1.60	1	1.60	
		Annular	1.20*	1	1.20	
		T-print	2.80	<u>5</u>	<u>14.00</u>	
				14	23.80	1.70

Index values taken from Miller (1991). Values marked with an asterisk (*) were extrapolated from Miller.

GLOSSARY

Terms in italic are defined elsewhere in the glossary.

absolute dating   A dating technique wherein one is able to assign a year or range of years to the archaeological material being dated.

adaptation   The strategy of survival of a group of people. How they adjust their behavior to a given set of environmental circumstances.

alidade   A telescopic device that sits on a *plane table* and is used, along with a *stadia rod*, for producing topographic maps.

alluvial   Soil deposited by flooding rivers. Alluvial soil often covers over ancient archaeological sites located near rivers.

anthropology   The study of the human species as biological and cultural creatures.

archaeological sites   The material remains of human existence reflecting a place where people lived and worked.

archaeology   The study of the material remains of human behavior. Archaeologists excavate and study the *artifacts, ecofacts,* and *features* that, together, constitute *archaeological sites.*

artifact   A constituent of an archaeological site. An artifact is any object a human being made and used.

assemblage   The entire collection of artifacts present at an archaeological site. The assemblage may be divided into constituent assemblages based on the type of artifacts present, for example, the ceramic assemblage, lithic assemblage, and pipe assemblage at a particular site.

association   Items found together at an archaeological site and believed to have been deposited together more or less simultaneously are said to be in association.

benefits records   Military records that include information on death or disability pensions and service pensions, as well as another kind of benefit, "bounty lands," provided to those who served in the U.S. military.

British Board of Trade   Arm of the British government whose primary responsibility was the administration of the colonies. The Board of Trade ordered the Connecticut censuses of 1756, 1762, and 1774.

broadcast refuse   A pattern of refuse disposal common in seventeenth-century New England, where trash was broadly distributed rather than concentrated in defined trash disposal areas, a method typical of the eighteenth and nineteenth centuries. Archaeologically, broadcast refuse appears as diffuse layers of trash rather than piles or mounds.

caching   The act of hiding something. The hiding place is called a "cache." Archaeologists sometimes excavate such caches.

ceramic   Generally, hard, brittle, heat-resistant objects formed from clay and then fired.

colluvium   Material deposited at the base of a mountain. Archaeological sites sometimes are covered with colluvium.

Council for Foreign Plantations   The governing body in Great Britain in charge of the colonies. The council was bureaucratically positioned beneath the *Privy Council* and above the *British Board of Trade.*

cranial suture closure   At birth the human skull is made up of a number of cranial bones separated by sutures. These sutures fuse during the life of the individual.

creamware   Ceramic with a yellowish or buff body and a clear lead glaze with a yellow cast. Creamware was introduced in about 1740, dropped in popularity by 1820, and was largely replaced with *whiteware* by 1830.

cultural dating   A technique for dating an object or site based on cultural comparisons and processes of culture change.

datum   Fixed point from which all other points at a site are measured. The 0,0 location of the two-dimensional grid superimposed over a site.

demographic   Relating to the population statistics of a group of people, for example, population size, male-to-female ratio, birth rate, longevity, and health status.

dendrochronology   Tree ring dating. Dating sites by reference to the sequence of rings found in logs used by the site inhabitants through comparison to the *master sequence* of tree rings for an area.

discard   A process by which archaeological sites come into existence; in this case, simply when people throw material away. Discard can be *primary* or *secondary.*

dower right   The legal right of a woman to a claim of, generally, one-third of all of the land owned by her husband upon his death—regardless of the stipulations in his will—and, in some states, a right to land sold by the husband during his life.

earthenware   *Ceramic* class made from common clays, fired to a temperature up to 1100°C (2000°F). Unrefined earthenwares include unglazed or glazed redwares and tin-glazed earthenwares (delft, faïence, and majolica). Refined earthenwares include *creamware, pearlware,* and *whiteware.*

ecofact   Material item found at an archaeological site exhibiting human activity but not manufacture or use. Examples are bones of animals killed, butchered, and eaten by site inhabitants, collected seeds and nuts, and wood burned in a fireplace.

economy   That element of culture concerning how people provide for their material needs.

enamel hypoplasia   Horizontal cracks in tooth enamel that result from dietary deficiencies.

ethnography   The process of living with a group of people to gain as complete an understanding as possible of their way of life. A subfield of anthropology.

excavation   The process of extracting from the ground the raw data of archaeology: *artifacts, ecofacts,* and *features* present at *archaeological sites.*

faunal   Relating to animal life. Faunal remains are the remains of animals, usually bones, found at archaeological sites.

feature   A constituent of archaeological sites consisting of artifacts, ecofacts, or both, reflecting an activity or set of activities conducted by site residents at a particular place.

federal mortality schedules   A statistical record of deaths kept in conjunction with the federal censuses in 1850, 1860, 1870, and 1880. These schedules list the names of people who died before June 30 within the census year.

frizzen   The part of a flintlock gun against which the flint strikes, making the necessary spark to produce the energy to propel the shot.

genealogical research   Broad term covering the study of family lines by reference to family, institutional, and official public records.

graniteware   A hard, white, plain ceramic type produced from 1805 to 1900. Similar to *ironstone.*

grantee   In a land transaction, the person who is buying the property.

grantor   In a land transaction, the person who is selling the property.

gunflint   Small, worked pieces of flint used in flintlock firearms to make the spark that ignites the powder, producing the energy that propels the shot.

half-life   In archaeological dating techniques involving the rate of decay of a radioactive isotope, the half-life is the known, constant length of time it takes for half the amount of a particular radioactive isotope to decay into some other isotope or element.

historical archaeology   The archaeological study of sites that date to the historical period. The term is usually used for the study of sites in the United States that date to the period during and after European colonization.

human osteology   The study of the human skeleton. In this context, the study of human bones found at archaeological sites.

index value   A statistic developed by historical archaeologist George Miller (1980, 1991) to express the value or cost of a ceramic object relative to the value of a creamware object of the same time period. A mean index value for a structure or a site is a relative indication of the wealth of the residents, as implied by the value of the ceramics.

in situ   Term meaning, literally, "in place." When artifacts are found by archaeologists in what is presumed to be their original place of deposition by site inhabitants, they are said to be "*in situ.*"

ironstone   A dense, vitrified or semi-vitrified ware first made in 1800. Heavily decorated prior to 1830. Usual designs copied Chinese porcelains. Ironstone is still manufactured.

isopleth   A line drawn on a map connecting points of equal value. A contour line on a topographic map is an isopleth that connects points of equal elevation.

law of superposition   Law in stratigraphic analysis, stating that because stratigraphic layers or *strata* are superimposed one on top of another through time, the relative age of an object found in archaeological excavation can be determined from its position in that sequence of soil layers.

letter of administration   When a person left no will, the probate court issued a letter of administration that ordered an accounting of the deceased's estate.

loss   A process by which archaeological sites come into existence; in this case, simply when people lose material.

lowered skull base height   A cranial condition resulting from poor nutrition during the developing years.

maker's mark   A mark placed on ceramics by the manufacturer that may include the manufacturer's name and logo and the name of the type of ware. Such marks are very useful in dating historical sites.

master sequence   In dendrochronology, the regional sequence of tree ring widths against which all subsequent archaeological wood samples can be compared and dated.

mastoid process   Bony protrusion behind the ear. The size and configuration of the mastoid can be used in determining the sex of a skull.

mean ceramic date   A date for a site or structure within a site, mathematically determined by reference to the periods of manufacture of the ceramics found and their abundance.

midden   Trash pile found at an archaeological site usually consisting of organic residue.

minimum vessel count   A conservative estimate of the number of vessels of each functional or morphological type or pattern category recovered at a site. Sherds are analytically combined if, based on class, type, pattern, and color, they could belong to the same object.

paleopathology   The study of ancient disease. Often diseases leave diagnostic traces on the human skeleton and these can be assessed by the osteologist.

pearlware   Ceramic with a white body and bluish-white glaze introduced in 1779. It was popular in the late eighteenth and early nineteenth centuries, declined in popularity in the 1820s, and was replaced by *whiteware* by about 1830.

pedestrian survey   The process of searching for archaeological material by a walkover and visual inspection of an area or site. Pedestrian surveys are most useful where past people built durable structures and where natural processes have not served to cover up site remains.

petition for probate   The official request that the *will* and *testament* be probated, or proved; in other words, read and acted upon by the authorities.

plane table   Flat, level table mounted on a tripod, and upon which the *alidade* rests. A site map can be drawn on a large sheet of graph paper that can be placed directly on the plane table.

population   Here, in the statistical sense of the entire group of items: sites and artifacts. A *representative sample* is a subset of the population.

porcelain   Ceramic objects made from a translucent paste fired to a temperature of more than 1400°C (2500°F).

primary discard   Material thrown out right at its place of use, as opposed to *secondary discard* where material to be thrown away is brought to a separate dump, or *midden*.

primary documents   Those items in historical research that are contemporary with the time or place being studied.

Privy Council   Arm of the British government above that of the *Council for Foreign Plantations*.

probate   Legal procedure in which the deceased's last *will* and *testament* are read and their validity assessed.

provenience   The precise location where an archaeological artifact, ecofact, or feature was discovered.

pubic symphysis   Place of articulation of a human being's two pubic bones. The surfaces of the symphysis can assist in determining the age at the time of death.

Puritan captivity narrative   Literary genre, popular in the seventeenth and early eighteenth centuries, focusing on the lives of Europeans kidnapped by Indians.

radiometric   Dating techniques based on the known rates of decay of radioactive elements.

real estate   Property, including land and structures.

redware   Unrefined earthenware with a reddish-brown body, often covered with a clear lead glaze. Redware was widely manufactured in America for domestic use from about 1620 to 1840.

relative dating   Dating techniques in which no year or range of years can be applied, but archaeological material can be placed in an order of occurrence.

remote sensing   Procedures where sites are searched for, examined, or both, using noninvasive techniques where no soil is moved; for example, aerial photography or proton magnetometry.

representative sample   A portion of a population (for example, a population of all of the archaeological sites in a region) where the proportions of various elements (site sizes, ages, kinds of sites) in the sample match those in the population.

sciatic notch   Notch in the pelvic bones across which the sciatic nerve is located. A wide notch is indicative of a female because it allows for a wide birth canal.

secondary discard   Process where material to be thrown away is brought to a separate dump or *midden;* as opposed to *primary discard,* where material is thrown out right at its place of use.

seriation   Process in *relative dating* based on the pattern of replacement of styles of an artifact type through time.

service records   Official list of the names of individuals who served in the wars conducted by the United States.

settlement pattern   The distribution of archaeological sites and analysis of their functions in relation to each other and features of the environment.

sheet refuse   See *broadcast refuse.*

sherd   Fragment of a *ceramic* object.

signature literacy   A minimal level of literacy signifying the ability to read and write one's own name. Among those who could not otherwise read or write, the ability to sign one's name was an important skill that enabled an individual to more easily enter into legal agreements such as *wills*, contracts, or deed transferals.

site survey   The process of looking for archaeological sites, including their preliminary investigation once located.

spatial context   Where an archaeological object is found in relation to a fixed point in space, other objects, artifacts, ecofacts, and features.

stadia rod   Long, ruled rod used in mapping. The rod is sighted through the *alidade* and a measurement can be taken of the elevation of the point upon which the rod is resting.

stoneware   Dense, heavy ceramic characterized by a gray, brown, or buff body. Salt-glaze finish with an orange peel texture was common until the 1800s. After 1810 brown Albany slip was common on vessel interiors. Stoneware dates to the sixteenth century in Europe and was manufactured in North America by the middle of the eighteenth century.

stratigraphic analysis   The study of layers at an archaeological site. Useful in producing a relative chronological sequence at a site and among sites.

stratigraphy   The layering of the earth.

stratum (pl., **strata**)   A layer in a stratigraphic sequence.

surface survey   Searching for sites by investigation of the surface of the ground. A *pedestrian survey* is a part of a surface survey.

talus   The material (*colluvium*) that accumulates at the base of a slope.

technology   How a people manufacture the items used in their culture.

terminus ante quem   Date based on using the most recent artifact found at a site as an estimate of the end date of the occupation.

terminus post quem   Date based on the recognition that a site must date to sometime after the age of the oldest artifact found there.

testament   The legal statement by which an individual disposes of his or her personal property; in distinction to the *will* wherein a person disposes of his or her *real estate*.

test pit   Shovel-dug holes or borings, usually about 50 cm on a side, useful in testing an area for the presence of subsurface archaeological remains. The soil is passed through hardware cloth or screening.

tibial bowing   A curving of the large bone of the lower leg resulting from poor nutrition. Seen in the skeletal remains of poor individuals with inadequate diets.

transfer print   A process patented in 1796; used on English porcelain by 1760, on unrefined earthenware by 1780, and as an underglaze on refined earthenware in 1783. A design in ink is transferred from an engraved copper plate to transfer paper and then to a ceramic vessel. The vessel is then glazed. Dark blue transfer prints were popular in America from 1818 through the 1820s. Other colors, including red, green, brown, and purple, were popular from the late 1820s through the 1840s. Since this time, transfer printing has continued to have periods of popularity.

vital records   Records of births, marriages, and deaths kept by towns, counties, states, and the federal government.

white granite   A hard, white, vitrified or semi-vitrified *ceramic* type that evolved from *ironstone* in the latter half of the nineteenth century. White granite is still manufactured.

whiteware   A *ceramic* ware characterized by a white body and a clear glaze. In some whitewares, cobalt blue was added to the glaze. Whiteware was first produced in 1820 and is still produced today.

will   The legal statement by which an individual disposes of his or her *real estate* in distinction to the *testament*, where an individual disposes of his or her personal property.

yellowware   *Ceramic* with a yellowish body covered in a clear glaze. It was produced between about 1830 and 1940.

REFERENCES

1818. March 24. Death Notices. *Hartford Times.*

1818. March 30. Death Notices. *Connecticut Mirror.*

1818. March 31. Death Notices. *Connecticut Courant.*

1818. March 31. Death Notices. *Connecticut Herald.*

1854. September 30. The Barkhamsted Lighthouse. *Mountain County Herald.*

1894. February 9. Barkhamsted Hollow. *Winsted Herald.*

1900. January 29. The Old Lighthouse. *Connecticut Courant.*

1933. March 3. Lighthouse Tribe Descendants Have Long Resided in Winsted; Several Generations Are Found. *Winsted Evening Citizen.*

1952. The Barkhamsted Lighthouse. *Lure of the Litchfield Hills,* 12(1).

1965. March 8. Obituaries: Lewis Mills. *Hartford Times.*

Abbe, E. 1984. Connecticut genealogical research: sources and suggestions. In *Genealogical Research in New England,* edited by R. J. Crandall, pp. 115–138. Baltimore: Genealogical Publishing.

Adams, N. 1968. Jesse Ives Tavern—Now The Old Riverton Inn. *Lure of the Litchfield Hills,* 28(2), pp. 9–10.

Adams, S. W., and H. R. Stiles. 1859. *The History of Ancient Wethersfield.* 2 vols. Reprint 1975. New York: Grafton Press.

Angel, J. L., J. O. Kelley, M. Parrington, and S. Pinter. 1987. Life stresses of the free black community as represented by the First African Baptist Church, Philadelphia, 1823–1841. *American Journal of Physical Anthropology,* 74, pp. 213–229.

Ascher, R., and C. Fairbanks. 1971. Excavation of a slave cabin in Georgia, U.S.A. *Historical Archaeology,* 5, pp. 3–17.

Baker, V. G. 1978. *Historical Archaeology at Black Lucy's Garden, Andover, Massachusetts: Ceramics from the Site of a Nineteenth Century Afro-American.* Andover, Mass.: Robert S. Peabody Foundation for Archaeology.

Barber, J. W. 1838. *Connecticut Historical Collections.* New Haven, Conn.: Durne and Peck and Barber.

Benes, P. 1977. Puritan gravestone art. In *The Dublin Seminar for New England Folklife: Annual Proceedings 1976,* edited by P. Benes. Dublin, N.H.: Boston University.

———. 1978. Puritan gravestone art II. In *The Dublin Seminar for New England Folklife: Annual Proceedings 1978,* edited by P. Benes. Dublin, N.H.: Boston University.

Benes, P., and J. M. Benes. 1989. Introduction: Unlocking the semantic and quantitative doors. In *Early American Probate Inventories,* edited by P. Benes, pp. 5–16. Boston: Boston University.

Bickford, C. 1979. The Connecticut census of 1762 found. *Connecticut Historical Society Bulletin,* 44(2), pp. 33–43.

Bierce, A. 1911. *The Devil's Dictionary.* Reprint 1958. New York: Dover.

Binford, L. 1962. A new method of calculating dates from kaolin pipe stem fragments. *Southeastern Archaeological Conference Newsletter*, 9(1), pp. 19–21.

Bower, B. A. 1991. Material culture in Boston: The black experience. In *The Archaeology of Inequality,* edited by R. H. McGuire and R. Paynter, pp. 55–63. Cambridge, Mass.: Blackwell.

Boyd, J. 1873. *Annals and Family Records of Winchester, Connecticut with Exercises of the Centenial Celebration.* Hartford, Conn.: Case, Lockwood, and Brainard.

Brothwell, D. R. 1971. *Digging Up Bones: The Excavation, Treatment, and Study of Human Skeletal Remains.* London: British Museum (Natural History).

Brown, A. R. 1982. *Historic Ceramic Typology with Principal Dates of Manufacture and Descriptive Characteristics for Identification.* Wilmington, Del.: Delaware Department of Transportation.

Buikstra, J. E., and D. D. Cook. 1980. Paleopathology. *Annual Review of Anthropology,* 9, pp. 433–470.

Bullen, A. K., and R. P. Bullen. 1945. Black Lucy's garden. *Bulletin of the Massachusetts Archaeological Society,* 6(2), pp. 17–28.

Bureau of the Census. 1909. *A Century of Population Growth: From the First Census of the United States to the Twelfth, 1790–1900.* Washington, D.C.: Department of Commerce and Labor.

Campbell, M. 1988. *The Witness and the Other World: Exotic European Travel Writings 400–1600.* Ithaca, N.Y.: Cornell University.

Cott, N. F. 1977. *The Bonds of Womanhood: "Women's Sphere" in New England 1780–1835.* New Haven, Conn.: Yale University.

Cramb, I. 1992. *The Art of the Stonemason.* White Hall, Va.: Betterway Publications.

Crandall, R. 1986. *Shaking Your Family Tree: A Basic Guide to Tracing Your Family Genealogy.* Dublin, N.H.: Yankee.

Davis, W. T., ed. 1971. *Bradford's History of Plymouth Plantation 1606–1646.* Reprint 1908. New York: Barnes and Noble.

Deagan, K. 1991. Historical archaeology's contribution to our understanding of early America. In *Historical Archaeology in Global Perspective,* edited by L. Falk, pp. 97–112. Washington, D.C.: Smithsonian Institution.

Deetz, J. 1969. The reality of the Pilgrim fathers. *Natural History,* 78(9), pp. 32–45.

———. 1971. Late man in North America: Archaeology of European Americans. In *Man's Imprint from the Past,* edited by J. Deetz, pp. 208–218. Boston: Little Brown.

———. 1973. *Invitation to Archaeology.* Garden City, N.Y.: Anchor Books.

———. 1977. *In Small Things Forgotten: The Archaeology of Early American Life.* Garden City, N.Y.: Anchor Books.

———. 1980. "Other People's Garbage." Public Broadcasting System: "Odyssey." Television program.

———. 1991. Introduction: Archaeological evidence of sixteenth- and seventeenth-century encounters. In *Historical Archaeology in Global Perspective,* edited by L. Falk, Washington, D.C.: Smithsonian Institution.

Dethlefsen, E., and J. Deetz. 1966. Death's heads, cherubs, and willow trees: Experimental archaeology in colonial cemeteries. *American Antiquity*, 31, pp. 502–510.

Ditz, T. L. 1986. *Property and Kinship: Inheritance in Early Connecticut 1750–1820*. Princeton, N.J.: Princeton University.

Duval, F. Y., and I. B. Rigby. 1978. *Early American Gravestone Art in Photographs*. New York: Dover Publications.

Etler, P. 1980. West coast Chinese and opium smoking. In *Archaeological Perspectives on Ethnicity in America: Afro-American and Asian American Culture History*, edited by R. C. Schuyoler, pp. 97–101. Farmingdale, N.Y.: Baywood.

Fagan, B. 1991. *In the Beginning*. Boston: Little Brown.

Fairbanks, C. 1976. Spaniards, planters, ships, and slaves. *Archaeology*, 29, pp. 164–172.

Feder, K. L., and M. A. Park. 1993. *Human Antiquity: An Introduction to Physical Anthropology and Archaeology* (2d ed.). Mountain View, Calif.: Mayfield Publishing.

Ferguson, L. 1991. Struggling with pots in colonial South Carolina. In *The Archaeology of Inequality*, edited by R. H. McGuire and R. Paynter, pp. 28–39. Cambridge, Mass.: Blackwell.

———. 1992. *Uncommon Ground: Archaeology and Early African America, 1650–1800*. Washington, D.C.: Smithsonian Institution.

Fogelman, G. L. 1991. *Glass Trade Beads of the Northeast*. Turbotville, Pa.: Fogelman Publishing.

Frurip, D., R. Malewicki, and D. P. Heldman. 1983. *Colonial Nails from Michilimackinac: Differentiation by Chemical and Statistical Analysis*. Mackinac Island, Mich.: Mackinac Island State Park Commission.

Frye, L., et al. 1991. *Coding System Manual for the East Liverpool, Ohio Urban Archaeology Project*. Columbus: Ohio Department of Transportation.

Galeener-Moore, L. 1987. *Collecting Dead Relatives*. Baltimore: Genealogical Publishing.

Geismar, J. 1982. *The Archaeology of Social Disintegration in Skunk Hollow: A Nineteenth Century Rural Black Community*. New York: Academic Press.

Gill, G. W., J. W. Fisher, and G. M. Zeimens. 1984. A pioneer burial near the historic Bordeaux trading post. *Plains Anthropologist*, 29, pp. 229–238.

Gilmore, W. J. 1982. Elementary literacy on the eve of the Industrial Revolution: Trends in rural New England, 1760–1830. *Proceedings of the American Antiquarian Society*, 92, pp. 87–178.

Glassie, H. 1968. *Pattern in the Material Folk Culture of the Eastern United States*. Philadelphia: University of Pennsylvania Press.

———. 1975. *Folk Housing in Middle Virginia*. Knoxville, Tenn.: University of Tennessee Press.

Godden, G. 1964. *Encyclopaedia of British Pottery and Porcelain Marks*. New York: Bonanza Books.

Gradie, R. F. 1992. Personal communication.

Graham, W. A. 1953. *The Custer Myth: A Source Book of Custeriana*. New York: Bonanza Books.

Greene, E., and V. Harrington. 1932. *American Population Before the Federal Census of 1790.* Reprint 1966. Gloucester, Mass.: Peter Smith.

Greenwood, V. 1973. *The Researcher's Guide to American Genealogy.* Baltimore: Genealogical Publishing.

Halacy, D. 1980. *Census: 190 Years of Counting Americans.* New York: Elsezier-Nelson.

Handsman, R. 1990. The Weantinock Indian homeland was not a "desert." *Artifacts,* 18(2), pp. 3–7.

Harrington, J. C. 1954. Dating stem fragments of seventeenth and eighteenth century clay tobacco pipes. *Quarterly Bulletin of the Archaeological Society of Virginia,* 9(1).

Hart, M. 1883, July 6. Barkhamsted Reminiscences. *Winsted Herald.*

Hester, T., H. Shafer, and K. L. Feder. *Field Methods in Archaeology.* Mountain View, Calif.: Mayfield Publishing. In preparation.

Hoadley, C., ed. 1880. *Public Records of the Colony of Connecticut.* Hartford, Conn.: State of Connecticut.

Jacobus, D. 1960. Connecticut. In *Genealogical Research Methods and Sources,* edited by M. Rubincam, pp. 124–133. Washington, D.C.: American Society of Genealogists.

Jones, H. R. 1881. Barkhamsted. In *History of Litchfield County, Connecticut,* edited by J. W. Lewis. Philadelphia: J. W. Lewis & Co.

Jones, O., and C. Sullivan. 1985. *The Parks Canada Glass Glossary for the Description of Containers, Tableware, Flat Glass, and Closures.* Ottawa: Parks Canada.

Jones, S. L. 1985. The African-American tradition in vernacular architecture. In *The Archaeology of Slavery and Plantation Life,* edited by T. Singleton, pp. 195–213. New York: Academic Press.

Kelley, J. O., and J. L. Angel. 1987. Life stresses of slavery. *American Journal of Physical Anthropology,* 74, pp. 199–211.

Kemper, J. n.d. *American Charcoal Making in the Era of the Cold-blast Furnace.* n.p.: Hopewell Village National Historic Site.

Kennedy, S. M. 1988. *Practical Stonemasonry Made Easy.* Blue Ridge Summit, Pa.: Tab Books.

Ketchum, W. C. 1975. *The Treasury of American Bottles.* New York: Rutledge.

Kidd, K. E. 1970. *A Classification System for Glass Beads for the Use of Field Archaeologists.* Ottawa: Parks Canada.

Kovel, R., and T. Kovel. 1953. *Dictionary of Marks: Pottery and Porcelain.* New York: Crown Publishers.

———. 1986. *Kovel's New Dictionary of Marks.* New York: Crown Publishers.

Krogman, W. M. 1973. *The Human Skeleton in Forensic Medicine.* Springfield, Ill.: Charles C. Thomas.

Landgraff, W. 1992. Personal communication.

Larsen, C. S. 1987. Bioarchaeological interpretations of subsistence economy and behavior from human skeletal remains. In *Advances in Archaeological Method and Theory,* edited by M. B. Schiffer, pp. 395–474. New York: Academic Press.

Lee, W. W. 1868, May 22. Barkhamsted Lighthouse: Origin of the Title, History, Incidents, etc. *Winsted Herald*, p. 2.

———. 1881. *Barkhamsted, Connecticut and Its Centenial 1879.* Meriden, Conn.: W. W. Lee.

———. 1897. *Catalogue of Barkhamsted Men Who Served in Various Wars 1775–1865.* Meriden, Conn.: W. W. Lee.

Lehner, L. 1988. *Lehner's Encyclopedia of U.S. Marks on Pottery, Porcelain, and Clay.* Paducah, Ky.: Collector Books.

Lewis, J. W. 1881. *History of Litchfield County, Connecticut, with Illustrations and Biographical Sketches of Its Prominent Men and Pioneers.* Philadelphia: J. W. Lewis.

Mason, J. E. 1855, June 23. Barkhamsted Lighthouse. *Mountain County Herald,* p. 2.

———. 1855, June 30. Barkhamsted Lighthouse. *Mountain County Herald,* p. 1.

McBride, K. 1990a. The historical archaeology of the Mashantucket Pequots, 1637–1900. In *The Pequots in Southern New England: The Fall and Rise of an American Indian Nation,* edited by L. M. Hauptman and J. D. Wherry, pp. 96–116. Norman, Okla.: University of Oklahoma Press.

———. 1990b. Personal communication.

———. 1993. Personal communication.

McCormick, G. 1975. Early inns and taverns. In *Barkhamsted Heritage,* edited by R. G. Wheeler and G. Hilton, pp. 141–154. Barkhamsted, Conn.: Barkhamsted Historical Society.

McGuire, R. H., and R. Paynter, ed. 1991. *The Archaeology of Inequality.* Cambridge, Mass.: Blackwell.

McKearin, G., and H. McKearin. 1941. *American Glass.* New York: Crown.

McKearin, H., and K. M. Wilson. 1978. *American Bottles and Flasks and Their Ancestry.* New York: Crown.

McManamon, F. 1984. Discovering sites unseen. In *Advances in Archaeology,* edited by M. B. Schiffer, pp. 223–292. New York: Academic Press.

Miller, C. 1969. *Genealogical Research: A Basic Guide.* Technical Leaflet No. 14. American Association for State and Local History.

Miller, G. L. 1980. Classification and economic scaling of 19th-century ceramics. *Historical Archaeology,* 14, pp. 1–40.

———. 1991. A revised set of CC Index values for classification and economic scaling of English ceramics from 1787 to 1880. *Historical Archaeology,* 25(1), pp. 1–25.

Mills, L. S. 1952. *The Legend of the Barkhamsted Lighthouse.* Hartford, Conn.: L. S. Mills.

Mourt, G. 1622. *A Relation or Journal of the Beginning and Proceedings of the English Plantation Settled at Plimoth in New England.* Reprint 1966. Readex Microprint.

Nelson, L. H. 1968. Nail chronology as an aid to dating old buildings. *History News,* 24(11)

Noël Hume, I. 1969. *A Guide to Artifacts of Colonial America.* New York: Vintage Books.

————. 1973. From creamware to pearlware. In *Ceramics in America,* edited by I. Quimby, pp. 217–254. Charlottesville, Va.: University Press of Virginia.

O'Brien, J. A. 1992, Dec. 27. Giving Peoples Forest Back to the People. *Hartford Courant,* p. H1.

Orser, C. E., Jr., 1991. The continued pattern of dominance: Landlord and tenant on the postbellum cotton plantation. In *The Archaeology of Inequality,* edited by R. H. McGuire and R. Paynter, pp. 40–54. Cambridge, Mass.: Blackwell.

Ortner, D. J., and W. G. Putsher. 1981. *Identification of Pathological Conditions in Human Skeletal Remains.* Washington, D.C.: Smithsonian Institution.

Oswald, A. 1951. English clay tobacco pipes. *The Archaeological Newsletter,* 3(10), pp. 153–159.

Otto, J. S. 1977. Artifacts and status differences: A comparison of ceramics from planter, overseer, and slave sites on an antebellum plantation. In *Research Strategies in Historical Archaeology,* edited by S. South, pp. 91–118. New York: Academic Press.

————. 1984. *Cannon's Point Plantation, 1794–1860: Living Conditions and Status Patterns in the Old South.* New York: Academic Press.

Poirier, D. 1976. Camp Redding: Logistics of a Revolutionary War winter encampment. *Northeast Historical Archaeology,* 5(1–2), pp. 40–52.

Pugh, J. C. 1975. *Surveying for Field Scientists.* Pittsburgh: University of Pittsburgh Press.

Ramsay, J. 1976. *American Potters and Pottery.* Reprint 1939. Ann Arbor, Mich.: Ars Ceramica.

Rathbun, T. 1987. Health and disease at a South Carolina plantation. *American Journal of Physical Anthropology,* 74, pp. 239–253.

Reitz, E. J., T. Gibbs, and T. A. Rathbun. 1985. Archaeological evidence for subsistence on coastal plantations. In *The Archaeology of Slavery and Plantation Life,* edited by T. Singleton, pp. 163–191. New York: Academic Press.

Richmond, T. L. 1993. A native perception of history: The Schaghticoke nation, resistance and survival. Paper presented at the annual meeting of the Northeastern Anthropological Association, Danbury, Connecticut.

Ripley, K. 1942. Canova pottery. *Hobbies* (Jan.), p. 58.

Roberts, D. 1968. The Village of Riverton-Town of Barkhamsted. *Lure of the Litchfield Hills,* 28(2), pp. 18–20.

————. 1969. The Village of Riverton-Town of Barkhamsted. *Lure of the Litchfield Hills,* 29(1), pp. 26–28, 35.

Robinson, P., and G. Gustafson. 1982. A partially disturbed seventeenth century Indian burial ground in Rhode Island: Recovery, preliminary analysis and protection. *Bulletin of the Archaeological Society of Connecticut,* 45, pp. 41–50.

Robinson, P., M. A. Kelley, and P. Rubertone. 1985. Preliminary biocultural interpretations from a seventeenth century Narragansett Indian cemetery in Rhode Island. In *Cultures in Contact: European Impact on Native Cultural Institutions in Eastern North America, A.D. 1000–1800,* edited by W. Fitzhugh. Washington, D.C.: Smithsonian Institution.

Rolando, V. 1989. Industrial archaeology survey of Vermont furnaces and kilns completes eleventh year. *Society for Industrial Archaeology: New England Chapters*, 9(2), pp. 11–13.

Rubincam, M. 1960. *Genealogical Research: Methods and Sources*. Washington, D.C.: American Society of Genealogists.

Salmon, M. 1986. *Women and the Law of Property in Early America*. Chapel Hill, N.C.: University of North Carolina.

Salwen, B., and S. Bridges. 1976. Cultural differences and the interpretation of archaeological evidence: The problem of dating. Paper presented at the annual meeting of the Society for Historical Archaeology, Philadelphia.

Scott, D., and R. A. Fox, Jr. 1984. *Archaeological Insights into the Custer Battle*. Norman, Okla.: University of Oklahoma.

Scott, D., R. A. Fox, Jr., and M. Conner. 1989. *Archaeological Perspectives on the Battle of the Little Big Horn*. Norman, Okla.: University of Oklahoma.

Seaver, J., ed. 1918. *The Narrative of the Life of Mary Jemison*. New York: American Historical Preservation Society.

Sharer, R., and W. Ashmore. 1992. *Discovering Our Past*. (2d ed.). Mountain View, Calif.: Mayfield Publishing.

Sieminski, G. 1990. The Puritan captivity narrative and the politics of the American Revolution. *American Quarterly*, 42(1), pp. 35–56.

Singleton, T., ed. 1985. *The Archaeology of Slavery and Plantation Life*. New York: Academic Press.

Skowronek, R. 1991. Paintings and potsherds: How fine art helps scholars identify artifacts. *Archaeology*, 44(6), pp. 52–59.

Smiley, E. 1934. *Short History of Riverton, Connecticut*. Riverton, Conn.: Edmund Smiley.

South, S. 1964. Analysis of buttons from Brunswick Town and Fort Fisher. *Florida Anthropologist*, 17(2), 113–133.

———. 1977. *Method and Theory in Historical Archaeology*. New York: Academic Press.

Spalding, J. A. 1891. *Illustrated Popular Biography of Connecticut*. Hartford, Conn.: Case, Lockwood, and Brainard.

Spargo, J. 1974. *Early American Pottery and China*. Rutland, Vermont: Tuttle.

Spier, R. 1970. *Surveying and Mapping: A Manual of Simplified Techniques*. New York: Holt, Rinehart and Winston.

Stiles, H. R. 1892. *The History and Genealogies of Ancient Windsor Including East Windsor, South Windsor, Bloomfield, Windsor Locks, and Ellington for 1635–1895*. Hartford, Conn.: Case, Lockwood, and Brainard.

Stryker-Rodda, H. 1986. *Understanding Colonial Handwriting*. Baltimore: Genealogical Publishing Co.

Sussman, L. 1979. *Spode/Copeland Transfer Print Patterns Found at Twenty Hudson Bay Company Sites*. Ottawa: Parks Canada.

Tallman, L. 1993. Personal communication.

Thomas, D. H. 1991. *Archaeology: An Introduction*. New York: Holt, Rinehart and Winston.

Turnbaugh, S. P. 1983. Seventeenth and eighteenth century lead-glazed redwares in the Massachusetts Bay Colony. *Historical Archaeology,* 17(1), pp. 3–17.

———. 1985. Introduction. In *Domestic Pottery of the Northeastern United States: 1625–1850*, edited by S. P. Turnbaugh, pp. 1–26. New York: Academic Press.

Utley, R. 1969. *Custer Battlefield National Monument, Montana.* Washington, D.C.: National Park Service.

Wells, R. 1975. *The Population of the British Colonies in America Before 1776: A Survey of Census Data.* Princeton, N.J.: Princeton University.

Wheeler, R. G., and G. Hilton, eds. 1975. *Barkhamsted Heritage: Culture and Industry in a Rural Connecticut Town.* Barkhamsted, Conn.: Barkhamsted Historical Society.

White, T., and P. Folkens. 1991. *Human Osteology.* New York: Academic Press.

Williams, L. E. 1972. *Fort Shantok and Fort Corchaug: A Comparative Study of Seventeenth Century Culture Contact in the Long Island Sound Area.* Ph.D. dissertation. New York University.

Witthoft, J. 1966. A history of gunflints. *Pennsylvania Archaeologist,* 36(1–2), pp. 12–49.

Wood, F. J. 1919. *The Turnpikes of New England and the Evolution of the Same Through England, Virginia, and Maryland.* Boston: Marshall Jones.

Wright, N. E., and D. H. Pratt. 1967. *Genealogical Research Essentials.* Salt Lake City: Bookcraft.

INDEX